CRISIS IN THE VILLAGE

"Robert Franklin's *Crisis in the Village* is a bracing and bold call for spiritual and social healing in the black community. With characteristic clarity and eloquence, Franklin challenges the entire black world, and the broader society alike, to marshall its resources to address the critical issues confronting black folk today. Franklin's brilliant scholarly intervention is both timely and necessary, and should be read by all who desire to help bear, and relieve, the burden of the black vulnerable."

—Michael Eric Dyson
author of *Is Bill Cosby Right?*
Or Has the Black Middle Class Lost Its Mind?

"Franklin artfully petitions us to rediscover, reawaken and resume traditions and values of a cultural ethic that created generations of great thinkers and doers, and guided the African American community to overcome when it appeared, by most standards, there was no way out of our despair. *Crisis in the Village* is an inspiring strategic plan for rebuilding intra-community excellence and social accountability that promises to re-energize 'sleeping giants.'"

—Ambassador Andrew Young
President Goodworks International, Atlanta,
Past President of the National Council of Churches,
and author of *A Way Out of No Way*

CRISIS IN THE VILLAGE
Restoring Hope in
African American Communities
ROBERT M. FRANKLIN

FORTRESS PRESS
Minneapolis

Coretta Scott King
A servant-leader who embodied enduring Faith

Imani Renee, Robert Michael, III, and Julian Michael . . .
My children who symbolize tomorrow's Hope

My wife, Cheryl, extended family, and friends
Providers and practitioners of unconditional Love

CRISIS IN THE VILLAGE
Restoring Hope in African American Communities

Cover image: Robert M. Franklin © Jon Rou/Emory University Photography; background cityscape © Bernd Obermann / CORBIS
Cover design: Kevin van der Leek Design
Book design: Timothy W. Larson

Library of Congress Cataloging-in-Publication Data

Franklin, Robert Michael, 1954–
  Crisis in the village : restoring hope in African American communities / Robert M. Franklin.
    p. cm.
  Includes bibliographical references.
  ISBN-13: 978–0–8006–3887–0 (alk. paper)
  ISBN-10: 0–8006–3887–5 (alk. paper)
  1. African Americans—Social conditions—1975- 2. African American families. 3. African American churches. 4. African American universities and colleges. 5. Nonprofit organizations—United States. 6. Community life—United States. 7. Social problems—United States. 8. Social change—United States. 9. Hope—Social aspects—United States. 10. Hope—Religious aspects. I. Title.
  E185.86.F72 2007
  305.896'073009045—dc22   2006102560

The paper used in this publication meets the minimum requirements of American National Standard for Information Sciences — Permanence of Paper for Printed Library Materials, ANSI Z329.48-1984.

Manufactured in the U.S.A.
11   10   09   08   07   3   4   5   6   7   8   9   10   11

CONTENTS

117865

ACKNOWLEDGMENTS

ONE book comes into existence through the good will and support of many people. This work was completed with support from the PEW Charitable Trusts as part of a project on religion and the family at Emory University's Center for the Study of Law and Religion (formerly, the Center for the Inter-disciplinary Study of Religion). Carole Thompson of the Annie E. Casey Foundation has been a valued colleague over the years and encouraged me to keep these ideas "in the air and on the ground" by enabling me to work with and present ideas to many groups of leaders around the country. Linetta Gilbert of the Ford Foundation has supported and encouraged my research and work related to the Gulf Coast and in the international arena. Perhaps my most influential mentor and dialogue partner has been Lynn Jones Huntley of the Southern Educational Foundation. I am indebted to each of these extraordinary women. I am also grateful for the encouragement of Ralph Smith, vice president of the Annie E. Casey Foundation, Sherry Magill, president of the Jessie Ball duPont Fund where I serve as a trustee, and to my fellow trustees and foundation staff. I am grateful, too, for the supportive work of Fran Phillips-Calhoun, David Lott, and the publishing team at Fortress Press. The opinions expressed herein are mine and do not necessarily reflect the views of any of my donors, conversation partners, or supporters.

INTRODUCTION

This book, then, is not intended as a broadside against any particular person or class, but it is given as a corrective for methods which have not produced satisfactory results.

—*Carter G. Woodson,* The Mis-education of the Negro

What we need are books that hit us like a most painful misfortune, like the death of someone we loved more than we love ourselves, that make us feel as though we had been banished to the woods, far from any human presence, like a suicide. A book must be the ax for the frozen sea within us.

—*Franz Kafka*

READING a book is easy. Understanding it may be difficult. But, writing one is even harder, especially if you don't particularly want to write it. In fact, that can feel like the literary equivalent of a root canal. That was the case here. I did not want to write this book. I was waiting for someone else to do it. I waited for someone whom I respected for her or his penetrating insight, eloquent advocacy, impatience with organizational mediocrity, and capacity to mobilize others around an inspiring vision and core values. I knew it would need to be someone who understands the assets and the challenges in African American communities—what I call villages—and who is part of the larger public conversation about the good life and the just society. I waited, I searched, and I tried to read and inquire broadly. But I did not find the book for which I was searching. Mind you, I discovered an extensive list of relevant books from which I learned a great deal, and to which I later refer. And many of my mentors—including Marian Wright Edelman, Hugh Price, Cornel West, and Tavis Smiley—wrote versions of the book that I felt was

1

needed. But even their excellent books and efforts left me feeling something slightly different was needed.

Then, while waiting and searching, I heard Marian Wright Edelman deliver a speech in which she quoted Mahatma Gandhi's bracing words, "We must be the change that we seek." And not long thereafter, I heard Jim Wallis of *Sojourners* magazine and Call to Renewal quote the young African American organizer Lisa Sullivan, who used to say, "We are the ones we've been waiting for." Soon I felt compelled to do more than complain about the lack of such a book.

At the same time, comedian Bill Cosby began to weigh in, candidly, courageously, and disturbingly, on some of the challenges in urban black communities. But he didn't seem to talk enough about black community assets for reversing the problems or about the magnitude of the external forces (the economy, institutional racism, poor education) that often suffocate personal initiative. Tavis Smiley and the talented colleagues who produced the 2006 "Covenant with Black America" raised my expectations even higher. But even after these flashes of hope and promise, I still found something missing.

I found myself waiting for a call to strategic action and the outline of an actionable plan that:

1. Enlists specific institutions,
2. Assigns specific roles to them,
3. Elaborates an accountability framework,
4. Incorporates a developmental approach to action mobilization,
5. Appeals for broad public support, and
6. Mobilizes every willing and able person to tackle the problems that now threaten our families, our communities, and our democracy.

I did not find these elements combined in any single book, essay, or action plan. I realized that I might have to take a stab at writing the book for which I was waiting. And in writing, hopefully others would find it to be the message that they, too, had been awaiting. Although I have trepidation about whether or not anyone will respond to this call, I am certain that issuing this call to compassion and beyond to moral action and leadership is worth the effort. So this is my contribution to releasing the "frozen sea within us."

VILLAGES AND ANCHOR INSTITUTIONS

This is a contribution to the conversation about what can and must be done to do a better job of "people-making," especially "child-making."[1] And ultimately, we must discover and implement the science and art of making better families, communities, and, we hope, a better nation and global community. This is the work that Dr. King referred to as building the "beloved community." It is work that will require the collective efforts, cooperation, and investment of the entire nation.

A few years ago, Senator Hillary Rodham Clinton called attention to these concerns in her celebrated book, *It Takes a Village*.[2] She borrowed an African proverb's evocative metaphor of "village" to remind us all of the collective responsibilities of every village to nurture its next generation. Marian Wright Edelman and the Children's Defense Fund later popularized the village metaphor. Despite its insights and useful recommendations, however, I do not perceive that Senator Clinton's book became a guidebook for the community leaders whom I know. I use the same village metaphor because I also believe that authentic restorative action happens at the local neighborhood level. The village metaphor may seem a bit odd for most of us who reside in or near cities. But it is intended to jar us into thinking about how we can take responsibility for changing our communities for the better. Neighborhoods become villages when all of the adults step up to show care and concern for all of the children. Villages need real grown-ups. Moreover, the hard and slow work of healing and reconciling broken people and fractured relationships that will in turn restore larger institutions must begin with these grown-ups (no matter what their age) inside local institutions. As I use the term *village*, I am referring primarily to local neighborhoods and communities with predominantly black populations. On occasion, I assume that these local communities share features in common and can be thought of as constituting a national village despite the artificiality of that construct. But, secondarily, I have Senator Clinton's meaning in mind. That is, villages are the neighborhoods and communities in which all Americans reside. In the final analysis, we all live in villages and we all should aspire to transform them into beloved communities. Village has a more intimate and inclusive emotional tone than its alternatives and, as I interpret it, requires justice as the precondition for peace, prosperity, and human fulfillment.

I refer to the central local institutions in villages as "anchor institutions"—the institutions that have an enduring presence and operate to stabilize people amidst chaos and rapid transition. When Hurricane Katrina struck the Gulf Coast in the middle of my writing this book, the "anchor" metaphor took on new life for me, as did the image of an anchor within a seaside village that prevents it from drifting into dangerous waters. During a visit to New Orleans a few months after Hurricane Katrina, I found myself riding for hours past thousands of devastated homes and vast neighborhoods laid waste by storm and flood. The stench and the silence became heavy and oppressive; nothing stirred. A place known for its vibrancy and high energy stood stagnant like an urban swampland.

Then, in the distance, a strange sound echoed. It was the sound of laughing, resilient children packed into the local school. The only institution filled with people that we had seen all day was this neighborhood school. As our bus filled with an interracial group of clergy and community organizers passed the school, all the kids ran to the window to wave at us. It was haunting to see this school functioning in the middle of what looked like a war zone. But, it was now an *anchor* to which the children of the neighborhood had returned to continue their long, long journey of learning, rebuilding, and healing.

Our guide was Joe Givens, a community organizer and New Orleans native. He offered advice that decision makers should heed: "Instead of trying to rebuild houses one at a time—a slow and lonely process—we should first restore our institutions where masses of people can gather and draw strength from each other." With those words, he captured the core mission of anchor institutions.

They gather us and, while binding us together in community, unleash creativity and possibilities for renewal that we could not have discovered acting alone, building alone, bowling alone, or going it alone.

I situate my voice within the context of my own village of origin with the hope of discussing the larger story of village transition and turbulence that we now face. Throughout the book, I will weave my story and voice into this effort to provide some analysis of the issues that need attention and the action that should follow.

I should note that this book assumed many forms since I first conceived it. Initially, I thought that a dispassionate, academic treatise would be the appropriate voice through which to articulate this case. Then, fearing that an excessively academic voice would be quickly ignored, I began rewriting in a style that was more terse and similar to a strategic plan or blueprint. Boring! Even I could not stand to reread it. It was like some of my earlier writings—once you put it down, you couldn't pick it up again. Finally, I decided that the method and style must convey a more personal dimension, a story in which I have "skin" invested. So I decided to write in a more conversational, autobiographical style to convey that there is much at stake and everyone needs to be brought into the conversation. I try to draw upon academic resources and data when necessary. After all, our analysis and plans for action must be grounded in reality. But it is important to preserve the human dimension of this crisis. And as a person of faith, I also pay attention to the spiritual or divine dimension of the solution. Since I am a minister and aspire to be one of what James Weldon Johnson called "God's trombones," as a partial tribute to Dr. Johnson, I decided to include the sermon that inspired the book.

THE AUTOBIOGRAPHY OF A VILLAGE

I was born into an extraordinary extended family network within the kind of "old-fashioned" village that was common throughout America during the 1940s, '50s and '60s, back when there were more real neighborhoods. Indeed, during and after the Great Depression, the steady migration of black people from the south to the north accelerated. With job opportunities opened by the wars in Europe and Korea, black people began to make strides in the economy and culture of America. I watched all of this as a child, a child of Mississippi migrants who found their way to the broad-shouldered city of Chicago. After years on Chicago's southside near 47th Street, years of smelling the nearby stockyards and watching the construction of the world's largest housing project (Robert Taylor Homes), my grandmother, Martha, and her twin sister, Mary, purchased a pair of two-story wood-frame houses next door to each other in the far southside neighborhood of Morgan Park. We lived on 118th and Watkins, one block from the city boundary on the south and one block west of Vincennes Avenue, the dividing line between white and black Chicago in our neighborhood. How different could this urban world have been from the small towns and farms they left behind in places called Clarksdale, Grenada, Watervalley, Holly Springs, and Battle, Mississippi?

The neighborhood was referred to as "the Jungle" because of its lush trees and thick green foliage. There were two amazing things about that little neighborhood. First, it had a marsh area that we called "the swamp." Today, a large industrial plant sits on that land and a few homes on my old block remain. As kids, we loved the swamp because we could catch tadpoles and other forms of life that had no business thriving on the southside of Chicago. But, second, my grandmother cleared an empty lot and planted a garden next to our house. I could write an entire story about a grandma, a garden, and a ghetto. There she planted corn, tomatoes, greens, onions, peppers, and green beans. I used to help her in the garden and marvel at how she could grow this "country stuff" right here in the city. (Now, more urban neighborhoods are discovering the wisdom of planting gardens in the 'hood.) As kids, we built tree houses, played hopscotch in the street, raced bicycles, and watched the neighborhood teenaged boys race cars along 119th Street, which we affectionately called "the strip."

In our extended family, most of the men were married and divorce was a rare and terrifying word. As some of the couples told me, "Look, we survived Jim Crow and sharecropping in the South, and we've survived poverty and racism Chicago-style, we're not about to let anything destroy our families now." They all went to church, they all worked hard, and enjoyed good relations with Jews, Italians, Irish, Eastern Europeans, and the few Mexican families with whom they interacted. I recall that our greatest tensions were with members of the Polish community. Remember, this was Chicago and that meant that the melting pot was brewing during the post–World War II years.

Our household always felt crowded. Two of Grandma Martha McCann's six sons and two daughters (one of them my mother) plus my father all lived together in a dynamic working unit. Nearly every day one or more of my other uncles came by to visit or eat. That's six adults, all of whom worked and pooled their resources. My dad worked over thirty-five years at the Campbell Soup Company plant on Chicago's westside. Living for a few years in Grandma's house, my parents saved money for a down payment for our first house miles away in the Mt. Vernon community, a community where we were one of the first black families.

Because Grandma was a church mother and home missionary at the St. Paul Church of God in Christ, she utilized her consummate culinary skills to do ministry throughout the city. I can still recall my three brothers and me being loaded into the backseat of our rickety 1956 green-and-white Chevy to drive into the "inner city," delivering pots of collard greens and corn bread. We hated having to ride that far in a nonair-conditioned car (except for the holes in the floorboard) in Chicago's summer heat to deliver a hot pot of greens, despite the award of a Tastee-Freez soft ice cream on the way home. But we always felt gratified by the shouts of joy that met my grandmother's arrival with the greens and a prayer for the family. We observed the little kids who seemed to live in squalor and despair in these ghetto buildings that were called tenements, buildings our family had left behind just years earlier. Grandma did not forget the people she left there. Now she had a garden and she could give them something they could not provide for themselves—fresh produce. She used to comment on how this was the first generation of black people who had no land, lost touch with the therapy of gardening, and who were forced to eat vegetables packed in aluminum cans.

In our household, before we owned a television set and before we discovered the world of theaters and movies, we had a set of encyclopedias and an illustrated Bible commentary to feed our imaginations. When we were bored, if weather permitted we went out to imitate the Chicago Bears, preferably in the dead of winter with plenty of snow on the ground. In the spring, we went out to catch tadpoles, race our bicycles along the city streets, build and retreat to our tree houses, and watch the "big boys" pitch pennies on the sidewalk. We heard women in the neighborhood discuss where they could find good bargains on children's clothes, and we heard the men discuss (or, rather, argue about) Martin Luther King's residing in a slum apartment on the westside of Chicago or Cassius Clay's (later Muhammad Ali) next fight. Nearly everyone attended church but few people drove as far as we did to worship in my parents' old neighborhood on the southside of the city.

The most vivid memory of my young life in the Jungle occurred the day a group of boys from outside our neighborhood showed up with a friend to visit a local girl. Several of the local boys gathered to prevent the visit and to end the relationship. As the voices of both groups of boys escalated, neighbors gathered on their porches or behind closed curtains to observe the muscle-bound urban gladiators. Suddenly, before a blow was thrown, my grandma, a church lady, ran into the street with her apron flowing and stood in between these gangsters. She began talking to them and reminding them that she knew their mothers and had fed many of them from her little garden. She asked, "How would your mother feel if she heard that one of you was shot over nothing? I had sons in the army who were shot, and there's nothing like a mother hearing those words. You think about that." Amazingly, these tough boys from the 'hood looked at her, looked at each other, backed away, and walked away, perhaps to do battle another day.

Another memory that informs my perspective goes back to my grandma's house, which had a very southern-style front porch. During the summer we screened it in so we could sit and sleep all night, seeking relief from the relentless Chicago heat. But during the day Grandma's friends, "the church ladies," would come over to visit and break bread. At the same time, my uncles' friends, affectionately called the "wine-ohs," also gathered for the fried chicken, yams, collard greens, and peach cobbler. Sometimes all of them would gather on the porch at the same time. Oh, the sights, sounds, and aromas! Guys who reeked of cheap wine and who talked too much and too loud sat next to these "praying women of the church" who were heavily perfumed and decked out in starched white dresses and nurses' shoes. It was wonderful—a zone where everyone could gather, break bread, and feel accepted. It was the beloved village.

Grandma was the virtual pastor of a house church that was far more inclusive than the St. Paul Church where we gathered two or three times per week. Taken together, her home visits to the infirm, her street courage with the homeboys, and her hospitality to saints and sinners alike demonstrated to me, a little kid, the power and the surprising possibilities that lurked within the religion of Jesus.

One moral leader intervened and made a difference. One woman acted with integrity and moral authority to benefit the entire village. I lived with her and watched her example until she died in August 1973. This book is inspired, in large measure, from watching her life, eating her collard greens, and listening to her wisdom.

NAMING OUR PAIN

I have had the privilege of expressing my vocational aspirations as a teacher, a hospital chaplain, an ordained minister, a seminary president, a foundation program officer, and a radio commentator. All of the threads of my identity inform the perspectives and positions I present. Of course, this is the case for everyone who writes but, unfortunately, we rarely learn much about the "rooted-ness" or social location of most writers and leaders. Feminists and scholars of color have critiqued the tradition that encouraged Anglo and European males to regard their voices and experience as the universal human norm. All other cultures and peoples were expected either to conform to that norm or explain why they did not. Thanks to those critiques, this practice is changing rapidly. Indeed, those of us in the academy now feel greater responsibility and external pressure to identify the sources of our perspective and authority. Ultimately, such honesty could lead to greater humility by all who wish to offer and to embrace proposals for how the human family may live peacefully with justice.

Looking into black communities scattered across America with the eyes of my grandmother, I feel pain. I also feel lots of hope. But let me stay with the pain, her pain, for a moment. Indeed, I think that one of the reasons many village leaders fail to connect with the community is, in the words of a Carly Simon song (and popular pain-relief commercial), they "haven't got time for the pain." There are times when we should study the pain, and times when we should share and feel the pain. Then there are times we should mobilize to end the pain. *But leaders who are unaware of, or uncomfortable with engaging and addressing, the pain of the people are unlikely to mobilize the power of the people.* Underneath our pain lays our power. But someone must name our pain and guide us through the common pains and the occasional deeper traumas of human existence.

The African American communities that I know best are facing serious challenges. So are non-African American communities. America is a nation of villages, of neighborhoods and larger groupings, and many of them are in crisis. Many black families are in distress and crisis, as are many white and Hispanic families. We are a hurting multitude. Increasing numbers of black students are not taking advantage of the opportunity of education. So are many white and Hispanic American youth, who fail to see the importance of academic excellence in the fields of science and math. America is a nation divided and in turmoil. We are red states and blue states and the public rhetoric of our most visible politicians and of our invisible but very audible radio talk-show hosts suggests that the culture wars cannot be reconciled. All of this at a time when a "global war against terror" centered in Iraq is unfolding on the global stage where America is a key player. The world needs strong moral leadership, but our national leaders continue to miss opportunities to provide it. The stakes are too high for apathy and for amateurs. By virtue of being the only remaining international superpower (for now), America has enormous responsibilities (and possibilities) that must be carefully and thoughtfully dispatched if we are to see any hope for fostering a global community among the community of nations.

Clearly, there are multiple spheres of crisis and challenge. I'd like to be attentive to all of them but, within the confines of a small book, I recognize that humility and realism must guide the choices I make. As Ralph Ellison once commented, "Trying to deal with the Negro problem apart from dealing with America's problem is like trying to do brain surgery with a switchblade."[3] Heeding Ellison, I will attempt to speak directly to the crisis within African American villages. This makes sense because most of the black population is now urbanized and, unfortunately, those urban centers are highly segregated by race and class. In response to the occasionally asked question, What is the black community today? I respond: wherever people of African descent are in the majority, whether by choice or circumstance, and they identify with the historical struggle for freedom, that is a black village. But while focusing on black communities and experiences, I'd like to peer further and more deeply into those dimensions of crisis that African Americans share with other communities. Again, the big conversation is about common ground. Some challenges are distinctive to the black community but most are not. And I would argue that our shared, common ground must become the basis for collective action on behalf of the larger public good. Indeed, whatever common ground we can find or claim in this troubled time is a high moral achievement.

This book could focus on issues pertaining to personal responsibility and the many things that individuals can and must do to improve their lot and to build healthier communities. Or this book could focus on the need for large sectors and structures like the economy or government to change in order to help people live better. Both issues are important and will certainly be acknowledged here. But there are already truckloads of good books that address both those dimensions of this struggle. Instead, I focus on the middle ground between individuals and social structures, the realm we refer to as "civil society" and its "mediating institutions." Mediating institutions stand between individuals and the market or government institutions. They are the people's networks of support and vehicles for social change. I'm calling them the "anchor institutions" because they are the creations and cultural products of courageous black mothers and fathers that have anchored black being, black identity, and black dignity amidst the horrors of history.

ENDURING INSTITUTIONS

Since I make the case for crisis within the anchor institutions in the black community with an eye toward how those institutions may be transformed, it is important to think about the characteristics of enduring institutions. Each of the anchors I discuss has endured precisely because they possess certain characteristics. And in order to sustain best practices and eliminate unproductive ones, organization leaders and their governors should be attentive to these strengths and weaknesses.

In a fascinating 2005 report titled "The World's Most Enduring Institutions," the organizational development and management consulting firm Booz Allen Hamilton identify the world's ten most enduring institutions of the twentieth and twenty-first centuries, based upon the analysis of leading experts. Their analysis includes institutions within the arts, entertainment, business, government, nonprofits, and academia "that have remained market leaders over a relatively long period of time, despite significant changes in their operating environments."[4] Their specific criteria or determinants included:

> *Innovative capabilities.* The capacity to create and modify strategies based on market opportunities and threats.
>
> *Governance and leadership.* A leadership structure and senior management team that promote an organization-wide commitment to enterprise resilience.
>
> *Information flow.* A continual flow of information regarding an organization's operations and markets that is evaluated by senior management in making strategic decisions.
>
> *Culture and values.* A working environment in which the adaptive qualities required for enterprise resilience are cultivated.

Adaptive response. The ability to withstand operational disruptions, market risks, and other threats without significantly compromising an organization's effectiveness.

Risk structure. A system for managing risk that doesn't encumber or limit an organization's operations.

Legitimacy. The undisputed, withstanding credibility of an organization within its market.

These criteria will be relevant to our assessment of why some of our anchor institutions appear to have lost touch with their constituents, and how they can regain their standing.

I want to focus here on three institutions that have played a heroic role in serving black communities in the past. Of course, every ethnic community has these same institutions. What's important is that these are institutions that African Americans control and for which they set the agenda, determine priorities, and pursue solutions with the necessary or available energy and resources. They are the church, the family, and the school. If the potential and power of just these institutions were properly aligned and mobilized, no matter who occupies the White House and no matter what Wall Street is up (or down) to, African Americans could make the lives of their children significantly better. This really is the power of the people. This is what we can decide, what we can do while other institutions and resources are sorting out their priorities and, we hope, standing and working in solidarity with us in this heroic human endeavor.

By focusing in this way on these three anchor institutions, I make a deliberate choice not to highlight the public sector or government, and the market sector of private capitalist activity. Of course, these sectors are vitally important and to a large extent determine the life prospects and opportunities for many people. But other worthy books deal with this subject matter far better than I could.

In the pages that follow, I discuss the crisis in each institutional sector—the familial, religious, and educational—and at the end, lay out more specifics on a call to strategic action. I organize the chapters in the following way. First, I begin with a suggestive story, a kind of *parable* that points to the larger crisis behind the story. Second, I provide a short list of *"what every educated person should know"* about this particular institution. I hope that this will go a long way toward helping black youth to understand more of their history and their responsibility for sustaining that history. Also, it will help non-African Americans to appreciate what is important about the black experience in America. Third, I outline *"what's wrong"* that needs fixing. And finally, I provide a brief look at *"what's right"* that should be preserved and provides the foundation for next steps and corrective interventions. These include the assets, promising practices, and leaders that hold great promise for the future, if and only if, they change their *modus operandi*. It is that change of style and heart and agenda that I address in the final chapter. As noted earlier, I include a sermon based on my favorite biblical story. I hope that the lessons that emerge from that story will illustrate how the smaller, local dramas unfolding in all of our communities viewed from a wide angle lens can point to exciting possibilities that unleash hope for the least advantaged members of our village.

One other note about my choice of racial identification language. I use the terms *black* and *African American* interchangeably as they are now commonly used. However, I understand the designation "black" is more inclusive of people of African ancestry who live throughout the African diaspora. By contrast, "African American" as a label that has rapidly entered the rhetorical mainstream, refers more specifically to the ensemble of histories, experiences, and identities of Africans who reside in the United States. This is an important distinction as we strive to respect the diversity of the "black experience" and avoid making unfounded claims predicated on monolithic assumptions.

This book issues an invitation, even a *call,* to strategic action (for those who like or need to be "called" to things). There are things that all of us can do to reverse the decline of families and child well-being, the erosion of moral authority in churches, and the moral drift in many schools and colleges.

In my judgment, the things that need doing in our time should be preceded by an intermediate action agenda. That agenda includes a few *rituals of personal and village renewal* (I elaborate on those rituals in my conclusion). One of the most important and potentially controversial rituals is the practice of holding each other accountable for doing what is needed. Here's a clue about the kind of simple action available to all of us that could begin to make a difference. *Every African American and all of our allies could devote just thirty minutes every week to the village-renewal agenda.* How that time would be spent would vary. I would suggest prayer, meditation, study, or actual service aimed at fostering a collective sense of "exodus," of moving out of bondage together. That is a place to start. But my hope is that it would become the baseline action for a journey that might demand a bit more from all of us. That thirty minutes could expand into many hours, days, and perhaps a lifetime of mentoring, volunteerism, giving and sharing resources, holding leaders accountable, and building the beloved community. But thirty minutes is a good place to start. It would be that developmental first step on a journey of a thousand miles.

Here's one other practical note: the rituals of renewal process will be centered around the agency of young people, generally those twenty-five years old and younger, similar to the civil rights movement. Armed with their ubiquitous cell phones and wireless technology, and animated by the hip-hop virtue of "keeping it real," young people could play a critical role in helping to renew a sense of village accountability and mobility. What might it do for a local pastor, or parent, or school teacher to receive a weekly or monthly call from a student who respectfully but persistently asks, "Yo, Rev, how are you doing this week with your village-renewal assignment? And how can we help you get back on track?" or, "Thank you for doing this. It means a lot to me and my generation. And we will honor you long after you're gone." But recruiting these young people will require the cooperation of school educators and officials and some resources from the philanthropic community. These are components of a vision and plan I will sketch in the final chapter.

If we perform these rituals and join this conversation, we could make a major step toward giving all of our children, including the children far from American shores, the gift of possibility.

SHOCK DOCS DON'T WORK

I've noticed that many authors who call attention to problems in the village do so by prefacing and sprinkling their concerns with long lists of depressing and "shocking" statistics. You have seen these documents. I call them "shock docs." They earnestly and passionately make the case for national concern about—well, pick an issue: youth violence, HIV-AIDS among black women, the "down-low" phenomenon among black men, the swelling prison population, kids orphaned by crack-addicted parents, racial profiling, and so on. I've written my share of shock docs and I now see that they are of limited value. The village has become numb to the pinch of the data. You can no longer shock us enough to get involved. We're not listening, we're "not feeling" the numbers anymore. We all know things are bad. So what? Or worse, we think, "Whatever!" We're a bit like the fictional Frankenstein's inert body that his doctor-creator repeatedly jolted with high volts of electricity to no avail. We will not be moved. But recall that in Mary Shelley's novel, the creature did finally move. The power to quicken dead flesh came from a bolt of lightning, from divine electricity. And once he began to move, he began to express his pain and alienation. And he began to express his rage over rejection. We know him now for his rage and bad behavior, not for the tender heart that lay underneath the anger. Expressing his existential predicament, he says to his creator,

> I am malicious because I am miserable. Am I not shunned and hated by all mankind? You, my creator, would tear me to pieces and triumph; remember that and tell me why I should pity man more than he pities me. I will revenge my injuries; if I cannot inspire love, I will cause fear. . . .[5]

In making the point about the limited effectiveness of "shock docs" to stimulate our overloaded sensory systems, I do not wish to suggest that data and stories are not important. Indeed, I am heeding the advice of George Orwell who said, "We have now sunk to such a depth, that sometimes the first duty of intelligent men (and women) is restatement of the obvious." On occasion I will cite statistics and use anecdotes to help place what appears to be obvious in sharper perspective.

RESPONSES TO THE EMERGING CRISIS

A long and rich literature exists on the history of African American debates about, and responses to the African American place in American society. My focus, however, is on what has been said about conditions that only emerged during the post–civil rights movement or the 1970s and thereafter. As years passed and village leaders focused on the legal, political, and symbolic battles in the public square, few seemed to notice that something was awry within the African American village itself. Village leaders in the 1970s, successors to Dr. King, rightly assumed that African Americans would continue to follow King's exhortations to "struggle with dignity, unity, and hopefulness."[6] But a new mood and a different attitude about America was spreading throughout the village, a mood that might threaten the very gains made following the civil rights movement. It was not the defiant and suspicious mood that Malcolm X had expressed in eloquent contrast to King. Malcolm, of course, had adopted this social lens from his predecessors Marcus Garvey, Elijah Muhammad, and his own father, the black nationalist Reverend Earl Little. Nor was that mood guided by the Black Panthers and other militants determined to wrest respect and possibly reparations from a hostile nation.

No, this was something new and something very threatening because of its growing influence. It was the descent of a more profound despair than the sons and daughters of Booker T. Washington and W. E. B. Du Bois had encountered before. The old, familiar desperation of people living on the margins of society seemed to find new depths. The new desperation found crack-addicted mothers neglecting and abusing their innocent, dependent children. And the old and familiar rage that occasionally found expression by joining a grassroots political movement for change seemed to find expression through increasingly gruesome forms of homicide, street violence and suicide. And, tragically, society with all of its prosperity and collective genius could not find ways to transform these trends into second chances.

Alongside the noteworthy material and symbolic progress that black citizens made in the post–civil rights era was the disturbing reality of a large (25 percent) segment of the black population that seemed mired in poverty.[7] Many of the poor youth also showed signs of a frustrated rage that could find no conventional or productive means of expression. Consequently, many poor, black communities ceased to be villages of care and accountability and degraded into corridors of lawlessness, violence, addiction, and self-hatred. Although "faith and family" continued to be important values for most African Americans, a growing percentage of people seemed to dismiss them. Worse yet, they seemed to embrace an alternative set of values (uncritical assimilation, individualism, materialism, violence, disinterest in educational excellence, and so forth) that would, in time, threaten to erode past progress and sentence countless young people to lives of misery, violence, and despair.

Several black social observers (often called "neoconservatives"), such as Shelby Steele, Glenn Loury, and John McWhorter, called attention to these issues, emphasizing that culture is as important as economic changes and urged blacks do more to ameliorate their own situation.[8] Standing in the self-help tradition established by Booker T. Washington, they have insisted that blacks look less for government-sponsored solutions and work to retrieve the eroded communal strengths and personal resources that enabled their ancestors to thrive amidst even harsher social conditions. Other observers, (sometimes called "liberals") such as Cornel West, Lani Guinier, and Michael Eric Dyson have often construed these analyses to suggest that the black community should "let the government and nation off the hook" while blacks struggle heroically to repair neighborhoods and cultures that others helped to compromise and corrupt. Unfortunately, these conversations do little to move the community closer to the kind of reconciliation that I think is needed to forge a united and coordinated mobilization on behalf of the most vulnerable members of our community.

Attempting to avoid such politically counterproductive debates, social scientists like William Julius Wilson sought to emphasize that structural changes in the economy of the nation, not the personal irresponsibility of any particular group, caused the material and resulting cultural deterioration in urban poor communities that occurred during the mid-1970s.[9] Well-paying, low-skill jobs in the manufacturing sector were disappearing and in their place came low-skill, low-paying jobs in the service sector, often many miles outside the city. And increasingly, the better jobs required education and technical skills that were virtually out of reach for most of the urban poor. America had ceased to be a place of opportunity, upward mobility, and personal improvement. Moreover, America seemed to be a nation that tolerated the death of childhood innocence, even the death of children themselves. The chilling portrait of inner-city schools depicted in Jonathan Kozol's 1967 classic, *Death at an Early Age*,[10] continues to haunt many people today.

Kozol's heartrending account of life in Boston public schools depicts the acute symptoms of a nation's failure to invest in the education and opportunities of its poorest children.

Death at an Early Age

Corresponding to the lack of jobs and the decline of hope in urban communities, a variety of negative alternatives rose to fill the vacuum. Among them were the street organizations (that is, gangs) like the Crips and Bloods that offered work, income, status, and protection to cooperative youth. As these groups grew in influence, they began to displace the icons of traditional neighborhood civic life like the Boy Scouts, Girl Scouts, church youth programs, and athletic leagues. I came of age in Chicago at a time when the Blackstone Rangers were boldly "drafting" new members. It was a crazy time because the U.S. military was drafting young people to serve in Vietnam. I heard mothers at church say that they'd rather have their sons serve in the jungles of Southeast Asia than be churned into the urban gang and crime subculture. To many people, both were tragic options. I managed to navigate between them and the church culture that demanded ever more of our time.

As these groups participated in the distribution of narcotics and acquired weapons that exceeded the firepower of local police, local communities were held hostage to a new reign of violence. As neighborhood elders and children huddled behind closed doors and found entertainment in excessive television viewing and consuming unhealthy, cheap junk food, they yielded the streets to the young gangsters. Ironically, collateral damage resulted, as those reasonable efforts to be safe fueled an epidemic of obesity-related health crises that generated a new public-health burden for the village and the state.

Scholars began to call attention to a crisis among young men who were increasingly susceptible to the depredations of street life. Some began to refer to these young brothers as an "endangered species." The evening news seemed full of images of these young men being hauled away in handcuffs, shirtless and defiant of all conventional norms. They were fully prepared to go to prison where they could "get big" (build muscular bodies and grow tough through prison fights). Many youths also adopted the "gangster" styles and poses in partial imitation of the movie images of the mafia—except these young brothers failed to imitate the codes of restraint and respect for the innocent observed by most organized mobsters. Even their postrelease behavior established models of fashion for youth who had no desire to pursue a lawless lifestyle. The sagging, baggy pants that white, Asian, Hispanic, and black youth proudly displayed mimicked the sagging trousers of inmates whose belts were confiscated upon entry to prison in order to discourage suicide attempts. Young kids were adopting local gangsters and criminals as their role models, yet few leaders at the time seemed to regard this as a developing national crisis and a threat to the future of African American villages.

What Kozol's book did to illumine the ecology of urban, poor schools in the '70s, a new generation of young black filmmakers accomplished cinematically in the 1990s and thereafter in films such as *New Jack City, Boys 'n' the Hood, Menace 2 Society*, and *Do the Right Thing*. More recently, the delightful and disturbing film *Akeelah and the Bee* portrays with piercing urgency the need to repair and rebuild local schools and the families that rely upon them.

But there has been another voice "crying in the wilderness" on behalf of the kids who die at an early age. And her argument is simple: if adults act, kids will live. Sounds like my grandmother—but it isn't. The speaker is Marion Wright Edelman, founder of the Children's Defense Fund:

> We are at risk of letting our children drown in the bathwater of American materialism, greed, and violence. We must regain

our spiritual bearings and roots and help America recover hers before millions more children—Black, Brown, and white, poor, middle-class, and rich—self-destruct or grow up thinking life is about acquiring rather than sharing, selfishness rather than sacrifice, and material rather than spiritual wealth. And even as so much progress has been made, for too many Black children and families, progress is not coming quickly enough or at all.

Consider these recent statistics about Black children living in the U.S.

Every five seconds during the school day, a Black public school student is suspended, and

Every forty-six seconds during the school day, a Black high school student drops out.

Every minute, a Black child is arrested and a Black baby is born to an unmarried mother.

Every three minutes, a Black child is born into poverty.

Every hour, a Black baby dies.

Every four hours a Black child or youth under twenty dies from an accident, and

Every five hours, one is a homicide victim. And

Every day, a Black young person under twenty-five dies from HIV infection and

A Black child or youth under twenty commits suicide.[11]

We must learn to reweave the rich fabric of community for our children and to re-instill the values and sense of purpose our elders and mentors have always embraced. . . . A massive new movement must well up from every nook, cranny, and place in our community involving millions of parents; religious, civic, educational, business, and political leaders; and youths themselves.[12]

I will say more of her work and her vision later, but I will say here that Mrs. Edelman may very well be the most overlooked but redemptive visionary restoring hope and speaking truth to black communities and the nation since the departure of Dr. King.

The Strange Silence

As increasing numbers of young people resorted to criminal means of support and recreation, community leaders began to see that these men would not be available candidates for marriage or for rearing the children they sired. Men and women, preachers, civil rights leaders, and professors seemed to reconcile themselves to the fact that black women, despite playing by the rules, would probably never be married, would rear children without a man, and/or would engage in the "love games" some people play when they see no alternatives for fulfilling their longings for companionship.

As statistics on the rising rates of nonmarital black births escalated year by year, few leaders treated this as a reason to revise dramatically the priorities on their agendas. One would think that with mounting empirical evidence, artistic presentations, and anecdotes about our "lost generation" of youth and the "endangered species" of young black men, influential leaders would have stopped doing business as usual to understand and halt the madness. Surely, mature, morally serious people would want to explore the potential long-term ramifications of these dramatic changes in our anchor institutions—families, churches, and schools. Indeed, the challenges facing these village youth (and adults) would seem to constitute sufficient reason to convene a series of leadership summits to grapple with this apparent internal decay. Why weren't the most influential leaders in the community speaking with urgency and impatience about this emerging tragedy? Why didn't these themes become the body of the annual addresses of major civil rights leaders and denominational presidents and bishops rather than passing, perfunctory references? Why didn't the DJs (disc jockeys) turn up the volume and rage through the airwaves asking tough questions about where we were headed? Why didn't the pulpits of America thunder with words of love and moral instruction for prodigal children who had lost their way?

To be fair, there were a few noteworthy efforts to convene and converse, such as a 1993 summit meeting at the Baltimore headquarters of the NAACP. Near the end of the two-day convocation, the organization's president, Reverend Benjamin Chavis, appointed three task forces on politics, economics, and religion, each charged with meeting and developing an action plan for the entire group's review and debate. I served on the religious task force, along with denominational presidents, bishops, megachurch pastors, Jesse Jackson, and Louis Farrakhan. It was an exciting and promising process, but one that soon expended its energy, never to be heard from again. In the end, our work lacked an urgent case statement, a strategic focus and direction, and the accountability that might have kept us moving toward a goal. Without these elements, people soon lose interest in projects fueled solely by boundless idealism.

Despite occasional efforts to convene organizational leaders to deliberate about the future of the village, there has not been a sustained and visible strategic effort with specific institutional assignments that might garner broad support from within and outside the community. Summit meetings aimed at building coalitions and developing working collaborative relationships only make sense to those who are aware of their limitations and conscious of the potential good that might result from cooperation with others, including competitors. Most village leaders have devoted themselves understandably to working within a single paradigm, the political or the economic or the faith-based, with little attention to alternative and multidimensional paradigms. This is understandable for busy leaders who have too much on the plate already. By focusing, one has a chance of achieving some results and making an impact. This enables us to sleep better at night. But the downside of that approach is that it can blind us to the actual complexity of any given issue. And for leaders who have been focused on social justice and public advocacy, it may obscure the capacity to perceive distress in the realm of family stability, quality interpersonal relationships, and child well-being. For instance, Representative Jesse Jackson Jr. says this on the topic of liberation and struggle:

> Many avenues of struggle are necessary for our liberation as a people and to become full citizens of the United States—religious and moral values, education, access to capital and economic development. None, however, is more important than the full use of our potential political power. Why politics? Political rights are protective of all other rights. There is no other single act than full political participation—registering, voting, educating, and involving ourselves in the public policy debates and issues that confront us every day—that would make as much difference in our material lives as politics.[13]

Of course, Mr. Jackson is a politician (and an intellectual child of Du Bois) and makes a case for the primacy of his field or approach to village liberation. But, remarkably, Jackson acknowledges the "many avenues of struggle" that are necessary and decides to marginalize the others by elevating his preferred strategy of uplift. And although there is much good that may be accomplished for children (and much harm that can be prevented) through political processes and behavior, many of the most important things kids need are not subject to the political process.

The love, nurture, mentoring, and discipline that children require are in the hands of parents and other steady and sturdy ordinary souls in the community. But can the village be mobilized to make these issues and goods a community priority? I'm ready for us to roll up our sleeves and begin the work of teaching, preaching, guiding, inspiring, encouraging, and reinforcing behavior associated with healthy relationships, marriages, and parenting. Yet, while our sleeves are rolled up, some of us should also devote attention to negotiating opportunities for the young people who try to take us up on all the good moral rhetoric. And a few of us will need to continue to protest to ensure that the nation never be permitted to ignore the continued existence of racism and classism. Also, this good and great nation must never permit hard-working people to do all the right things—get married, work hard, and care for their kids—and still slip further into poverty.

In reviewing the speeches and writings of many of these leaders, it is surprising that so little "high priority" and urgent attention has been given to concrete, specific proposals for reviving the very institutions, values, and practices that facilitated black progress in earlier decades. Everyone noticed problems in families, churches, and schools, but exceedingly few thinkers applied their practical wisdom to effecting a change of direction. In fact, I would argue that, as a group, village leaders have not been sufficiently specific and strategic about coordinating, sequencing, funding, and continually revising their efforts to ensure a better future for our children. Further, in order to restore hope to African American communities, these leaders should now initiate a village renewal process that begins with convening a community-wide conversation about the future of our children, the institutions that form them, and the practical steps, values, practices, and organizations that are needed for our renewal.

My purpose is not to question the sincerity, integrity, or wisdom of any existing leaders or scholars, unless that is justified. Carter G. Woodson, commenting on his book that was certain to ruffle feathers, *The Mis-education of the Negro*, put it this way: "This book, then, is not intended as a broadside against any particular person or class, but it is given as a corrective for methods which have not produced satisfactory results."[14]

It would be easy to note the shortcomings in the approaches of other leaders and to scoff at them for not being omniscient. For that matter, it would be easy to focus on my own shortcomings and not bother with this larger project. Instead, I'd like to acknowledge and celebrate their service and contributions. Their good and faithful service is responsible for the achievements and progress accomplished to date. But I'd like to invite and challenge these and other emerging leaders to consider a different approach to addressing and solving our village problems. *We do not have the luxury of leaders who are not strategic and capable of leading change and producing results.*

I prefer to call attention to the promising starts and elements of a future agenda that are already on the table. I can best do this by examining a few of the pronouncements and plans of Du Bois's intellectual protégés. This genre of discourse (spoken and written) could be characterized as the African American "improvement industry." In its written form, the most serious articulations of village uplift have been produced by some of America's best-known public intellectuals—people like Cornel West, Henry Louis Gates Jr., bell hooks, Julianne Malveaux, Nell Painter, Peter Paris, Michael Eric Dyson, and many others. A more popular version of the same project has been produced by radio and television personality Tavis Smiley (formerly of Black Entertainment Television [BET], and National Public Radio), who has published a collection of essays on how to improve the village. In audio-visual form, Tavis Smiley and radio DJ Tom Joyner have hosted an annual "State of the Black Union" conference in which twenty-five or more thought-leaders comment on the theme of the day. Themes have included the black political agenda, economics, education, and, in 2004, "Strengthening the Black Family." The focus on family issues will be pertinent to much of what I wish to set forth later.

THE IMPROVEMENT INDUSTRY

The "improvement industry" is extensive. Its practitioners include grassroots leaders, pastors, community activists, television personalities and politicians who may write a book. The most visible members of the industry are motivational speakers, many of them clergy, or present themselves as quasi-spiritual leaders on a mission from God. They tend to be more devoted to the market and its rewards than other mission-centered servant leaders. But most of the advocates for human betterment are unsung, unknown heroes and heroines who will never be rich and famous.

I acknowledge this class and vocational divide and try to be sensitive to those grassroots voices that are out there. My grandmother was one of them. At the same time, I'd like to invite heightened attention to those thought leaders and change agents who have produced books or other texts that provide us with the benefit of studying their visions and plans carefully, a more daunting task when we have to rely solely upon the oral pronouncements of these leaders.

Speaking of African American thought leaders, I must acknowledge the extraordinary influence and accomplishments of television host and quasi-pastoral counselor, Oprah Winfrey. Perhaps more than any other African American alive today, she has become an icon who has deep roots in the black community and transcends those roots to relate to every segment of the society. With the possible exception of Bill Cosby, no other African American has been viewed as widely in American households and respected for their intellectual and cultural contributions to the mainstream of popular culture. Although Ms. Winfrey has not yet written a book that sketches a plan for community renewal, through her numerous publications and sponsorship of other helping professionals, her impact is felt in the larger human improvement industry.

I am interested in that subset of books that go beyond describing problems and/or analyzing them, but rather set forth practical proposals and agendas for action. Some authors are especially gifted at describing social problems and providing very important accounts of the situation at hand. Often, they provide accounts of the origins of the problem bolstered by statistical data to help us appreciate its magnitude, such as we see in Morehouse Research Institute director Obie Clayton Jr.'s fine volume, *An American Dilemma Revisited*.[15]

By contrast, other authors are keen at providing incisive analysis of social problems. They build upon the descriptive, historical, narrative, and statistical framework of others. But their distinctive value is to help us understand the meaning of the data; that is, they move from "what is" to "what it means." The great ethicist Reinhold Niebuhr said that any effective ethical work must begin with an accurate description of what is going on (descriptive ethics precedes normative ethics). Or, in the words of his brother, theologian H. Richard Niebuhr, we should first ask, "What is God doing?" and then, "How shall we respond?" He wrote about this "ethics of responsibility" in his book *The Responsible Self*.[16] Perhaps the best-known example of analytic discourse is found in Du Bois's famous "two-ness" discussion of black identity. It goes beyond describing to looking below the surface:

> Here, then is the dilemma, and it is a puzzling one, I admit. No Negro who has given earnest thought to the situation of his people in America has failed, at some time in life, to find himself (or herself) at these crossroads; has failed to ask himself at some time; what, after all, am I? Am I an American or am I a Negro? Can I be both? Or is it my duty to cease to be a Negro as soon as possible and be an American? ... Here, it seems to me, is the reading of the riddle that puzzles so many of us. We are Americans, not only by birth and by citizenship, but by our political ideals, our language, our religion. Farther than that, our Americanism does not go. At that point, we are Negroes, members of a vast historic race that from the very dawn of creation has slept, but half awakening in the dark forests of its African fatherland. We are the first fruits of this new nation, the harbinger of that black tomorrow....
>
> One ever feels his twoness—an American, a Negro; two souls, two thoughts, two unreconciled strivings; two warring ideals in one dark body, whose dogged strength alone keeps it from being torn asunder.

> The history of the American Negro is the history of this strife—
> this longing to attain self-conscious manhood (personhood), to
> merge his double self into a better and truer self.[17]

The purpose of analysis is to help us to look beneath the surface
of reality and to understand underlying root causes and issues. But
there is another segment of the "advancement genre" that I refer to
as "moral agency literature" or black normative discourse. In the
field of ethics, "normative" refers to language about what "ought to
be." Black normative discourse is more prescriptive than its descriptive and analytic partners, but it depends upon them for its authenticity. Thus, some books describe problems, some analyze problems,
and others offer practical strategies and solutions to problems.

To illustrate the broad range of important texts in that third
category, I'd like to mention several that I have found to be compelling. I will sample from some but not all of them. My short list of
books that attempt to move beyond describing and analyzing the
crisis to providing practical and constructive responses includes
(in the order in which I discuss them):

> Tavis Smiley, ed., *How to Make Black America Better:*
> *Leading African Americans Speak Out.*
>
> John McWhorter, *Winning the Race: Beyond the Crisis*
> *in Black America.*
>
> Juan Williams, *Enough: The Phony Leaders, Dead-End*
> *Movements, and Culture of Failure That Are Undermin-*
> *ing Black America—and What We Can Do About It.*
>
> Jawanza Kunjufu, *Solutions for Black America.*
>
> Tavis Smiley, ed. *The Covenant with Black America.*

Although there are many other important and worthy books
that might be reviewed here,[18] I highlight these because they contain statements, testimonies, and proposals from a virtual "who's
who" of the current black leadership class.

The first observation that could be made about these texts is
their titles. The titles convey the importance but not the urgency

of the topic at hand. Consequently, they may not succeed in arousing the initial interest of a busy reading public. They state their mission and focus with admirable moral seriousness. Consider again the language we find there: "restoring hope," "the future of the race," "winning the race," "how to make black America better," "African American solutions to African American problems," and "a moral, political and economic imperative for the twenty-first century." Each assumes the need for practical moral wisdom about achieving transformation within the village. Each is forward looking and promises to provide strategic, practical insights for creating a better future. Each adopts a "big picture" perspective as opposed to a narrow, issue–based focus. Finally, with the exception of the McWhorter and Kunjufu books, each is a collection of essays, interviews, and speeches from a variety of voices, some prominent, some lesser known. Taken together, they express the state of "the conversation" in the African American village today. But, despite their insight and wisdom, when I read them against the background of our contemporary crisis, I find something missing.

How to Make Black America Better

Tavis Smiley's opening essay in *How to Make Black America Better* is noteworthy because he moves to a very practical set of exhortations on how to improve the group. He calls them "Ten Challenges to Black America." Writing like a benevolent big brother, he urges:

1. Think Black First, 100 Percent of the Time,
2. Look Past What Whites Are Doing to Us to See What We Are Doing to Ourselves,
3. Every Black American Should Put Family First,
4. Black Americans Must Consider the Consequences of Their Actions,
5. Every Black American Should See Him or Herself as Part of a Larger Black Community,

6. Every Black American Must Preserve His or Her Health—Physically, Emotionally, Psychologically, and Spiritually,

7. Every Black American Should Develop an Economic Plan,

8. Make Education the Number-One Priority for Every Black American,

9. Encourage the Black Church to Do More,

10. Every Black American Should Establish a Black American Legacy.[19]

Of course, this list resembles every other "black improvement checklist," including the Congressional Black Caucus agenda, the Million Man March agenda, and the agendas of nearly all the civil rights organizations. It is both interesting and promising that there is widespread consensus about the basic priorities for action among these organizations. I wish leaders would acknowledge this more and take the next logical step of talking more about collaboration, consolidation, and possibilities for improving efficiency and stewardship. It is unacceptable that these organizations do not achieve their maximum impact due to their separate and poorly coordinated labors.

Perhaps the most notable feature of Mr. Smiley's list is the "putting family first" component. As stated above, few leaders have made healthy relationships, marriage, and family life a central and explicit cause for collective action. The other thing I find interesting about the list is the absence of a major plank devoted to international linkages and placing the black struggle for justice into a global context. Such internationalism has become more prominent in African American organizations in recent years, fueled by various crises in African nations—genocide in Sudan, AIDS throughout the continent, famine and political conflict—as well as the occasional triumphs, such as the election of the first female head of state, President Ellen Johnson Sirleaf of Liberia. We should also credit the effective advocacy on behalf of Africa by Ambassador Andrew Young, Randall Robinson, and a host of advocacy organizations such as the African American Institute led by Mora McLean. And we should acknowledge that President George W. Bush appointed two African Americans—Colin Powell and Condolezza Rice—to serve as U.S. Secretary of State, representing all Americans in the global community.

Elsewhere in this book, in his essay "Leveraging Our Power," Earl Graves, editor of *Black Enterprise* magazine, offers a compelling call to action. Graves writes:

> There will be no further interest in our demand for moral justice until we command the significance that only economic power can engender. It is also clear that we must stop looking outside of ourselves—individually and collectively—for the leadership that will create that economic shift. Nobody's going to do it for us. We need to practice leadership on a daily basis as individuals. We need teachers, doctors, ministers, fund-raisers, business owners, and workers everywhere to practice leadership by acting for the good of their fellow African Americans wherever necessary.[20]

This is Graves's call to action, and commendably, he names the leadership and professional categories that must respond for effectiveness. Note, however, that two groups are missing: students or young people who are not yet accomplished professionals, and grassroots people, many of whom are employed part time. Then, sounding like a latter-day Booker T. Washington, Graves shifts into moral rhetoric or "moral agency" talk, the kind of speech that moves people to act.

> How does that translate into your day-to-day reality? The answers are really quite simple. If you are in a position to hire or promote people, look out for your own. Help them get where they deserve to be. That's leadership. If you are a minister, preach self-preservation and self-determination rather than simply exhorting the faithful to count on personal salvation in the next life. That's leadership. If you are a parent—a mother or a father—be the absolute best parent that you can be. That's leadership, possibly at its purest and most powerful. If you are on the board of directors of a company that isn't doing all it can to hire and promote African Americans, stand up and tell the board what they need

to do. If necessary, show them how to do it. Inform them that it makes good business sense to hire us, not because it's the right thing to do from a social perspective, but because it's the right thing to do from a business perspective. . . . Use your perspective, your experience, your guidance to improve the lives of other Blacks within your sphere of influence. That's leadership. If more of us lived our lives like that, no one would have to ask where our leaders of the future were going to come from. If more of us lived like that, the battle for economic parity along racial lines would be far closer to its conclusion.

If more of us lived like that, not only would Black America be better, all America would be better.[21]

Graves is a skilled public communicator and knows how to frame his case for the public. You can easily imagine his words as a powerful commencement address. But, despite the virtue of his call for leadership, especially framing good parenting as leadership "in its purest form," he issues the call without a strategy for holding his hearers accountable. This is symptomatic of where our best efforts continue to fall short. I want to push the discourse to the next level, to name the specific stewards of our anchor institutions, and pose strategies for how they could be held accountable for effective service.

Winning the Race

In his provocative *Winning the Race: Beyond the Crisis in Black America*, John McWhorter urges black people to cease taking comfort in, or defining their identity in terms of, past victimization. And he calls for a "new black leadership for new Negroes." McWhorter is often characterized as a neoconservative, but I think that we should not allow the labels to prevent a fair assessment of the ideas offered by any thinker.

McWhorter is transparent about the kind of leadership he'd like to see in his "Scorecard for Black Leadership." In it, he contrasts "Black Leader A" and "Black Leader B." Black Leader A "celebrates our victories" while Black Leader B "celebrates our victories only in parentheses under the impression that trumpeting our failures is more important because it lets whites know they are "on the hook,"[22] Leader A is also: "committed to eventually getting past race," "interested in cultural hybridity as evidence of progress," "identifies racism and discrimination after careful consideration," "interested in blacks succeeding in the system as it is and considers us capable of doing so," and finally, "considers the equation between alienation and black identity a problem."

By contrast, "Black Leader B" (and we can almost hear him calling the names of some of the old-guard Civil Rights leadership and clergy here) "is committed to delineating us as a race apart, seemingly hoping that whites and other races will blend together but blacks will remain a separate group since we were brought here against our will," "interested in cultural hybridity as evidence that whites "appropriate" blackness and sell it back to us," "identifies racism and discrimination as the cause of all statistical discrepancies between blacks and whites," "is interested in blacks succeeding in a system transformed by a revolution and considers us incapable of doing so otherwise," and "considers the equation between alienation and black identity a "wake up call" to a benighted white Establishment by a people "denied love" McWhorter declares that "black leaders and thinkers should be ranked on that scorecard. Some will prefer Black Leader B, but people of this kind will have no influence on the future of black America. No one ever got ahead by getting back."[23]

Apart from the somewhat haughty tone of Mr. McWhorter, who is comfortable declaring that some "people of this kind" are marginal to the process of village renewal, I am disturbed by the harsh dichotomy he seems to draw between these social and philosophical outlooks. If I read him correctly, he is uninterested in attempting to find common ground between them. I think that this view is shortsighted and plays into the culture wars and mean-spirited politics that now grip our nation.

Enough

Similar to McWhorter in his impatience with traditional black leadership, journalist Juan Williams agrees that contemporary leaders represent a decline from the noble leadership of the civil rights movement. Although the book is titled to trigger controversy and sell books—*Enough: The Phony Leaders, Dead-End Movements, and Culture of Failure That Are Undermining Black America—and What We Can Do About It*—his final chapter enumerates practical steps for remediation and repair.[24] He writes:

> Arriving at real solutions to help the poor get out of poverty is not hard as it seems. What is hard is getting the message out. It is especially hard when a deafening batch of shrill voices is shouting excuses for why the poor remain poor. . . .
>
> The good news is that there is a formula for getting out of poverty today. The magical steps begin with finishing high school, but finishing college is much better. Step number two is taking a job and holding it. Step number three is marrying after finishing school and while you have a job. And the final step to give yourself the best chance to avoid poverty is to have children only after you are twenty-one and married. This formula applies to black people and white people alike.[25]

Williams's book is a lively defense of Bill Cosby's message about parental and youthful irresponsibility that stands in counterpoint to Michael Eric Dyson's book on Cosby. Reading Dyson and Williams's books prompted me to imagine overhearing two rabbis argue vigorously over the proper interpretation and ethical application of a sacred text. But, at the end of the day, both brilliant authors leave me wanting just a bit more with respect to what must be done by whom, when, where, and how. We all know why this is critical.

Solutions for Black America

In a sparkling, but too brief, essay titled "Solutions for Black America," Afrocentric educator Jawanza Kunjufu begins by identifying the usual "problems and causes" of our social crisis before proceeding to a concluding chapter titled "Implementation/Models of Success."[26] To his credit, he includes family issues in his assessment of the problem noting (without citation) that "only 32 percent of African American children have fathers in the home. And the divorce rate in Black America is 66 percent."[27]

He recommends that the "Black Leadership Forum" emerge as the lead player in convening future gatherings of leaders in the community. The Forum is a venue where major civil rights and non-profit organization leaders convene regularly to share information, explore and implement collaborative projects usually aimed at the political and economic progress of African Americans. However, a member of the Forum whom I interviewed felt that in the past it had not focused on the topic of healthy relationships, marriages, and families, and probably would not do so given its focus on more political and civic issues. In my final chapter, I will nominate a different institution to serve as the convener of all institutions that are committed to changing the script and reversing the trend lines for the most disadvantaged people in our communities.

The Covenant with Black America

Without question, the most significant recent example of the black improvement genre is *The Covenant with Black America*, edited by Tavis Smiley. It is especially exciting to have witnessed (via C-SPAN) the evolution of the project as it emerged organically from town-hall meetings, community conversations, and nationally televised annual panels of experts. For several weeks, the book occupied the number one position on the *New York Times* nonfiction best-seller booklist. It contains ten chapters that set forth and analyze major challenges in black communities. They include:

1. Securing the Right to Healthcare and Well-Being
2. Establishing a System of Public Education in Which All Children Achieve at High Levels and Reach Their Full Potential
3. Correcting the System of Unequal Justice
4. Fostering Accountable Community-Centered Policing
5. Ensuring Broad Access to Affordable Neighborhoods That Connect to Opportunity
6. Claiming Our Democracy

Unlike many of its predecessors in the improvement industry that are long on describing and analyzing problems but short on conceptualizing actionable solutions, each chapter of Smiley's book begins with a framing essay and set of facts concerning the problem. Then the chapters unfold with user-friendly notes on "what the community can do," "what every individual can do now," and "what works now." Also, each chapter contains the urgent highlighted note: "Most of All: Hold all leaders and elected officials responsible and demand that they change current policy." In many ways it is a milestone text that I have urged people to read, debate, and act upon.

But, for all of its virtues, I think that the book has a few noteworthy shortcomings. First, it does not contain a chapter devoted solely to an analysis of the situation of healthy African American relationships, marriages, and families, and the steps that should be taken to repair what is broken. The admirable prioritizing of the family in Smiley's earlier essay, "How to Make Black America Better," is missing here. Many authors appear to assume that children are being reared in households where parents and guardians can and are providing what children need. They do not pause to ask, "What if the household in which our reader lives is in a state of conflict, even chaos? How should we reformulate our advice for the adults and children living under such circumstances?" In view of the difficult condition of so many black families it seems odd and unfortunate that the primary unit of socialization does not receive its own distinctive and discrete treatment. The personal zone of intimacy and commitment is one where many people, blacks and all others, are hurting but one that receives inadequate attention from most thought leaders.

Also, no one seems to apprehend the nexus between the personal and the public—that is, the connection between unhealthy relationships and dysfunctional families and the political apathy, bad economic decisions, and diminished educational aspirations that most black leaders bemoan. I often thought of this as Jesse Jackson and others recited the astounding statistics on the number of black people who are not registered to vote, along with the numbers who are registered but not casting votes. (Others have commented on the many votes that have been cast but gone uncounted in the two history-making presidential elections that began this millennium, so I need not say more.)

Second, by addressing their suggestions to individuals, the authors seem to reinforce the fallacy of an Enlightenment view of people as relatively detached agents motivated primarily by rational self-interest. Although that description may fit large numbers of affluent, educated black people, it has not been the experience for most contemporary working and poor people nor has it been part of the historical experience and narrative of the African American pursuit of freedom, justice, and opportunity. Indeed, the song by Sister Sledge captures the romanticized group solidarity and "fictive kinship" familiar to most blacks, as they sang, "We are family, I've got all my sisters with me." It is that wonderful sense of "all my sisters and me" that offers hope of overcoming the most destructive features of hyperindividualism and materialism that blacks have assimilated and recapitulated deep into their own cultures.

Third, the Covenant mentions "holding all leaders responsible for change" but immediately becomes timid by not venturing further to specify *how* such leaders should or might be held responsible. What if the leaders do not wish to take risks in acting on these ambitious and demanding issues? What should every community do in that case? Although the authors acknowledge the potential power of the community by citing "what works" in each chapter, they do not specify the ethical duties of community-based institutions that have the capacity to strengthen or harm African American civil society. Black clergy, churches, mosques, denominations, community organizations, nonprofit organizations, fraternities, and sororities are not challenged specifically as one might expect in the face of a great and growing crisis. Why let these community change agents off the hook so easily when many of them would be amenable to considering new approaches to old problems?

Finally, the book is thinner than I would have expected on surprise and soul. No doubt this is a consequence of the "multiple parent birthing" of edited texts. Written by a group of smart and committed people, the book reads a bit too much like a "white paper" from a Washington think tank. Ironically, the "afterword" penned by publisher and brilliant poet Haki R. Madhubuti begins, "There is music in our lives. Seldom has a partnership of such political, economic, and cultural significance taken place than that of Tavis Smiley and Third World Press."[29] Although it is substantive, strategic, hopeful, and wise, for my taste Smiley's book lacks precisely that music, that jazz, and the soul-stirring inspiration that animated the live town-hall meetings he and Joyner convened.

As a book, the Covenant resembles the well-researched sermons delivered in monotones by learned ministers in silk-stocking bourgeois churches—the kind of sermons Dr. King felt compelled to preach at Dexter Avenue and Ebenezer Baptist Churches. But he knew that such sermons, although valuable for conveying information and analysis, rarely moved the moral will, or evoked sufficient joy to lift his listeners to celebrate their potential and to march toward victory. We know from the sermons King preached at the mass meetings at the beginning of the Montgomery bus boycott that he had another voice; a voice different from his usual Sunday morning liturgical voice. It was the earthy and sensuous voice of a grassroots poet expressing the misery and the hope of his village. He sang their blues and he lifted them with hymns of change and possibility. That was the voice that moved America closer to the beloved community.

CROSS-REFERENCING AS A CLUE TO COLLABORATION

One final comment about the advancement genre and industry. This insight derives from an exciting exercise undertaken by a class I taught at Emory University in 2006 on "African American Moral Leadership." If you lay side by side documents such as the NAACP's Agenda, the National Urban League's "Opportunity Compact," Tavis Smiley's "Covenant with Black America," Louis Farrakhan's "Ten Point Plan from the Millions More March," the Congressional

Black Caucus's Agenda for the 109th Congress titled, "Closing Disparities and Creating Opportunity," and the road-map documents for Operation PUSH and SCLC (that's just seven texts), you will find something striking. For the most part, they all say the same thing, diagnose the same maladies. But, with few exceptions, they do not refer to each other. For instance, the public documents and Web sites of the NAACP don't talk much about the good work of the Urban League or of PUSH/Rainbow.

There is a long history of black leaders collaborating to advance the cause of civil rights, especially when the "big five" lobbied President Lyndon Johnson and were present when he signed the Civil Rights Act of 1964. Many of these same organizational leaders sat at the table together in the Black Leadership Forum and provided valuable leadership for extending the Voting Rights Act. But they have not called for or sponsored a national initiative to revitalize black families, churches, and colleges.

All seem to be working in parallel silos without evidence of learning from each other, without combining their "brand name equity" to increase visibility of their work, without acknowledging their relative strengths and expertise, and without sharing volunteers and resources to sustain and deepen their impact.

HOW THIS BOOK IS DIFFERENT

I want to join this conversation about reversing the crisis in black communities by adding three distinctive contributions. First, I offer a *developmental approach to framing solutions and strategies.* Most suggestions articulate a primary strategy or response without acknowledging the differing starting points of various readers. I think that it will be important to frame suggestions for a diverse audience, some of whom are new to the issue and require "first steps," while others are familiar and committed and can heed more challenging suggestions. Still others are at an advanced stage that enables them to intervene in more sophisticated and strategic ways. Leaders should address that diversity in an intentional manner.

Second, I'd like to promote a *culture of accountability* that may sustain more of the "good starts" that are often launched after an initial spark of inspiration. I'd like to outline an innovative approach that enlists and empowers young people and their ubiquitous personal technologies to assist with the accountability of village individuals and institutions as well as public officials and institutions.

Finally, I will present the *theological foundation* that informs and guides my perspective. I believe that it is a perspective that could be widely shared even by those who are not Christian. It is a theology of reconciliation that suggests that any effective village-renewal process must be rooted in a deeper spiritual process or movement that has the capacity to transform lives. Reconciliation is the art of restoring right relationships between parties that are or have been estranged. This theological rationale renders intelligible and satisfactory even the smallest gestures of voluntary action, personal sacrifice, and sharing.

Together, these features constitute the "soul" I think is sorely needed in discussions about how to heal, restore, and mobilize black America. This is one way we may be able to mobilize the beloved community of which Dr. King spoke.

1
FAMILIES
A CRISIS OF COMMITMENT

ON 17, May 2004, during the fiftieth anniversary commemoration of the Supreme Court decision in *Brown vs. Board of Education* that declared segregated schools unconstitutional, a switch deep inside comedian Bill Cosby flicked on. Three thousand prominent citizens, both black and white, had gathered inside Constitution Hall in Washington, D.C., to celebrate their toil and progress in racial justice since the *Brown* decision. Cosby, the featured guest, decided not to offer the usual polite, perfunctory, or humorous comments. He decided to be courageously inappropriate. Fearing that the achievements of the civil rights movement might be squandered and remain unavailable to the black urban poor (the population that Dr. King sought to empower most through his final mission, the Poor People's Campaign), he launched into a jeremiad, an evocative, indignant sermon against what he took to be the "bad faith" of some urban black and low-income parents whom he believed had not done their best to rear kids with love and discipline. His subsequent campaign has sought to revive a culture of personal and parental responsibility, especially in low-income communities. What Cosby has done is stimulate, even provoke, some vigorous conversation about the condition of black people and families living in poverty.

I'll return to Cosby's "campaign" shortly, after I begin with a bold, unqualified ethical assertion: *African American communities and leaders should immediately cease "business as usual" and devote time, attention, and resources to convening an inclusive and strategic community conversation about the future of our relationships, marriages, families, parenting, and child well-being. And they should enter that conversation with a commitment to undertaking every appropriate action that is in the best interest of our children and families.* If we fail to get the family agenda right, we will take a tragic step backward in our heroic movement for justice and opportunity. In other words, much of the progress made during the post–civil rights movement years could be jeopardized by our inattention to the health of this primary anchor institution. But before talking further about families, we should begin with a quick consideration of what every educated person should know about black families in America, and why Bill Cosby is so concerned about this issue.

WHAT EVERYONE SHOULD KNOW ABOUT BLACK FAMILIES

1. *Africans were brought to the United States to work. Their owners never intended them to experience conventional family bonds.* The early African population in the United States was predominantly male because most of the prisoners of war and others who were initially sold or traded into servitude for hard labor were men. The women who were sold into slavery worked as hard as men and pregnancy did not relieve them from back-breaking farm and household work. Tools of labor and capital do not need families.

2. *After the Atlantic slave trade came to an end in the United States in 1808, and no new Africans could be brought to America, a fascinating thing occurred: the native-born U.S. slave population skyrocketed.* High birth rates among native-born black people became a matter of economic practice (capital creation). The compulsory impregnation of black women (breeding) did not involve human bonds of commitment, romantic intimacy, or sustained care. Indeed, most of the population growth was the result of rape and coercion by Euro-American masters, their sons, and male slaves.[1] The wombs of black

women became a commodity for driving the engine of capitalism by supplying it with a steady supply of new laborers.

3. *Although marriage between black female and male slaves was generally prohibited by law, this did not prevent these slaves from performing their own secret rituals of commitment, love, and fidelity.* Secret slave marriages occurred, often with the simple but touching ritual of "jumping the broom." Although we are uncertain of the origins of the practice, following the exchange of vows, the bride and groom joined hands and jumped over a broom to signify "crossing over" to a new status and life together.[2] America's official public policy toward black adults was to prevent marriage while encouraging and rewarding sexual behavior and high rates of unwed pregnancy. The slave industry actively discouraged, and often punished, romantic commitment, permanent bonding, and healthy relationships. This policy illustrates how the public sector could intervene and interfere with the intimate lives of black people.

4. *Despite the frequent breakup of black families on plantations, many fathers and mothers succeeded in maintaining lasting relationships.* Still, they lived with the constant, terrifying awareness that their closest human bonds could be violated and severed at any moment without legal recourse.[3] Marriage and family love survived against all the odds. This is an example of what I call "heroic bonding and commitment" amidst tragic circumstances.

5. *During some of the most difficult years of black life in America, marriage rates were high and adults took parenting seriously.* In 1880, just fifteen years after the abolition of slavery, years when lynching and harassment were commonplace, 56.3 percent of African American households were nuclear households and 23.5 percent were extended family households (truly heroic commitment). Marriage rates were high and black churches and colleges actively encouraged an increase of committed, permanent relationships and responsible parenting. But one hundred years later, only 33.2 percent of African American children lived with both parents, a drop from 75.8 percent in 1940.[4] During World War II, the marriage rate among young African

Americans was higher than the marriage rate of their white counter-parts. Blacks understood and embraced the personal and financial benefits of marriage. In 1950, 78 percent of African Americans were married. But by 1996, that number had dropped to 34 percent.[5]

6. *African American men and women have been pioneers in the marriage game. They were engaged in "modern marriage" long before their white counterparts.* That is, marriages in which men and women both worked and cared for children were a necessity in black families before white women entered the workforce en masse.[6] Ironically, many black women left their homes and children in order to work as nannies and housekeepers in white households. Black families contributed some of their own nurturing energies to support the health of white families.

7. *Black families are typically "extended" families rather then simply nuclear families, a family pattern that has helped African Americans to survive amidst difficult and uncertain social conditions.* Most black families include some "fictive kin" or people who are not biologically related but who regard one another as permanent and real family members. In recent years, grandmothers have played a significant role in supporting family members who are absent or disabled by drugs, prison, or other circumstances.

8. *For families living in extreme poverty, the burdens on marriage, parenting, and family life in general have been devastating.* Until reforms in the 1980s, low-income single mothers faced numerous incentives for keeping fathers out of the household. Now father absence (men who have not seen their children during the past year or more) in poor communities is approximately 40 percent,[7] and the nonmarital birthrate in African American communities hovers around 70 percent[8] Ongoing research is underway about the status of these "fragile families."

9. *Black children, like all children, thrive best when their married biological parents rear them. But when that is not possible, they*

can do well in other family forms so long as they are loved, supported financially, and given the safest, most nurturing environment possible. There is abundant research now available that reminds us of the importance of healthy relationships between fathers, mothers, and their children. Of course, when the ideal is not available, the village and the public can and should support the healthy development of children as if these were investments essential to the health and security of the nation. Today, grandmothers, single parents, adoptive parents, and foster parents are doing an extraordinary job of providing what it takes to make healthy children and citizens.

10. *Historically, black communities have practiced an "ethic of family pluralism" that included some tolerance for gay and lesbian members of their families, churches, and villages.* This is noteworthy in view of the difficulty of having candid, informed conversations about sexuality in most black churches and communities. Respectful tolerance toward homosexuals seemed to be rooted in a folk wisdom about the difficulty, if not impossibility, of simply changing the target of one's romantic affection. Some believed that religion, therapy, or punishment could change sexual orientation. But most seemed to be uncertain about the construction of sexual orientation and love and did not spend much time thinking about whether or not it was possible and how to change a person's identity. Although black homosexuals lived in the closet, witch-hunt campaigns to expose and harm them were uncommon. This past culture of sexual secrecy and quiet tolerance has eroded significantly in recent years as black clergy and church members have been challenged to be more explicit about their support or opposition to homosexuality and same-sex marriage. Some black church leaders have been enlisted by politically motivated "family values conservatives" to use their moral authority (earned during the civil rights movement) to oppose homosexual leaders who have framed their struggle also as a civil rights issue. In short, black communities have been challenged to prioritize this topic and to frame their response as far more conservative and intolerant than their previous "pluralistic" practices seem to warrant. Despite some empathy for homosexual village

members, generally, African Americans have been considerably less understanding and tolerant of bisexual and transgendered people.

11. *Recently, many black families and institutions have reacted to the national family-values debate by promoting an "ethic of family survival" that is in tension with its past ethic of family pluralism.* Black leaders and families who feel that the traditional heterosexual black family is losing its normative status are taking action to prevent further regression. With growing anxiety about the future of black marriage, families, and children, many religious blacks have grown more strident and conservative in hopes that this stance will halt further erosion of nuclear and extended families. Consequently, voting against same-gendered marriage may reflect village anxiety about families in general more than a rational moral argument about human nature, creation, and sexuality.

WHAT'S WRONG?

What's wrong? More than anything, the community's most responsible and influential leaders and institutions have not yet convened a sustained, national, strategic action-focused conversation about the future of black families, especially about what children need to thrive in our society. I would submit that all of us should be addressing the topic of reviving a culture of healthy relationships and restoring an ethic of commitment in our village. Healthy relationships that lead to healthy marriages, parenting, children, and families are the building blocks of a healthy society. If our children and families are not well, larger and exceedingly expensive crises in the public arena will result, including higher rates of school delinquency and drop out, crime, suicide, incarceration, emotional illness, and substance addictions. For instance, Dr. James Comer, an esteemed Yale University child psychologist, frames the "social impact" case for caring about children and schools (one core component of the larger issue) in this way:

> Any understanding of the present plight of schools is helped by widening the frame for a moment to discuss the impact of U.S. economic and social trends over the last several decades. Children who underachieved in school and left school without

adequate cognitive skills and knowledge were not in significant trouble in our society until about three decades ago. Only within the last decade has widespread attention been given to the detrimental impact these unsuccessful students will have on the nation's future.[9]

Cosby's Call and Our Response: A Conversation Starter

I think that the conversation about what's wrong in black families, whether framed as a "crisis of commitment" or not, should begin by wrestling with some of these stark realities. As I noted above, Bill Cosby has already sounded an alarm about the crisis in some black families. Despite the problems in the way he first addressed the topic of family and child well-being by targeting parental irresponsibility, a youth culture that seems to encourage rude, violent, and anti-intellectual behavior, all future conversations about the black family will now reference Cosby's pronouncements as a rhetorical ground zero. Much like the Moynihan Report of the 1960s, Cosby's message has become the diagnosis to be reckoned with. In 1965, Assistant Secretary of Labor Daniel Patrick Moynihan released a policy paper titled, "The Negro Family: The Case for National Action," that came to be known as, "the Moynihan Report." In it, he advanced controversial claims regarding the decline of male roles in black families, and the persistence of racial disparities in economic status despite recent Civil Rights legislation.

Given his recent role as a cultural commentator, it would be easy to forget that Cosby is a comedian. He's supposed to make people laugh and forget about their problems. But for the past few years he has been trying to make people mad. A consummate entertainer, he has lost his appetite for amusing us. He has indicted some African American adults for accepting a culture of mediocrity, materialism, and moral indifference. He has scolded the churches for failing to regard this crisis as a threat significant enough to change business as usual radically. He has even chided popular versions of black spirituality that focus superficially on "Jesus," while ignoring the social problems in the community that Jesus would certainly have engaged. He has chastised the American middle class and institutions of civil society for not being sufficiently angry to coalesce and change this situation. He, like minister, culture critic, and radio personality Michael Eric Dyson (who has been openly critical of Cosby), seems to think that the black middle class appears to be in a crisis of some sort. He acknowledges that government and the market could do more to support fragile families and promote better citizenship, but he places the weight of his analysis on individual and community self-determination. In essence, the wonderful statement made by Rabbi Joachim Prinz at the historic March on Washington in 1963 captures Cosby's outlook. In reference to the Holocaust, to slavery, and other historical outrages, Rabbi Prinz declared, "Few were guilty, all are responsible."

In other words, relatively few parents are guilty of the behavior that Cosby has targeted. Fortunately, a majority of people and families living in poverty make good decisions, rear children, and behave responsibly. All who bemoan multigenerational poverty as a social phenomenon must also bemoan and condemn the policies that make it difficult to escape poverty, including tax policy, housing policies, criminal-justice and wage-labor policies. If we limit our analysis and indignation to the most visible manifestations of poverty, inadequate education, impoverished dreams, and crude or rude behavior, then we risk blaming the victims of failed economic and political policies. Some of Cosby's harshest critics, most notably Dyson, have articulated this concern. Ultimately, we must demand and design public policies and business practices that support people who make an honest effort to improve their lives. It is immoral and unacceptable that a person can work full time for minimum wage and still live below the poverty level. How can this be in a society with so many billionaires? Our fellow neighbors deserve the assistance of a society that has a moral commitment to supporting individuals and families along the journey toward self-sufficiency. Few of the people living in poverty whom Cosby scolds played a role in designing wretched school systems. Few of them made the decisions about locating businesses and new jobs in faraway suburbs, or commissioned the housing that no average working people can afford. Few of us are guilty. But all are now responsible for this new and more selfish version of the American dream.

He Paid for the Microphone

As many have already observed, Cosby is not the first "public moralist" to call attention to the underside of urban village culture. Scores of preachers, teachers, scholars, and artists have weighed in on these issues before, often more systematically, often more colorfully. But at a time when a growing number of African Americans are "unchurched," it may take an unconventional public moralist to reach this generation. And, ironically, allegations of moral failure in the moralist's own personal life don't necessarily disqualify the person. In fact, such resumé items can enhance his or her credibility or "street rep" in communities that are accustomed to imperfect messengers.

I would submit that there are four reasons why Cosby's underlying goal of starting a conversation about family and child well-being is commendable despite its shortcomings. The first of them is that, paraphrasing Ronald Reagan, "He paid for this microphone" (or is it a megaphone?). Bill Cosby created an award-winning, long-running television program, "The Cosby Show," which revolutionized the way America and the world perceived black families by relativizing the usual focus on black family pathology. Cosby became a consummate marketing expert and advocate for the modern black family of hard-working, accomplished mother-father professionals who rear great kids and enjoy affluent lifestyles. "The Cosby Show" was a stunning success and has shown surprising "staying power" (my pre-teenaged kids during the 2000s loved the show in reruns as much as we enjoyed the originals twenty years earlier). Many black critics of the show complained that the fictional Huxtable family was a romantic ideal that bore little resemblance to the real black families they knew. Other young black professionals declared that finally a TV show depicted their experiences, values, and aspirations. They welcomed Cosby's effort to provide needed balance to the often comical and stereotypical family profiles that most Americans had come to expect and enjoy in such shows as "Good Times," "The Jeffersons," "Sanford and Son," and "Julia." Given that divergent portraits of black families have emerged both in popular culture and in reality, it is important to let that broaden our perspective on

African American families. But how ready is America—both blacks and whites—to entertain a variety of black family forms?

Second, Cosby is one of the few visible, multimillionaire black celebrities who has put his money (lots of it) where his mouth is. Before it was in vogue to do so, he and his wife Camille were philanthropic leaders, making generous gifts to historically black colleges (especially Spelman and Morehouse) and other institutions. The Cosbys' example of family philanthropy should inspire a new generation of the black *nouveau riche* to give more to the institutions that are holding our communities intact.

Third, he has written books that express his understanding of romance, effective parenting, and educational excellence, thereby demonstrating his theoretical sophistication in the fields of social psychology, culture, and education, and his gift for expressing this knowledge in an accessible manner. These books include the best-selling *Fatherhood, Love and Marriage,* and *Time Flies.* Moreover, he has enjoyed a long friendship and collaboration with Harvard psychiatrist Dr. Alvin F. Pouissant, which has raised his awareness of cutting-edge research in childhood development on what works and what does not work. The opening page of *Fatherhood,* expresses well Cosby's rationale for leadership on this topic:

> I am not a psychologist or a sociologist. I do have a doctorate in education, but much more important than my doctorate is my delight in kids. I devote a part of my professional life to entertaining and educating them. I like children. Nothing I've ever done has given me more joys and rewards than being a father to my five. In between these joys and rewards, of course, has come the natural strife of family life, the little tensions and conflicts that are part of trying to bring civilization to children. The more I have talked about such problems, the more I have found that all other parents had the very same ones and are relieved to hear me turning them into laughter. Yes, every parent knows the source of this laughter. Comes share more of it with me now."[10]

And, finally, tragically, he has stood over the gravesite of his own murdered son (the one about whom he writes so poignantly throughout his books) and watched years of effort, excellence, and investment laid to final, premature rest, something no parent should ever have to do. He is in a small class of other celebrities who take up campaigns for social change—Harry Belafonte, Ruby and Ossie Davis, Stevie Wonder—yet he stands apart from them because he has aggressively challenged African American individual and community shortcomings and not simply the shortcomings of the dominant society. And he has aggressively opened a dialogue on some of the most sensitive topics in black life, including marriage, family, sexuality, and moral obligation. And speaking of moral obligation, his own personal moral challenges testify to the fact that one doesn't have to be perfect to commit oneself to noble goals and to work to improve the lives of people living in poverty. If this is true, then there is hope for many people, including me, who have made our share of errors in the continuing journey toward healthier relationships.

Cosby and His Critics, Right and Wrong

In response to Cosby's sermon, there have been numerous critics. As noted above, Michael Eric Dyson has written a book-length response, *Is Bill Cosby Right? Or Has the Black Middle Class Lost Its Mind?* in which he critically examines Cosby's speeches, critiques Cosby's observations of the urban black poor.[11] Dyson also offers alternative interpretations and data regarding the same concerns that alarmed Cosby.

Cosby's critics are correct about one significant point. His use of "signifying language," or a folk rhetorical style of calling people out and shaming them to improve, may not achieve its intended result. It is more difficult today to shame people to exert greater responsibility and effort in the cause of better parenting, frugality, and self-esteem. Maybe in the past when bonds of social attachment and trust were stronger, shame worked, but not any more. Hence, Cosby gives the impression of joining those distant and self-righteous, affluent Americans who commonly blame poor people for their misfortunes. With so much energy and lots of resources already mobilized, and with rising expectations that the process he has begun will actually have a positive impact on the misery of unparented, unsupervised young people and irresponsible parents, it would be a shame not to move the needle in the direction of constructive solutions.

Here again is part of what's wrong. Despite the fact that Cosby has broken the village silence or community veil and started a public conversation, neither he nor his major critics have generated response strategies that are practical, strategic, and comprehensive. While he and his detractors allude to the church, for instance, so far I have heard no systematic call to action by America's approximately fifty thousand black Christian churches, its hundreds of Muslim mosques, or its many other houses of worship. These people of faith have something valuable to offer to what Cosby hopes to achieve, particularly if they were to work in concert with nonprofit organizations like the Children's Defense Fund, Boys and Girls Clubs, Big Brothers and Big Sisters, the YMCA and YWCA, scouting organizations, and so on. Together, all of these organizational assets possess the expertise and muscle needed to make a lasting, positive impact on our kids. What they all lack are armies of volunteers who could act to reverse negative child and family trends.

And while we're worrying about the plight of urban poor black people, we should also pay attention to the plight of all middle-class and affluent families that face distresses of a different kind. They may not live on the financial edge of disaster like their poor counterparts. But they, too, face challenges and threats that need attention and intervention. These include parental stress, child activity overload, inadequate sleep and fatigue, and declining leisure time together to heal and nurture their own souls and their relationships. Writer and cultural critic Barbara Ehrenreich suggests that businesses and corporations that demand ever more evening and weekend hours from working parents should also be indicted for their "home-wrecking" behavior.[12]

What I would prefer to hear or see from all of these dedicated and thoughtful leaders is a plan that might offer hope to the very parents and kids that are in trouble today. I'll have more to say about that in this book's conclusion when I turn to action that is practical, developmental and strategic, comprehensive, and includes accountability to the larger community.

Healthy Relationships and Commitments

Historically, the African American struggle for freedom, justice, and opportunity has inspired the world and earned considerable moral authority. That is the result both of our goal, namely, to participate fully in American society, and the means we employed to achieve it: nonviolent, dignified, collaborative strategies that enlisted the good will of fellow citizens regardless of race, ethnicity, class, or creed. That was part of the genius of Dr. King.

But as growing numbers of African American young people appear to lag farther behind in the journey toward full participation in society—an issue that is Cosby's passion—I fear that we risk losing the moral authority that compelled the nation to comply with legal and moral principles of justice and to express good will and support for the aspiration of black people for freedom and inclusion. And as I've already suggested, the future of many post–civil rights movement gains—political, economic, cultural and so on—may be threatened by the cynicism, alienation, and disengagement of a growing number of our children and youth. If this occurs, it will be the fault of the adults in the village, not our children. This means that while we struggle to protect and extend voting rights, expand job opportunities, alleviate poverty, improve public health, and create safer streets, we must do the unglamorous work of improving the quality of relationships, all relationships, in our communities. Doing so will ensure that we produce healthier and better children, healthier and better parents, and healthier and better adults who act with integrity on behalf of the common good. In fact, that is my definition of a *moral agent*: one who behaves with integrity on behalf of all people. Hence, my focus on healthy relationships will help us to become moral agents and, perhaps, moral leaders.

Humbly and hopefully, I am calling the village to stop business as usual and to begin a national conversation on the subject of healthy relationships. *Healthy relationships are interpersonal bonds and interactions that are characterized by mutuality, trust, respect, nonviolence, and sharing.* Some social-psychologists refer to these as "other-regarding" relationships. Healthy relationships foster greater and deeper levels of interdependence and personal fulfillment. But, in order to sustain such relationships, a broader culture for, and public commitment to, supporting families is necessary. I maintain this because poverty often undermines social trust; lack of opportunity erodes personal responsibility; dramatic inequalities in wealth negate a broad sense of the common good; and crime and violence compromise mutual respect, sharing, and the possibility of community. Hence, there is a public dimension even to our personal relationships.

Here are the major reasons why I think we should start the village conversation with the topic of healthy relationships:

1. *Relationships matter.* Almost all people care about the quality of their relationships with others. If they don't care, other people will certainly bring that neglect to their attention. This "healthy relationships" focus helps us to think about and assess the quality of all kinds of interpersonal interaction in our communities. Whereas many people have no interest in the specific topic or institution of marriage, everyone has an interest and an investment in healthy relationships, or, as the coaches say, everyone has "skin in the game."

2. *Dating matters.* A growing chorus of experts agree that we should approach the topic of reviving a culture of commitment and healthy marriage in low-income minority communities from the vantage point of viewing marriage as a point (ideally, an end point) along a developmental continuum of relationships. The continuum begins with what children learn from parents and caregivers about gender, roles, responsibilities, and relationships. But as adolescence arrives, a time when dating usually occurs, many young people operate without a script for healthy dating. One evening while I was writing in the family room and my kids were taking advantage of their allotted television time, I realized that nearly every program depicted attractive young people engaged in casual dating that included sex, living together, getting drunk, being rude, and making jokes about it all. After about three of these shows I began to pay closer attention and realized that a more positive, responsible, and moral alternative would not be heard unless we said something. Our side was losing before even taking the field. Thus, I'd like to

emphasize the need to *revive a culture of healthy dating*, a concern shared by many community leaders.

3. *Ideals and norms matter.* As previously noted, research strongly indicates that children do best when they are reared by their own responsible and caring parents. That is an historical ideal that has undergone difficult times during the past thirty years. It is clear, however, that *few influential voices are making the case for healthy marriage.* Community-based organizations need to reassert that ideal on behalf of the best interests of our children. This is not a mean-spirited, right-wing conservative diatribe or agenda; it is fundamentally an African point of view and a responsible, religious alternative to the chaos that now reigns.

District of Columbia Delegate Eleanor Holmes Norton has founded the Commission on Black Men and Boys. She declares: "The virtual disappearance of marriage among many young African Americans of every income level and the devastating effects on children demand all the help we can get to draw attention to the responsibility all of us must assume."[13] She, along with many others, would call attention to the following research findings:

- Married people are economically better off when they pool their resources.
- Married men earn significantly more than their never-married, cohabiting, and widowed peers (the efficiencies, scales, and bargains of marriage almost always benefit men more than women).
- Married people live longer and enjoy better health.
- Married people enjoy more frequent sex and are happier with their sex lives than single people.
- The children of married people tend to fare better in life, especially in educational attainment and avoiding risky behaviors.
- Married men take fewer life-threatening risks (excessive drinking and drug use) compared with their single counterparts. And,

- Married people are generally able to rely on their extended families as an informal insurance policy or network that provides temporary help during tough times.[14]

4. *Healthy alternatives matter.* The traditional "marriage ideal" may not be available to every adult, especially in lower-income African American communities. But *children can do well in other family forms* (single parents, extended families, and the like) if they are nurtured in the context of healthy relationships marked by mutuality, respect, nonviolence, and sharing, and where there is broad public support for these norms. Community-based organizations, especially houses of worship, should play a lead role in celebrating these effective and successful alternatives even as they reassert their ideals and norms. It seems both cynical and counterproductive to place exclusive emphasis on a noble ideal that may be elusive for many. As the philosophers say, "We must not allow the perfect or ideal to become an enemy of the good."

5. *Policy matters.* As shown above, from its earliest days American public policy intentionally harmed black families, prevented black marriages, prohibited parental roles and authority, discouraged intact families, and violated the autonomy of black bodies and voluntary sexual behavior. During the traditional welfare era, public policy penalized married poor couples and imposed disincentives to male (father) presence in families. Only recently has public policy attempted to be more marriage- and family-friendly for African Americans. Advocates for personal responsibility should acknowledge this history of systematic harm against the black family.

6. *Ethics matter.* The healthy-relationships focus also represents an ethical challenge to all forms of oppressive and humiliating language, behavior, customs, and policy. In other words, it is good and right for human beings to be concerned with, and constantly working to improve, their own effectiveness as healthy relationship partners. That is part of what distinguishes humans from the rest of the natural order. Over time, relationships should help us to become better people who are more responsive to other people's needs and

thus better able to anticipate them. Dr. King spoke of this as being part of an "inescapable network of interdependence."

7. *Fathers matter.* Again, research suggests that kids do better in a variety of indicators when there is a positive relationship with their fathers, even if those fathers do not live with their kids (non-custodial fathering). Fathers in our culture bring distinctive goods that are worth reclaiming. Fortunately, there is a vibrant "fatherhood movement" in this country that has made strides and will continue with our help. I talk more about this movement at the end of this chapter.

8. *Faith matters.* We are persuaded that faith leaders have distinctive goods to bring to the process of improving the well-being of children, adults, and neighborhoods that struggle with disadvantages. Again, a continuum is helpful to organize their contributions. All are necessary for strengthening village relationships.

charity —> counseling —> social service delivery —> advocacy —> community development.

But, there is also a menu of substantive, theological goods (concepts, practices, symbols, messages) such as forgiveness, redemption, reconciliation, community, and the importance of children and community service that can assist.

9. *Collaboration matters.* All of the separate and valuable organizations in these communities will have limited impact unless they puzzle out a way to work together more effectively. Collaboration is difficult. Former U.S. Surgeon General Jocelyn Elders says humorously,"Collaboration is an unnatural act between two nonconsenting adults." But we should be inspired to subsume our institutional agendas for the good of our children. That is the highest expression of moral goodness and maturity.

10. *Violence shatters.* Research indicates that there is a tragically high level of relationship violence in all communities, including

intimate violence in relationships and marriages. Communities must be empowered to break the silence about this difficult topic. Here again, a variety of organizations are attempting to raise the community's awareness and ability to intervene here. One of the most difficult dimensions of this tough problem emerges when the clergy are the abusers or sexual predators toward their church members. I have served on the board of a Seattle-based nonprofit organization, Faith Trust Institute, that addresses this and other issues from an interfaith and multicultural perspective.

Several black church leaders have weighed in on family concerns that both scholars and comedians have framed. For instance, in July 2005 at the National Press Club in Washington, D.C., a group of twenty-five pastors led by Reverend Eugene Rivers issued an open letter to black church leaders calling on them to break their silence on the sinking condition of black families. Even as they affirmed the past strength of churches that led the civil rights movement, the group bemoaned those churches' withdrawal from community problem-solving in subsequent years. They also called attention to the moral hypocrisy and failings among some prominent black church leaders, exhorting them to reform their own conduct while teaching others to "live up to the biblical standards of sexual purity" by offering premarital counseling for engaged couples and other resources to help preserve marriages.[15] Elaborating on the message of the letter, Rivers and the William J. Seymour Institute for Advanced Christian Studies in Boston (of which he is president) have prepared a thoughtful report titled "God's Gift: A Christian Vision of Marriage and the Black Family."[16]

In another well-publicized "family crisis event" in 2005, the New Birth Full Gospel Baptist Church outside Atlanta staged a march (along Auburn Avenue where Dr. King's historic church is located) in support of civil rights, economic opportunity, and protecting the traditional family. Some estimates suggest that over fifteen thousand people responded to pastor Bishop Eddie Long's invitation to register their concern about the future of the village. Many observers felt that the bishop and his congregation were sending a clear signal to state legislators who were contemplating the legalization of same-sex marriage, a measure that failed. (I have more to say about how the village should frame the same-sex marriage conversation later in this chapter.)

It is important and encouraging that many people are talking, even marching, out of concern for the future of families and communities. It would be even better to ensure that a critical reading of the Bible, solid social-science data, and the testimony of community members inform those discussions and occasions for public witness.

Reviving a Culture of Commitment

Cosby has clearly brought fresh attention to an old issue, anxiety about black families. But it is now time to frame the issues in a constructive way that move us beyond blaming victims and polarizing the community that needs to be reconciled. So I'd like to suggest that the conversation begin with the following issues. The one big question for village discussion should be: *How can African Americans, working in partnership with allies, renew a culture of commitment that fosters healthy relationships, dating, marriage, and parenting?*

Although that is the primary question that should be engaged by every segment of the village and the nation, other important related issues deserve, and may require, attention. For instance:

1. Which historical factors are relevant to the culture of commitment in black families today?

2. What is the state of dating among young people and how can it be improved?

3. Why are fewer African Americans getting married and how do the attitudes of men and women differ and coincide regarding relationships, marriage, and parenting?

4. How can we revive the culture of good parenting and collective responsibility for children?

5. What do we know about the extent of violence in relationships today?

6. How should the village deal constructively with the challenging subjects of human sexuality, homosexuality, and same-sex marriage?

7. What resources are in place to help us accomplish this work?

My hope is that local community-based organizations will seize the moment to sponsor village-wide conversations that cover these and other topics. I'd love to see every church, every black college, every community organization, all of our sororities and fraternities, and family reunions to discuss these issues first. Then, after discussing them, they should commit themselves to practical change activity.

Obviously, I cannot insist that every community address this particular set of questions, but I have no doubt that people in every community are asking these questions. And people are responding to them in all sorts of venues, such as barber shops and beauty salons. I would like to see these conversations occur in more ways that are more *intentional, informed, and ongoing*.

Which historical factors are relevant to understanding the decline of commitment in many black families today?

Slavery's Impact on Commitment

I debated whether or not to include the issue of slavery in a contemporary discussion on how to renew a culture of healthy relationships. I feared that the volatile topic might threaten or prevent moving beyond its known harms and its many unknowable influences. When the topic of slavery arises, many people shut down or simply get "stuck in history." But Maya Angelou's extraordinary wisdom on this argues for inclusion. She writes, "History, despite its wrenching pain cannot be unlived but if faced with courage, need not be lived again."

One cannot talk very long about black families before the issue of slavery's legacy and continuing impact emerges. Some people assume that black family difficulties today are the direct result of the anti-family institution of American slavery. But the issue of slavery's legacy and impact is more complicated than that. I think it would help the conversation if we could acknowledge this, understand its probable and possible impacts, and then move on to the work at hand.

In a powerful essay on the contemporary debate about family issues and urban poverty, Brown University economist Glenn Loury observes that conservatives now dominate the discussion. He writes:

> These [right of center] voices seem decidedly unfriendly to black aspirations, and progressive sociologists studying the life of low-income urban communities cannot be unaffected by this. With great fanfare, conservatives now declare the historic battle against racial caste to have been won. They go on to say that, but for the behavioral dysfunction of the black poor, and the misguided demands for affirmative action from a race-obsessed black middle-class, our "problem of the color line" could be put behind us. Abigail and Stephan Thernstrom with their book, *America in Black and White: One Nation, Indivisible,* offer a prime example of this mode of assessment. This line of argument should not be permitted to shape our national understanding of these matters.[17]

In contrast to most progressively inclined African American leaders who dismiss and discredit nearly all conservative analysis and opinion, Loury acknowledges that there may be a "grain of truth in the conservatives' insistence that cultural differences lie at the root of racial inequality in America."[18] Just when one thinks Loury is about to take too large a conciliatory step toward this "unfriendly" camp, he pulls off the gloves and continues:

> While there may be a grain of truth in the insistence by conservatives that cultural differences lie at the root of racial disparity in the United States, the deeper truth is that, for some three centuries now, political, social and economic institutions that by any measure must be seen as racially oppressive have distorted the communal experience of the slaves and their descendants. When we look at stigmatized "underclass culture" in American cities of today we are seeing a product of that oppressive history. . . . Consider the so-called black underclass—the poor central city dwellers who make up perhaps a quarter of the African American population. In the face of the despair, violence, and self-destructive folly of so many

of these people, it is morally superficial in the extreme to argue as many conservatives now do that "if those people would just get their acts together, like many of the poor immigrants, we would not have such a horrific problem in our cities. . . ." So, while we should not ignore the behavioral problems of this so-called underclass, we should discuss and react to them as if we were talking about our own children, neighbors and friends. This is an American tragedy. It is a national, not merely a communal disgrace.[19]

Contemporary discussions about race relations generally, and black family issues in particular, are frustrating and predictable. When the subject of slavery and its impact emerges, one is likely to encounter either a considerable ignorance of America's past, a lack of intellectual honesty about its consequences, or a contraction of the empathy necessary to work for change. Yet, after years of working on racial justice and reconciliation and participating in President Clinton's "One America: Race Initiative," I am convinced that Americans cannot have a productive, honest conversation about our contemporary challenges until we better understand that past. We must reckon with slavery, America's original sin, not simply to understand its possible lingering impact on black family dynamics but in order to discern continually what justice requires of a great nation that became great at the expense of an incalculable exploitation of humanity. The answer to the question, Who might we have been had slavery not occurred? is just a small portion of unknowable historical knowledge.

It might be useful to summarize the debate on the lingering effects of slavery on black families. When the famed Howard University sociologist E. Franklin Frazier argued that slavery was responsible for the troubles and instability of black families, many social scientists embraced his perspective. Indeed, Daniel Patrick Moynihan's report[20] that trumpeted the pathology of black families was essentially following Frazier's lead. As a white policy maker and academic, Moynihan was a more vulnerable target for those who resented the exposure of this "dirty laundry." However, more recent research has challenged and severely critiqued components of Frazier's perspective. Relying on census data, some historians have shown that the two-parent nuclear family was the predominant family form in the late nineteenth and early twentieth centuries for blacks as well as whites. For instance, during the final years of slavery at a time when one might have expected the greatest evidence of "family disorganization and pathology," Herbert G. Gutman found that 70 to 90 percent of black households were "male-present" and that a majority of them in the counties he examined were nuclear families.[21] African American families had demonstrated an extraordinary adaptive capacity that most researchers had underestimated. African American family scholars such as Andrew Billingsley have tried to replace the usual focus upon black family deficits with an emphasis on family assets and strengths such as extended family networks, fictive kin, and the veneration of grandmothers.[22]

Again, the picture is complex. Black women and men were marrying and attempting to build strong families, but significant social and economic forces were impeding their way. Given the migration of the black population between 1940 and 1970, one could say that African Americans were headed into the "jaws of modernity."

In his compelling study of African American gender relations, *Rituals of Blood: Consequences of Slavery in Two American Centuries*,[23] Harvard sociologist Orlando Patterson suggests that we not overemphasize slavery as an explanation (as Frazier did), but intellectual honesty and rigor require us to understand its most important features.

> After two hundred fifty years of forced adaptation to the extreme environment of slavery, African-American men and women developed a distinctive set of reproductive strategies in their struggle to survive. Tragically, the strategies that were most efficient for survival under the extreme environment of slavery were often the least adaptive to survival in a free, competitive social order.[24]

Patterson notes that the most devastating impact of the "centuries-long holocaust of slavery" was the "ethnocidal assault on gender roles, especially those of father and husband, leaving deep scars in the relations between African-American men and women."[25] He then traces the manner in which male slaves found it rational and expedient to have as many children as possible in order to "leave progeny who might survive to adulthood." Male slaves experienced the separation of two important processes that have been almost universally observed together in parenting: that is, calculating the number of children one could support financially, on the one hand, and then carefully proceeding to limit one's family size accordingly, on the other. During slavery, black men were prevented from exercising moral agency to participate in this parenting process; and after slavery they were not encouraged or rewarded for doing so.

Patterson presents a chilling analysis of how newly freed young black men and women began to have large numbers of children which suited them perfectly, but almost sentenced them to long-term dependence upon the southern sharecropping economy and "farm tenancy rather than farm ownership."[26] He declares that "Afro Americans and American society at large (like Afro-Caribbean and Afro-Latin societies) are *still living with the devastating consequences* of this male attitude toward reproduction."[27] Together with the phenomenon of very early marriages among African Americans as compared with others, and extremely high fertility rates, he notes that "this pattern was a recipe for chronic and persistent poverty."[28] Whether Patterson's interpretation is firmly supported by the data may be a matter of perspective and argument. But he has highlighted factors and dynamics from the slave past that have not been adequately theorized and thereby has served the conversation well. Going forward we should be attentive to these factors without engaging in deterministic analysis of human behavior.

Black Cultural Changes: For Better or Worse?

Another significant factor affecting the environment for black marriage and parenting has been the changing nature of social, cultural, and moral codes. During and immediately after the slave period, the black community did not stigmatize female-headed households. As Columbia University economics Ronald Mincy asks, "For who knew why such a woman was now alone? Who would dare judge her for this status if her fiancée or husband had been lynched? Or, perhaps she was with child because she had been raped by the master." Others were abandoned by husbands who migrated north, promising to send for the rest of the family, but ultimately were consumed by the streets of the city. Mincy observes,

> At certain times in the painful history of race relations in this country, desertion and victimization were as likely causes of single motherhood as moral failure. In any individual case, who

could know? Who would ask? In response, the black community developed a tradition of embracing all of its children, even the fair-skinned ones. Under these circumstances, stigmatizing unwed births was impossible.[29]

The famed sociologist Kenneth Clark noted how this change of moral code correlated with class identity.

> In the ghetto, the meaning of the illegitimate child is not ultimate disgrace. There is not the demand for abortion or for surrender of the child that one finds in more privileged communities. In the middle class, the disgrace of illegitimacy is tied to personal and family aspirations. In lower-class families, on the other hand, the girl loses only some of her already limited options by having an illegitimate child: she is not going to make a "better marriage" or improve her economic and social status either way. On the contrary, a child is a symbol of the fact that she is a woman, and she may gain from having something of her own.[30]

This practice is complex and merits more attention than we can provide here. However, we should note that the *ethic of toleration and acceptance* of single parenthood which the larger community developed has always lived in tension with the more powerful central norm of the traditional family that middle-class black church culture endorsed. The churches believed that the causes of out-of-wedlock birth and divorce could be changed. The larger community, however, assimilated the dominant culture's myths of individualism and moral relativism and made no special efforts to intervene.

Migration and Commitment

In his best-selling book, *The Promised Land: The Great Black Migration and How it Changed America*, Nicholas Lemann observes that

> between 1910 and 1970, six and a half million black Americans moved from the South to the North; five million of them moved after 1940, during the time of the mechanization of cotton farming. The black migration was one of the largest and most rapid mass internal movements of people in history perhaps the greatest

not caused by the immediate threat of execution or starvation. In sheer numbers it outranks the migration of any other ethnic group Italians or Irish or Jews or Poles to this country.[31]

William Julius Wilson reminds us that the earliest detailed national census information on family structure is available from the 1940 census:

> In 1940, female-headed families were more prevalent among blacks than among whites, and among urbanites than among rural residents for both groups. Yet, even in urban areas, 72 percent of black families with children under eighteen were male headed. Moreover, irrespective of race and residence, most women heading families were widows.[32]

Although African Americans embraced marriage once they were free to do so, especially between 1890s and the 1940s, something began to change after the 1950s. African American women began to marry later than their white counterparts, resulting in a "post-sixties reversal in which the proportion of single African-American women significantly exceeded that of single Euro-American women."[33]

Underscoring the impact of macroeconomic changes on black families that had survived slavery and sharecropping only to arrive in northern ghettos, Wilson insists that we recall that between 1947 and 1972 the central cities of the thirty-three most populous metropolitan areas lost 880,000 manufacturing jobs, while manufacturing employment in their suburbs grew by 2.5 million. The same cities lost 867,000 jobs in retail and wholesale trade at the same time that their suburbs gained millions of such positions. Wilson argues persuasively that we cannot ignore the impact of joblessness on the desire of men, especially urban black men, to pursue marriage.

This fact also reminds us of the need to keep both the public dimension and the village or communal dimension of the commitment crisis in mind. That is, pervasive social factors that were outside the control of the community, like joblessness and economic change, had an impact on adult (especially male) employment, which, in turn, had a negative impact on their desire to begin conventional families. The topic of male interest in committed relationships and the obstacles that discourage them is a topic that demands greater attention and intervention.

Healthy Dating

What is the state of dating among young people in the village?

In October 2003, I had the privilege of co-leading a consultation on clergy attitudes toward healthy relationships.[34] We wanted to know what black churches are saying and doing about healthy dating, marriage, and family relationships. One of the clergy, Reverend Jules Bagneris of Los Angeles, observed that "our kids don't know what it means to go on a healthy date. They don't know the difference between casual dating and dating to select a permanent life partner. They assume that all dates involve sex. And, in the church, we haven't talked about what a healthy date looks like. So, why do we come down so hard on them when they get it wrong?"[35] His comment riveted the attention of everyone present and forced us to admit that churches haven't done a very good job on this foundational topic, much less the more delicate subject of sex.

Most pastors agreed that dating is an appropriate place to begin the conversation about the future of healthy marriages and families. Young men and women need to be taught how to relate to one another in respectful, caring ways. This topic has very high stakes when one considers that if a low-income, minority, teenaged girl becomes pregnant, her chances of completing school, being employed in an upwardly mobile job, getting married, owning a home, and so forth are severely compromised. Indeed, it almost seems unfair that youthful, uncontrolled passion can trigger such a life-changing downward spiral, with rare exceptions, for such young people living in poverty. Of course, teens with greater family resources and income have more support for continuing to pursue their life potential. But with so much at stake, why aren't we approaching this conversation publicly, constantly, and urgently?

What is an unhealthy date? Unhealthy dates are those in which one or both parties disrespect the body, mind, emotions, and/or values of the dating partner. They lack honorable affection and the desire to see the other person fulfill their full potential. Unhealthy dates are charged with the negative energy and brooding potential for date rape and other forms of coercion and manipulation. Unhealthy dates also disregard the love and investment of the young person's parents and community who have worked hard to produce an attractive, responsible, and healthy individual.

It became clear to us that clergy were not being intentional about this important topic. Yet, many of the same clergy expressed public disapproval toward young people who made bad choices in the province of love, sex, and commitment.

Healthy Marriages

Why are fewer African Americans getting married and how do the attitudes of men and women differ and coincide regarding relationships, marriage and parenting?

Although the U.S. Census Bureau projects that 90 percent of all Americans will someday marry,[36] sociologist Orlando Patterson underscores a more discouraging reality for African Americans:

> There has been a sizeable decline in the marriage rate of African-American men since the forties. In 1940, the overall marriage rate of black men under twenty-four exceeded that of their white counterparts, as did the percentage of black men under thirty who were married. After 1950, the rate at which black men married plunged, although it still remains significantly higher than that for black women.[37]

Patterson then sets the stage for an animated debate by putting forth three provocative questions.

- Why are blacks refusing to get married?
- Why, when they do get married, do their marriages collapse at such unusually high rates? And,
- Why do African Americans choose to remain single when the social, psychological, and economic rewards of marriage or stable partnering are, especially in their case, so substantial?[38]

Three frequently cited explanations have been offered by informed observers and scholars. First, the "male marriage pool" thesis developed by Wilson suggests that black marriage rates deteriorated in the 1970s because of declining job prospects. Men who do not have work or the pride that derives from work are poor candidates for stable relationships and marriage. I refer to this as the "supply-side crisis" in black communities. Most women, unless they are social workers in search of new cases, are not interested in relationships with men who enter the relationship as economic dependents. As a popular blues tune declares, "I can do bad all by myself . . . don't need nobody's help."

Second, "the 'female independence" thesis argues that "the improved economic situation of women since the 1950s has made all women more independent of men. Women delay marriage in order to pursue their careers or because they do not feel as pressured to secure a marriage early, and when they do get married they are less reluctant to walk away from unhappy circumstances."[39]

And third, the "school enrollment" hypothesis maintains that "increased school enrollment accounts for the delay in marriage. Young black people are pursuing their education instead of going directly into the work force and getting married, as they might have done during earlier periods when there were fewer educational opportunities."[40] I can think of innumerable black female professionals who recall with some frustration the dual messages from their mothers: Stay in school, get as much education and then earn as much as you can without depending on a man, on the one hand; on the other hand, hurry and marry a good man and provide me with grandchildren before your biological time-clock runs out. This may constitute a normative crisis in which equally desirable goods compete for a woman's preference.[41]

Although Patterson employs demographic data to challenge and qualify each of these common explanations, for him the bottom line is that black men and women are "moving on very *different socioeconomic trajectories*":

Black women do considerably better than men on all the vital demographic indicators of health and physical survival. And they are fast closing the income gap between the genders and are already significantly ahead of African-American men in the acquisition of educational and occupational skills and positions.[42]

This parallel trajectory leaves Patterson close to despair about the future of black marriages, at least as we have traditionally thought about what constitutes a "black marriage." He offers a variety of additional data and insights documenting this discrepancy that are worth reviewing and must certainly be discussed throughout African American communities, including the following:

> • 83 percent of divorced or separated black men believe that a woman can do just fine bringing up a boy, but only two-thirds of divorced or separated black women think so.
>
> •Black men and women hold significantly different attitudes towards sexual morality. Much of the difference is traceable to the higher rate of female participation in the church resulting in a more conservative sexual ethic. Since so many divorces are the result of infidelity, it is significant that black women live by a norm of marital fidelity (83 percent had never been unfaithful to their spouse as compared with 57 percent of men, a 26-point gap).

The Marriage Mystery

Ronald B. Mincy and Hillard Pouncy of Rutgers University have investigated what they refer to as the "marriage mystery," namely, "Given the significant advantages to marriage for black adults and, with qualifications for children, why is this institution relatively underused by blacks?"[43] One would expect self-interested, economically rational agents to select life-plans that represent good investments and life choices. Why is that not happening among many educated, upwardly mobile black people who make smart decisions in other areas of their lives? Mincy and Pouncy ask: "Does marriage offer enough advantages to adults to motivate them to marry and remain married so that the interests of their children are also secured?"[44]

But, from my perspective, the question should be framed a different way, namely, "Why hasn't the best case for marriage been made to young African Americans?" And, "Who will make that case?" Who is going to pitch marriage to a skeptical audience? In a culture where marketing makes the difference in how we behave and in the choices we make, someone has to be an advocate for healthy relationships and for healthy marriages. I think that married men, both those who are happily married and those who are simply content, must become the leading street advocates and advertisers for the goods of marriage. The boys and girls in the village need to see and hear from people who are positive about marriage. But, people who have experienced disappointment, divorce and tragedy in relationships can also be advocates for healthy marriage. Often, they know better than anyone else what people need to know, feel, and do in order to be good relationship partners.

A growing body of research on marital assets may be useful in framing the case. According to a July 2002 Centers for Disease Control report,

> Compared with unmarried people, married men and women tend to have lower mortality, less risky behavior, more monitoring of health, more compliance with medical regimens, higher sexual frequency, more satisfaction with their sexual lives, more savings, and higher wages. . . . The differences between married and unmarried people may reflect a causal effect of marriage or a selection effect. Healthier people may be more likely than others to find mates and marry. Research has suggested that the benefits of marriage may be partially due to a selection effect and partially due to true benefits to be gained from being married as opposed to being unmarried.[45]

Talking to young men around the country, it has become clear to me that *no one in the village has made the case for marriage* in a way that impresses these young men. One young brother replied to my query with the memorable comment, "Why should I trade in my 'player's card' for a marriage license?" He saw no compelling reason to leave the "field of play" to sit on the bench with one partner in a monogamous relationship.[46] This represents a clear and present challenge to village institutions and leaders. How can the case for the goods of marriage be made to young men? Although I don't have a definitive answer to the question, I know what has worked in the past. Simply put, the husbands in the village have to engage the players and tell their stories.

The Magic Moment

The Fragile Families Study is a national research project tracking the experience of over three thousand low-income people in several states. One of the most surprising findings that has emerged from interviews is that 87 percent of young, unmarried men and women were romantically involved at the time of the child's birth. Even more surprising is when the young people were asked if they thought that their relationships would move toward marriage, the vast majority wanted to get married and were hopeful that that would occur. Some scholars began to refer to this relatively brief period as "the magic moment." But after one year, less than 20 percent of these individuals actually got married. And as more time passed, fewer and fewer moved toward marriage. So the question has now emerged, "If there are young unmarried parents who say they want to get married but ultimately fail to, is there something that the community, the church, and/or the government could do to support them in their own self-stated personal goals? Is it possible for the anchor institutions of the village—our congregations, colleges, nonprofit organizations, and local businesses—to step up and assist with this message development and dissemination?"

The relative absence of "marriage spokespeople and poster children" is confirmed by researcher W. Bradford Wilcox, who met with college-educated African American men and women in Atlanta. He notes that they reported that black churches and clergy generally do not talk about sex, dating, marriage, and divorce in church. Pastors know that their churches are populated by large percentages of single mothers and many do not wish to arouse pain and moral ambiguity that they do not feel competent to resolve. The gap between where people are hurting and what pastors choose to talk about represents important homework for theological seminaries, Bible colleges, and denominational leadership education programs.[47]

In an earlier study, Wilcox discovered that despite the fact that urban mothers who attend church place a very high value on marriage, there appears to be an "African American faith and family paradox" that involves the coexistence of "unusually high rates of church attendance and unusually low rates of marriage."[48] His data also confirm the impression that black churches sponsor few explicit premarital education or marriage promotion ministries.

> • Only three percent of African-American churches in Wilcox's research sample offer formal programs in marriage and parenting, compared with 18 percent in the general population. And 5 percent offer programs targeting unmarried people—singles, single-parents and so on.[49]

Finally, Wilcox suggests that church attendance plays a role in enhancing men's appreciation for, and acceptance of, marriage and family responsibilities, as opposed to the more carefree lifestyle of many urban single men. Given the apparent positive impact of religion on male attitudes about marriage and parenting, it would seem to be strategically important for churches to be more aggressive and intentional in promoting an institution that offers many goods to adults and their children.

The Wedding Ordeal

According to researcher Kathryn Edin, many young parents do not get married because they hold such a high view of marriage that they feel that they weren't anywhere near having the material goods they felt necessary for a good marriage. Many indicate that they want first to acquire a house, furniture, car, better job, and enough money to afford an "*Ebony* magazine wedding" before getting married. Many younger people also say that they feel it is okay to have children first, and only when everything else is in place should marriage occur. Professor Edin notes that women and men in low-income neighborhoods have higher views of marriage than their middle-class and affluent counterparts. I would add that many of these young people have unrealistic views of what must be in place before marriage, such as one commented: "I can't marry her, we still disagree about things. . . ." Would it not be appropriate for the anchor institutions in the village to explore ways in which they could help to reality-test and correct unrealistic expectations and alert them to the fact that people who have been married for thirty years still disagree, but they work things out together? And that the "working things out" process requires specific interpersonal skills such as communication and conflict resolution that can be taught?

Another interesting dimension of the marriage conversation has to do with the "wedding ordeal." Reverend Wilson Goode, the former mayor of Philadelphia, leads an organization known as AMACHI, which is devoted to increasing adult mentoring in children's lives. Like Edin, Goode has observed that some (who knows how many?) young people are postponing marriage until they can have that "*Ebony* magazine wedding"—an elaborate, expensive, eye-catching event that demonstrates and enhances the couple's socioeconomic status. Goode and others argue that the village should be promoting what he calls a "culture of simple weddings" that do not leave working and poor people further impoverished following the ceremony. Others agreed and suggested that young couples should be encouraged to pay less for a "great party" and devote more attention to planning a good honeymoon and a good family plan for the long haul. Even more exciting is his suggestion that, when young people come forward with an interest in marriage, the village would step forward to honor and celebrate their decision by helping to defray the cost of a modest wedding and reception.

This is a concrete way in which communities can begin to promote a culture of healthy relationships and marriage. Anchor institutions and responsible adults should communicate to young people that if they are sincere about marrying and are willing to undergo premarital counseling, the community or congregations will step up to subsidize the cost of the wedding and reception.

Marriage Benefits

There's another dimension to this conversation that may be surprising to people. The popular weekly black-format magazine, *Jet*, weighed in on the subject of differential marital benefits with an article titled, "Who Benefits More From Marriage—Men or Women?" (2001). Nearly all of the scholars who provided brief comments concurred that men are the winners (especially economically) in marriage. Howard University sociology professor Florence B. Bonner explained,

> Women may benefit from the resources being brought to the relationship like finances and status; however, in a dual-working family, women still end up with more of the responsibility for children, less of an opportunity to advance their careers than do men, and a lot more stress engaged in both at work and at home, because they are trying to negotiate those two spaces.
>
> If you document the number of things that women do within a week to help support a man's career, it is obvious that marriage benefits males in terms of career advancement. If you are working six to seven days a week, then you have almost no time to do laundry, make the trip to the cleaners or do grocery shopping. Men can step in and do that, and we treat it as if it's a wonderful example of progress, but they do not do that consistently.[50]

Despite the practical premium for men, Dr. Joyce A. Ladner argues that both "men and women need companionship; they need to be loved, to have someone to care about them and someone who is there for them."[51]

Some scholars have noted that men who are married more often avoid life's riskiest behavior (such as driving under the influence of alcohol) and benefit from having the spouse's family as an informal insurance policy that covers the gaps during financial challenges. By contrast, single men lack this menu of supports. Also, married men benefit from the sacrifice of spouses who help them focus on their work (while often neglecting the spouse and children), perform well, receive promotions, and earn greater pay.

Hence, both women and men are beneficiaries, even if in different ways. However, Patterson's research suggests that men value companionship at a considerably higher rate than women (49 percent of men vs. 19 percent of women), while women seem more focused on the "instrumental aspects of marriage," such as financial security.

These data remind me of a haunting question raised by theologian Jacquelyn Grant. Noting the variety of ways in which religious institutions both exclude women and utilize them to the point of exploitation, she asks, "Is religion good for women's health?" She urges women to reexamine the goods they derive from faith and to begin renegotiating with religious authorities for more inclusive and just practices. We might ask the same kinds of questions about marriage: Is marriage good for women? Do women really need marriage? The village will need to discuss honestly and patiently these and other provocative questions.[52]

Ultimately, Patterson has advice to give, somewhat unusual for a social scientist and historian, but advice that may contain a grain of hope for some black women.

> I urge African-Americans, especially African-American women, to engage more in out-marriage [i.e., interracial marriage]. This would immediately help to solve the marriage squeeze of African-American women. And with the sexual and marital competition of men from other ethnic groups African-American men may well be prompted to alter their own attitudes and behavior. Given that African-Americans are only thirteen percent of the population, even if only one in five men who are not African-Americans are interested in inter-marrying with them this would immediately double the market of available spouses for them. Hence, African-American women *should immediately* . . . extend the equal opportunity principle to the marriage market.[53]

Of course, African Americans for many decades have engaged in interracial partnering, especially males. Consider celebrated offspring such as Tiger Woods and Halle Berry. However, this path remains emotionally charged and politically complicated in most black communities. In the past, when the African Americans I know observed an interracial couple, they did so through the filters of history and power relations, rather than the lens of mutual affection and personal choice. In contemporary culture, especially with the strong influence of hip-hop culture's celebration of multiculturalism, sampling, and synthesis, anecdotal evidence suggests that these earlier patterns of caution are eroding.

If "out marriage" or interracial marriage is to become more common, I would urge that it become the topic for village discussions that focus on the realistic options for intimacy available to black women, and to the kinds of households that are best for children.

According to a U. S. Census Bureau study undertaken by sociologists Grace Kao of the University of Pennsylvania and Kara Joyner of Cornell University,

- In 1992, 8.9 percent of 18- and 19-year-olds said they were dating someone of a different race. A decade later, the figure was 19.7 percent.

- In 1992, 9 percent of 20 to 29 year old Americans were living with people of different races. A decade later 16 percent was.

- In 1980, 1.3 percent of marriages in the U.S. were interracial. By 2002, that had more than doubled to 3 percent.

- In 1987, 8 percent of adoptions were interracial. By 2000, 17 percent were.[54]

Researchers suggest a few reasons for this increasing openness to interracial coupling are the "white fraction of the U.S. population is shrinking."[55] Also, there appears to have been some softening of racial attitudes during the post–civil rights movement era. For instance, in 1990 two thirds of Americans polled said they opposed having a close relation or family member marry a black person. That number dropped to about one third a decade later. Third, some people speculate that "more integrated workplaces" have had an impact also. As one federal justice department official in Minneapolis noted, "The white-collar workers were all white when I started working at Detroit Radiant Products in the '70s. There were some other races in the shop but there was no commingling to speak of. Where I work now it's a lot different and a lot better."[56] This study suggests that "Americans age 21.5 are the likeliest of all to be living with people of another race." Researchers also noted that "while interracial couples who live together often marry, their relationships disintegrate short of the altar more often than those of same-race couples do."

The Impact of Public Policy on Black Families

In addition to the impacts of slavery as well as economic and cultural change on families, public policy has also been an important factor. Here, I will be exceedingly brief in noting that the black family has been acted upon with varying effects by a long history of law and public policy. Blacks have had to endure the indignity of a social system that did not permit legal marriages and contract-making among enslaved people. Blacks would not be recognized before law as citizens until passage of the Thirteenth and Fourteenth Amendments to the U.S. Constitution in 1865 and 1868. Later, the welfare system was implemented in ways that penalized women for allowing a man to be present in the household. *Law and policy have been enemies of the black family for a long time.*

One could examine the history of race law that impinged upon the black population which had a cumulative negative impact on black families, from the lynching laws that removed men from families and had a chilling effect upon men who stood up for their families, to the history of welfare policies that functionally drove men out of the lives of women and children. Perhaps legislators can now lend their authority and resources to strengthening fragile families.

Research has called attention to the fact that a higher percentage of children living in single-parent households also live in poverty compared with their counterparts in two-parent households. This has prompted policy makers to consider the public benefits of marriage as a social unit in which children tend to fare better. Other scholars have raised critical questions about using marriage as a virtual poverty alleviation strategy, particularly because women in unhealthy marriages are frequently subject to abuse and violence. Such households may have more financial resources available, but no one benefits from encouraging or perpetuating abusive marriages. Indeed, it would be immoral to do so. Consequently, the public debate has been framed as a movement to promote "healthy marriage," that is, committed and sustainable relationships where both adults feel safe and respected and are capable of providing love and guidance to their children.

A 2004 report puts it this way: "Both adults and children are better off living in communities where more children are raised by their own two married parents. Both adults and children live longer, have higher rates of physical health and lower rates of mental illness, experience poverty, crime and domestic abuse less often, and have warmer relationships on average, when parents get and stay married."[57]

Led by President George H. W. Bush, parts of the government have made marriage promotion among low-income people a high priority on the social-policy agenda. A host of privately run marriage promotion and enrichment organizations that have served primarily educated, suburban populations in the past have now been enlisted to deliver marriage support services to poor and minority communities. Taken as a whole, these organizations have given rise to what is often called the "marriage movement." The movement currently enjoys high visibility, access, and influence in federal and state policy-making circles. Some observers fear that segments of the marriage movement may translate their influence into policies that impose penalties on single mothers who do not (or cannot) get married. There is a call for a more balanced approach that promotes and supports marriage while also supporting single parents who are working toward self-sufficiency.

Most scholars and marriage promotion leaders seem to agree that it makes more sense for government to adopt what the Center on Law and Social Policy (CLASP) refers to as a "marriage plus" approach—that is, promote marriage but do not penalize people who cannot and will not be married. The government is charged with serving the common good and using our tax monies to help us accomplish things we could not easily accomplish alone. We need to support all kinds of people in committed, loving relationships who are rearing children, the nation's most important natural resource.

In an effort to discover how black churches might relate to the largely white marriage movement and to the Bush administration's marriage promotion efforts, the Annie E. Casey Foundation hosted a consultation of clergy and marriage education experts from around the nation in 2003. Said Foundation vice president Ralph Smith, "If marriage is a viable option for helping those children, then marriage needs to be at least on our radar screen for more study and analysis."[58]

Speaking for the federal government, Dr. Wade F. Horn, assistant secretary for the Administration for Children and Families (ACF) of the Department of Health and Human Services, declared, "Those of us who really care about the future and prospects for low-income children really have to confront this issue. So many children live in single-parent, single-income families, and the anecdotes and data are compelling. We have no social policy in play that is powerful enough to lift those children out of poverty. In many respects what brings us here is to figure out ways to work on this issue that are culturally competent, appropriate, and respectful to communities in which some of us live and some of us serve."

Prior to joining the Bush administration, Horn was a long-standing advocate for father involvement in the lives of children. He noted that he had learned from experience what government ought *not* to do. For instance, *government should not*:

- Seek to coerce people to get married
- Engage in stigmatizing and lecturing people about marriage
- Engage in the matchmaking business, especially if it might inadvertently trap people in abusive relationships
- Retreat from providing adequate supports to single-parent families.

Horn observed that "children live in single-parent as well as two-parent households and every child deserves to be supported and encouraged." Some pastors observed that Horn would do well to communicate this message more aggressively to the conservative segments of the faith community who may wish to use policy to penalize single parents. He went on to describe an ACF initiative to develop marriage promotion strategies for African Americans communities that recognize and address cultural sensitivities and the uniqueness of the African American community: "It's true that if you take two people not working and they get married and are still not working, they are still poor. So we believe work and work supports are the mechanism for overcoming poverty, but there is good reason to believe marriage is relevant to reducing poverty." The initiative aims to:

- Develop demonstration projects that illustrate effective collaboration between key community sectors, including local government, business, civic and non-profit organizations;
- Emphasize marriage in various federal programs, including Refugee Resettlement, the Children's Bureau, Community Services and Temporary Assistance for Needy Families (TANF);
- Conduct research on the efficacy of various programmatic approaches to marriage promotion and strengthening; and
- Provide training in this somewhat uncharted field for ACF staff.

Although marriage may be in a state of crisis throughout American society, Horn stressed that African American families are less likely to have access to marriage education services and less likely to be able to purchase them. "What we need to do is to make sure marriage education services are accessible and co-located in the same communities. Regardless of socioeconomic status, conflict is inevitable. What is not is how couples manage it."

In another effort, the African American Healthy Marriage Initiative is convening conferences around the country and busily making grants to churches and community organizations engaged in promoting healthy marriages. In addition, proposals are being considered in Congress for, and some states have already created, "marriage development accounts" that award bonus dollars to low-income women and men who wish to purchase a home, send a child to college, or start a business. During the three-year period of eligibility for funding, the individuals have to marry in order to receive the money. And while social conservatives have introduced many of these ideas, they have begun to win support from progressive black lawmakers. Recall Eleanor Holmes Norton's words cited earlier: "The virtual disappearance of marriage among many young African Americans of every income level and the devastating effects on children demand all the help we can get to draw attention to the responsibility all of us must assume."[59]

Despite their good intentions and accomplishments, many clergy and black community leaders regard the marriage promotion work with keen suspicion. Their suspicions are rooted in a protective posture toward black families that have often been the victims of government assistance (as we noted above) rather than beneficiaries. And they are suspicious of the political agenda of those who stand to claim success in encouraging more marriages. If good work is accomplished, it surely should be acknowledged. But, those efforts will be better served if they can be depoliticized.

Healthy Parenting

How can we create a culture of healthy parenting and collective responsibility for nurturing children?

Every African American over the age of forty has stories about how the entire village parented the children of the neighborhood. In this age of litigation, sexual abuse of children, kidnapping, and other outrages, it is difficult to recall that there was a time when the adults of the community provided care and discipline to all of the children. Since this collective practice disappeared only two generations ago, I wonder if it is possible to revive these practices. Here again, the village could and should convene to allow the elders in the village to tell stories about how "village parenting" was done. And as we ponder retrieving the tradition, we will need to revise our practices in light of new legal, cultural, and social realities.

The issue of parenting raises concerns about how the village can assist all of the parents who are not prepared to be effective parents.

"Baby Mama Drama" and Blended Families

While I was driving to the Children's Defense Fund's summer leadership program in 2004 in order to deliver presentations on healthy relationships, a song came onto the radio by a group of male "artists" whose name intentionally remains unknown to me. Its refrain went on and on for several minutes with little narrative to help us understand the vitriol and vehemence of their shouted words, "I hate my baby's mama. I hate, I hate, I hate my baby's mama."

This song was espousing a view of women, parenting, and relationships that suggested that the singer had reached the end of his wits in negotiating with the mother and co-parent of his child. Unfortunately, he did not seem to be aware of alternatives to expressing his resentment in such a humiliating manner.

With the majority of black babies born outside marriage, obviously large numbers of biological mothers and fathers of those children need to have focused conversations about the well-being of and provision for those children. Unfortunately, when the parents are unable to communicate effectively or resolve conflict peacefully, tension and sometimes open conflict emerge. This has come to be known informally as "Baby Mama Drama" and "Baby Daddy Drama." Typically, the drama emerges when expectations and obligations are not met. Once again, adults who have experienced and resolved challenges in this arena must assist the larger village in building healthy blended families and respectful relationships. I know first hand that respectful resolutions that serve the best interest of the children are possible.

As the village moves into the future, it will be necessary to assist people, especially young people, in the arts of communication, conflict resolution, and developing a rational plan for themselves and their families that places the best interest of children in the first and central position. This is a value that the entire village and its institutions and individuals can and should emphasize.

Going forward, more families will be blended families. Everyone recognizes that multiple-partner fertility represents real challenges to developing respectful and low-conflict relationships between the various adults involved. But the challenges can be overcome. Adults must remember that the children are not responsible for creating the complicated situations into which they were born; hence, it is morally wrong to penalize. The entire village should make it a priority to help people learn the skills of managing complicated, extended family dynamics in ways that best serve our children.

One of the most dynamic leaders of the African American marriage promotion and education movement is Nisa Muhammad, founder of the Wedded Bliss Foundation, who offers a hopeful assessment of the prospects here. In a volume she edited, *Raising the Bottom: Promoting Marriage in the Black Community*, Muhammad offers a snapshot based on her experience of how the marriage option is attractive to both young men and women who find themselves in complicated family situations:

> The single mother is faced with providing and parenting at the same time.
>
> Time is not on her side. There doesn't seem to be enough hours in the day for work, cooking, cleaning, childcare, homework, transportation to and from plus all the other things that go into just having a life. Most single women would welcome with open arms the help and support that a happy successful marriage offers.
>
> For single men, parenthood offers at worst "baby mama drama," child support nightmares such as wage garnishment, a trip to family court and often incarceration. From worst to best there is a tug of war between children of a previous life and starting a new life, which can include a woman and her children from a previous life. Who gets the money? How is it divided? There are now more children and responsibilities but not more income. It's a dreadful life. But it doesn't have to be that way. Most single men would also welcome with open arms the help and support that marriage offers.[60]

It would behoove our village anchor institutions to develop strategies and practical interventions to help young parents and their children who find themselves in unpleasant, and often unhealthy relationships negotiate their situations and develop plans for giving their kids a better chance. Churches, schools, and community organizations can and must offer these resources if we are to break the cycle of despair that these kids land in through no fault or choice of their own. Helping them is an act of moral maturity and of mercy.

The Impact of Divorce

Most people are aware that almost half of all marriages end in divorce, hence it is important to acknowledge divorce's presence in the proposed conversations. According to the CDC study of marriage, cohabitation, divorce, and remarriage,

> The proportion of time spent in marriage has varied across demographic subgroups. Since 1950, the marital patterns of white and black Americans have diverged considerably. About 91 percent of white women born in the 1950s are estimated to marry at some time in their lives, compared with only 75 percent of black women born in the 1950s. . . . Black married couples are more likely to break up than white married couples, and black divorcees are less likely to remarry than white divorcees. . . .[61]

A revealing report from the Institute of American Values, "Does Divorce Make People Happy? Findings from a Study of Unhappy Marriages," raises several relevant issues for discussion. Using data from a nationally representative survey of 5,232 married adults, the study focused on all spouses (645) who in the late 1980s rated their marriages as unhappy. Five years later these same adults were reinterviewed. Some had divorced, some separated, and others stayed married. The authors observed that "the conventional wisdom would argue that unhappily married adults who divorced would be better off: happier, less depressed, with greater self-esteem and a stronger sense of personal mastery, compared to those staying married."[62] They ask, "Was this true? Did unhappy spouses who divorced reap significant psychological and emotional benefits? Surprisingly, in this study, the answer was no. Among the findings were:

• Unhappily married adults who divorced or separated were no happier, on average, than unhappily married adults who stayed married. Even unhappy spouses who had divorced and remarried were no happier, on average, than unhappy spouses who stayed married. This was true even after controlling for race, age, gender, and income.

• Divorce did not reduce symptoms of depression for unhappily married adults, or raise their self-esteem, or increase their sense of mastery, on average, compared to unhappy spouses who stayed married. This was true even after controlling for race, age, gender, and income.

• The vast majority of divorces (74 percent) happened to adults who had been happily married five years previously. In this group, divorce was associated with dramatic declines in happiness and psychological well-being compared to those who stayed married.

• Unhappy marriages were less common than unhappy spouses. Three out of four unhappily married adults were married to someone who was happy with the marriage.

• Staying married did not typically trap unhappy spouses in violent relationships. Eighty-six percent of unhappily married adults reported no violence in their relationship (including 77 percent of unhappy spouses who later divorced or separated). Ninety-three percent of unhappy spouses who avoided divorce reported no violence in their marriage five years later.

• Two out of three unhappily married adults who avoided divorce or separation ended up happily married five years later. Just one out of five of unhappy spouses who divorced or separated had happily remarried in the same time period.

• While 64 percent of Americans agreed in a recent poll that divorce almost always or frequently harms children, just 33 percent agreed that "for the children's sake, parents should stay together and not get a divorce, even if the marriage isn't working."

Relationship Violence

What do we know about the extent of violence in relationships today? During the past several years, there have been numerous news accounts of individuals, almost always men, who have taken their children hostage, engaged police in shootouts, committed mass homicide and then suicide, or otherwise committed fatal crimes within their family systems, all in the name of love. In other words, these were not strangers engaged in domestic violence but rather people who had in the past been intimate acquaintances. Then, the relationship went bad, often connected to a downturn in the economy that left a family member unemployed or otherwise on hard financial times. For some reason, these individuals have resorted to violent means to resolve their problems.

Is it love that makes people this crazy? The great psychologist Carl Jung suggested that many people suffer emotional and mental illness due to a "disturbance in the province of love." Each time I hear these all-too-frequent news reports, I think, Which institutions in the community are helping people to understand, prevent, and get help with domestic violence? [63] What worries me is that the people who are "acting out" their "relationship rage" have few local places to turn for help. Yes, there are government and nonprofit agencies available for marital and familial distress in low-income communities. But in general, their intervention approach is more passive than is necessary. By contrast, local congregations often have the moral authority to enter the lives of community members in a bold and potentially redemptive way. If the pastors, specialized ministers, and laity were trained to respond to, and help prevent, relationship violence, many lives could be redeemed before things reach the point of no return.

Unfortunately, many churches and clergy are ill-equipped to help people deal with sexual and domestic violence. Referring to the issue of domestic violence within the religious community, Reverend Al Miles sees "complacency among many clergy with confronting abuse and the urgent need to address the problem as a pastoral duty."[64]

For the most part clergy have hindered rather than helped women break free from their abusive partners. Our apathy, denial, exhortations, ignorance, and misinterpretations of the Bible have added to women's pain and suffering and placed them in even greater danger. The time is long overdue for us pastors to stop turning our backs on domestic violence and begin speaking out against this sin. . . . We have a responsibility to preach and teach the biblical truths about God's love, which binds women and men together as equals rather than ordering them in a hierarchy. As long as we refuse to fully carry out our pastoral duties, victims of domestic violence will continue to crumble emotionally, psychologically, and spiritually underneath the weight of brutality and scriptural misinterpretations, which no human deserves.[65]

It is a double tragedy when people, usually women, approach pastors about abusive husbands or male partners only to be told by a trusted religious authority to return to the abusive man as an act of love, faithfulness, or obedience to God's Word.

Since religion can be both a resource for liberation and healing as well as an obstacle to health, it is absolutely vital that religious leaders have the appropriate knowledge and skill to counsel people appropriately. And in light of Miles's observation about clergy who may be complacent about breaking the silence on this issue, it is important for the entire village to educate itself about what our sacred Scriptures have to say and how the entire village should reinforce positive, life-giving messages.

In her groundbreaking research into relationship distress among low-income people, Kathryn Edin has interviewed poor women and mothers in Philadelphia.[66] She found that the single most oft-cited reason for the dissolution of a marriage or cohabiting relationship was relationship violence. This shocked those of us who have tried to follow the conversation and research about marriage and family life in poor communities. We assumed that the major reasons for break-up would be infidelity, drug addiction, or imprisonment. But, to our surprise, relationships and marriages are not hanging together because of violence by one or both of the partners. (It should be noted that drug use may precipitate much of the relationship violence, hence, that primary problem must be addressed.)[67]

Healthy Same-Gender Relationships

How should the black community approach the subject of homosexuality and same-gender marriage?

Toward Reconciliation and Healing

I am annoyed and embarrassed by the way in which many influential black church leaders have weighed in on the topic of homosexuality. In the process, many have poorly stewarded the moral capital and authority these churches earned during the civil rights movement. There is an alternative to the hostility, self-righteousness, and mean-spirited rhetoric some clergy have employed in the name of a Christ who was radical and revolutionary in his capacity to love and accept others. Indeed, Jesus often transgressed the religious and social conventions of his day just to demonstrate the power of God's love toward humanity. I think this is why we have the story of the "prodigal son." And it is why the Apostle Paul, who was not a very tolerant fellow, found himself declaring that "Nothing shall separate us from the love of God in Christ Jesus" (Romans 8).

It is now time for black churches and clergy to adopt a more redemptive approach to the issue of homosexuality and same-gender loving unions. As a way of moving beyond analysis and argument, I'd like to take the risk of presenting my perspective in the form of a resolution that churches and the community should consider and discuss and adopt.

A Resolution on Faith and Sexuality

Whereas:

- As leaders and members of the African American Christian church, we acknowledge one of the fundamental theological claims of historic Christianity, namely, all people are made in the image of God. Homosexuals are children of God and deserve the love and respect of every community member and authentic Christian.

• The black church community is diverse. Some of us regard homosexuality as sinful. Despite our perspective on sin, we are compelled by our faith to love all of God's children, even if we disagree with their sexual orientation and behavior. Love is greater than all sins and "nothing can separate us from the love of God."

• In our diverse black church community, some of us regard homosexuality as a natural and normal state and identity given by God just as heterosexuality is a gift from God. We do not feel compelled to condemn or change the lives of those who are different. Some of us affirm the right of gay and lesbian people to marry and enjoy the civil benefits of a legal union.

• We acknowledge that no matter what our theological and ethical position might be, homosexuals are here to stay, and that finding a way to live peaceably and respectfully is our moral duty. Our love for, and grace toward, others are closer to the nature of God than are our anger and pride.

• We acknowledge that homosexuals contribute to the well-being of the church and the society in a variety of ways. Whether we approve or not, we affirm that when homosexuals express their right to adopt and rear children, they serve the best interests of children who are often the most vulnerable people in our communities. Jesus often expressed his profound care and concern for the well-being of children.

• We acknowledge that homosexuals who cherish the quality of their relationships do not threaten the vitality of heterosexual marriages and relationships.

• We acknowledge that the black church's traditional teaching about homosexuality may have made it difficult for men who have sex with both men and women (the "down low" lifestyle) to be honest about their sexual preferences and practices. The down low phenomenon has threatened the well-being of many innocent wives, women, and their children. Insisting that anyone remain "in the closet" only prolongs their misery and delays their honest reckoning with themselves and their community. It would be a loving act to enable all adults to be fully and freely who they are before God. We invite those men to cease their selfish and dangerous behavior and be true to themselves and others. The truth will set you free.

• Heterosexual members of the community urge our gay, lesbian, bisexual, and transgendered neighbors to exhibit patience with the discernment and deliberation process that heterosexual church members need to undertake and are now engaging.

• Homosexual members of the community urge our heterosexual neighbors to respect us as equals and not ask us to compromise our identities, values, and expectations for the sake of your comfort. We have been the silent, invisible, sacrificial lambs long enough. We will not retreat into the closet. God sees us and God loves us.

"We hereby resolve that:

• We will not permit our religious and moral values to be manipulated by politicians or any parties that wish to capitalize on our family values and do not understand or respect our obligation to practice the ethic of love, forgiveness, and reconciliation.

• We will not use language that has the effect of stigmatizing any particular group of God's children any more than we wish to be stigmatized for our own personal sins and shortcomings.

• As citizens of both the church and of the secular state, we recognize that if the state approves of civil unions or

same-sex marriages or other actions that violate our conscience, we have the right to protest that state action.

• The state cannot legislate what our faith determines to
be good and right. However, we can and will disagree in
a respectful manner.

• And we resolve to engage patiently in a process of discernment, prayer, study, discussion that we hope will
lead us closer to what God is doing in our lives, in the
church, and in society."

During this period of discernment, I hope that churches will
draw upon biblical scholars, theologians, and ethicists who can help
to resource this vital conversation in the village.[68] Biblical scholar
Randall Bailey has expressed disappointment that many black
denominations have reached conclusions on homosexuality without
consulting the best minds in the black church community. And William Sinkford, president of the Unitarian Universalist Association,
suggests that as all churches and the society at large are engaged in
a discernment process about homosexuality, they should not force
premature closure on the process by attempting to impose constitutional amendments or other legal measures. Above all, as the dialogue continues, we should remember and practice the wisdom of
Augustine who observed, "In all things essential for the faith, Unity.
In all things nonessential, Liberty. But, in all things, Charity."

WHAT'S RIGHT?

I began the chapter by noting that leaders and communities are
not having an urgent and informed conversation about healthy
relationships. Actually, that is changing, but much too slowly given
the magnitude and seriousness of the challenges to our children
and families. Perhaps the most important fact that brings hope is
that we are starting to have a conversation about the long-neglected
issue of what can and must be done about black family distress.
What is surprising is that the conversation was jump-started by
a comedian.

Among the factors that I find to be most encouraging are:

1. an energetic debate about the future of black families is now already underway;

2. a tradition of proclaiming and practicing a complex message on family norms capable of strongly promoting heterosexual marriage while also affirming the good and loving work of most single parents who do not deserve to be penalized; and

3. a new literature and leaders who can help the community deal responsibly and lovingly with its homosexual members.

A Complex Message on Family Values

Black churches have a long history of managing the complexities, ambiguities, and tragedies of black family life. That tradition may be little known throughout the village, especially in the churches, but this would be a good time to retrieve some of its best features.[69]

Even before black people could legally marry, the churches sought to foster a climate of extended kinship networks that were tolerant of the variety of black family units in their midst. Their central family norm was the embrace of the mother-father parenting team. They taught a strong ethic of parental responsibility but did not embrace the paternalistic practices of their white counterparts—in part, because black women always worked outside their households, usually helping white families to remain intact and thrive. Black men understood what was necessary to sustain their own families, including tolerating the intrusion of nonfamily members for the sake of keeping a job. They also functioned as fathers and caregivers as well as disciplinarians when mothers had to be away. This points to a tradition of adaptive, flexible, and tolerant parenting practices that helped black families thrive against the societal odds.

In addition, black churches thought and talked about the tragedies that could affect black families. They understood that black women were victims of rape, interracial children often emerged from those unions, and many black men and fathers would not be present or able to rear these children for a variety of reasons. This is painful, perplexing, emotional material and those family and church leaders had to deal with it. Consequently, as economist Ron Mincy has noted, black churches and communities articulated a norm of family life that embraced all of the children in the slave community without questioning their lineage. And they embraced these kids without applying excessive stigma to mothers who were single. Still, when the congregation gathered on Sunday, they heard positive endorsements of marriage and responsible parenting. They held these two ideas and norms in creative, life-giving tension, one that has eroded under the pressure of eliminating ambiguity and asserting self-righteousness. We should not underestimate its sophistication and deep humanity.

This is an important cultural practice and moral acknowledgment that should be revived for our time. The complexities that now mark black families are such that not every heterosexual person will get married. Despite that fact, marriage should be promoted as the preferred context in which childbearing occurs. At the same time, village leaders should clearly declare, "But if marriage is not possible, then we will support those single or primary parents who wish to do what is best and right for their kids, indeed, for the good of the village and the entire society."[70]

Resources for Renewing a Culture of Healthy Dating, Relationships, and Marriages

Although there has been a marriage education and promotion movement in this country for many years, it is a relatively new phenomenon in African American communities.

In 2006, the Coalition for Marriage, Family and Couples Education, a group comprised of the nation's major marriage education and promotion organizations, convened its tenth annual conference under the theme, "Smart Marriages: Happy Families." In the past, the coalition and the conference were overwhelmingly represented by white, educated, and affluent people, many of them Christian.

But in recent years the complexion of the marriage movement has begun to change. A dynamic group of African American healthy relationship and marriage experts have emerged and are becoming national leaders in their own right; most of them are featured speakers at SmartMarriages conferences.[71]

I am also particularly impressed with a DVD series titled "Basic Training for Couples: A Black Marriage Education Curriculum." The joint product of Dr. Rozario Slack and Nisa Islam Muhammad, part of its value derives from the unlikely collaboration of a Christian man and a Muslim woman (both married to other spouses) reflecting on the challenges of marriage and offering practical advice on how to improve relationships. They do so in a lively, friendly, and often very insightful manner. Indeed, their workshop at SmartMarriages was one of the standing-room-only events that I attended, a fact that bodes well for village renewal.

Recommendations from Clergy

Earlier, I mentioned the Annie E. Casey Foundation consultation where clergy gathered in focus groups to discuss the issue of how to increase church leadership on healthy marriages and relationships. The leaders offer the following suggestions for future action:[72]

• *Marriage leaders and foundations should facilitate the preparation of user-friendly fact sheets and talking points* to get this issue onto the radar screens of key opinion leaders who are needed to raise public awareness.

• *Funding will be needed to train local marriage leaders* to ensure that low-income neighborhoods have an informed resource person available.

• *Community colleges are often overlooked resources that must be included in community marriage projects* to ensure ongoing institutional support for implementation. In some communities, the colleges and schools may be safer, more neutral sites for recruiting a diverse population to marriage education classes.

• *Ensure that relationship and marriage education begins in prisons and continues as people reenter neighborhoods.*

• *Partner with health-care providers* to reach both parents at the time of pregnancy and/or delivery. The Fragile Families research project reminds us of the "magic moment" for focusing on marriage promotion with young unmarried parents who may wish to marry but are uncertain about the necessary steps.

• *Establish a fifteen-year marriage and family commission* charged with monitoring the progress of the community in promoting healthy relationships.

• *Explore the role of African American national denominations* in supporting this work at the local level.

• *Develop ample opportunities for volunteers* and nonprofessionals to get involved.

• *Be certain to acknowledge generational differences* in attitudes and assumptions about marriage. Be sure that older volunteers do not impose their assumptions on young people.

• *Promote Black Marriage Day (March 28)* as an annual occasion for valuing marriages, similar to Mother's Day and Father's Day. This tradition was started by Nisa Muhammad and has been cited favorably in national African American magazines, such as *Essence*.

• *Link marriage promotion activities* to other familiar occasions and events, such as Women's History Month, Black History Month, Black Justice Day, Take Back Your Marriage Month, and so forth.

• *Consider using the consultation report as the basis for a publication* that could further raise consciousness among college and graduate students and other young people.

Supporting Healthy Fathers

The statistics on father absence are so troubling that they beg for com-munitywide discussion and action. Indeed, I believe that this topic must become an urgent priority for our nation's most important and influential institutions and leaders including government, business, media, education, philanthropy, the vast nonprofit sector and, espe-cially, houses of worship of all kinds—congregations and clergy.

In 1998, a historic conference, sponsored by the Morehouse Research Institute at Morehouse College in Atlanta, Georgia, almost succeeded in placing the issue of father absence on the national agenda, with its report "Turning the Corner on Father Absence in Black America."[73] Three things made this conference and report both promising and remarkable. First was the comprehensive way in which it defined the issues. The proceedings were informed by a variety of disciplines and brought together historical, global, and grassroots perspectives. Second was the diversity of its fifty signato-ries, who represented an impressive variety of academic disciplines, sectors, institutions, political persuasions, and ethnic-racial identi-ties, including four black preachers. And third was the audacity of its proposed ten-year strategic agenda in advocating specific policy ideas, expenditures, and collaborative public and private action aimed at reversing father absence.

Notwithstanding all this, I perceive that the important call of 1998 has gone unheeded in local communities and churches as well as university conferences. If there was community discussion of these issues at all, it was exceedingly episodic and short-lived. To revive and catalyze discussion of this issue, it makes sense to begin by highlight-ing, without repeating in detail, features of the report, and then to elaborate my own constructive proposal for moving forward.

"Turning the Corner on Father Absence in Black America" begins with several statements about the unity and vision of the conference organizers. It issues a "call to action" to fathers, churches, civil rights organizations, and the public sector to prioritize this issue for the next ten years. The wide-angled analysis of its section on "why fathers matter" identifies various economic, cultural, and policy challenges to fatherhood and marriage, and it wisely places the American family crisis within the context of global trends. The report finds that by fault of strident individualism and a weakened sense of obligation to the family, "fathers the world over, rich and poor alike, are increasingly disengaging from their children and from the mothers of their children."[74] The section on "spiritual dimensions to father absence" invokes African notions of the sacredness of being a father (creator), the idea of co-creatorship. The report concludes with ten recommendations for collaborative and self-empowering activity designed to reverse this crisis.

By way of providing a sense of the tone of the report and beginning to frame the state of the conversation, I include several brief passages here:

> We gathered together because of our shared concern about the national trend of father absence that is affecting nearly all races and ethnic groups in the United States, and because of our particular concern about father absence in the African-American community . . . [75]
>
> We gathered together because we believe that among the most urgent problems facing the African-American community, and the entire nation, is the reality that 70 percent of African-American children are born to unmarried mothers, and that at least 80 percent of all African-American children can now expect to spend at least a significant part of their childhood years living apart from their fathers . . . [76]
>
> Although we differ on the relative weight to be given to economic, cultural, and private and public policy factors in shaping the lives of African-American fathers, we agree that each of these factors is at work, and that comprehensive strategies are needed to confront the crisis of father absence in the African-American community. . . . [77]

Then, closer to the point of my concern about religious intervention on this issue, signatories affirmed that:

> We gathered knowing in our hearts that the estrangement of fathers from their children is wrong, that children need both their

fathers and their mothers, and that neither the African American community, nor the nation as a whole, can truly prosper unless and until we reverse the alarming trend of father absence . . . [78]

We agree that there are profound spiritual dimensions to this crisis, and that in order to make the way for nurturing relationships between fathers and their children, much healing must be done between fathers and mothers, men and women.[79]

I appreciate the report for its efforts to name the estrangement between fathers and their children as a moral wrong and that what is needed is a broad approach to healing.

One of the things I admire about this conference is that it brought together many of the local leaders and change agents who are making a difference in promoting responsible fatherhood. During the past fifteen years, fatherhood advocacy leaders and organizations have been, in the words of fatherhood scholar Ron Mincy, "expanding job placement services for fathers to focus on retention and wage and career growth. [They] have also been expanding the legal, educational, team parenting, substance abuse, physical and mental health and other services to meet the needs" of their clients, their neighbors, and their families.

Mincy worries that these important efforts could be discouraged by heavy-handed marriage promotion initiatives, especially those that enjoy the backing of the government. This is the sensitive ground we must all negotiate wisely. At the end of the day, we all want the same things. We want the kinds of relationships and families that contribute to the well-being of children, and to the flourishing of women and men, together and singly.

Mincy proposes that we think about father involvement in children's lives as a ladder that begins with "no father-child contact," moves up to "some father-contact," and, when possible, moves beyond the temporary, episodic contact to full-time presence predicated on a healthy relationship with the mother and, ideally, marriage.

Based on this research we know which things contribute to the probability that people will move up the ladder. The upward climb is most likely to occur when:

- Employment services are available
- Fathers are employed
- Men and women avoid multiple partner fertility
- Education about preventing nonmarital fertility is accessible

Based on my own experience, observations, and practice of ministry, I would add to this list:

- Both individuals possess, or are willing to develop, basic respect and care for each other. In other words, estranged lovers and relative strangers can learn and can try to become friends.

Just as there are dynamic leaders emerging in the healthy relationship and marriage promotion movement, there are several effective "fatherhood movement" leaders providing direction that can assist the entire village. I have worked with two of them that deserve mention here. Joseph Jones Jr. is president of the Center for Fathers, Families, and Workforce Development in Baltimore. He has developed a curriculum on helping young men and women learn to improve their communication and conflict resolution skills. Also, Reverend Dr. Clyde Williams is director of the Alabama Fatherhood Initiative and is integrating the focus on healthy relationships and marriages into the traditional one-dimensional focus on men and fatherhood. Each year, Dr. Williams convenes a statewide conference of public, private, and nonprofit professions to provide practical workshops on how they can assist people who want to have better families.

A Final Note on Love and Commitment

In an important conversation between Maya Angelou and Cornel West, West puts his finger on a core issue in the crisis of families, namely, the challenge of long-term, faithful commitment. He says: "One of the interesting things to me is what happens to love between men and women today. What are the conditions under which they're willing to be related and connected?"[80]

Angelou responds by reflecting on family role norms in West African culture and the ways in which slavery distorted stable family norms and practices, leading to the socially ambiguous and disabling dynamics observable today. Then West elaborates:

> For me there are three crucial dimensions in terms of trying to understand the problems with relationships these days. One is economics. No doubt, when you're unemployed or underemployed, or when you have a high level of job insecurity and anxiety, you're going to have trouble in your relationship. The second is political. That's when the movement that focuses on your suffering is relatively weak and feeble, you do feel debilitated, if not demoralized. . . . Then we've got another dimension, which is personal. Which is we're living in a society that is losing *the art of intimacy.* And by that what I mean is the *courage to be vulnerable and to accent longevity in your relationship.* We've got market moralities; we want disposable bodies. And so it takes time to be able to really be vulnerable, to get to know a person the way Adam knew Eve. That is to say, to know in the sense of dealing with their insecurities and incongruities and contradictions and tensions, and they get to know yours. Now one of the things about folks in the past, they weren't perfect, but they knew they were in this thing together.... That doesn't mean that you permit patriarchal subordination. But it does mean that it's not going to be meeting somebody on Monday and making the final decision on Friday. You've got to work some things through. That's how intimacy is cultivated. . . .[81]

These are valuable insights that should be discussed in local communities as we critically examine our working definition of quality relationships.

In the volume *Black Genius: African American Solutions to African American Problems,* co-editor and novelist Walter Mosley offers wisdom in an important essay titled "Giving Back." His reflections on the nature of love contribute further to the kind of intimacy and courage to be vulnerable that West espouses.

It is my claim that real love, the love of others and love of self, is often painful and sometimes seems harsh. If we do love each other and we love our race, then we have to be critical of ourselves and honest. We don't need charity or self-pity or defense. We can't expect our brothers and sisters to crucify themselves for us. We can't reach out to someone who is not putting out his hand. Love is an act of recognition, empathy, and sharing. Love is not the act of giving, but is, in itself, a gift. We can't go to Africa with empty suitcases hoping to load up on a culture that we left behind four centuries ago. We must go with full hearts hoping to share what we've learned, which is quite a bit, with what our ancestors have become. We can't expect our children to have pride in themselves if we can't give them a stake in building their own lives.[82]

CONCLUSION

I have penned the words of this chapter not as a disinterested scholar or idealistic advocate. I write as a flawed and grateful man, father, brother, son, and friend. And "with a little help from my friends," I have grown and learned much (and still learning) about the dynamics of commitment and sharing, and the vulnerability that love demands. I know that I could not have experienced the joy, love, and hopefulness that I have known without the forgiveness, patience, and graceful generosity of my friends and family.

In this chapter, I have highlighted several prominent issues that merit attention as a village-wide conversation is considered and developed. I have noted several basic facts and observations about black families that I believe are important for informing the public's understanding of black family concerns and for framing the point of departure for the villagewide conversations that need to occur. I conclude here with a set of questions that I hope may stimulate discussion and, ultimately, lead to redemptive action immediately.

QUESTIONS FOR DISCUSSION

1. What practical steps can you take to promote a culture of healthy relationships?

2. What concrete actions can you and your friends undertake to promote the art of healthy dating?

3. If there is a love deficit in some African American communities, what can be done to reverse it starting tomorrow? How can we revive the "art of intimacy"?

4. What have you heard black community leaders say about this topic?

5. Reverend Jesse Jackson has said, "What began as a problem has deteriorated into a condition. Problems require solving; conditions require healing." What steps should now be taken to begin healing in black families? Who should take these steps? What are you prepared to do to support family and relationship healing?

6. When it comes to divorce and the well-being of children, what should the community expect of each partner as they go separate ways?

7. With respect to nonmarital birth, what should the village expect from both partners before, during, and after the birth of a new child?

8. How will you and your friends, family, and neighbors express your commitments to all children?

9. How will you initiate a productive conversation concerning the topic of homosexuality and same-sex marriage? What are the safest places to have this conversation?

10. In light of apparent strong African American opposition to legalizing same-sex relationships, should local communities encourage tolerance and respect for village members with different sexual orientations and lifestyles? If so, how can that be accomplished?

11. What is the role of economics and public policy (jobs, income, assets) in promoting a culture of healthy relationships, marriages, and families? What can we do to influence the debate?

12. What concrete actions should local village leadership initiate in the next six months to improve life for all families, married people, cohabiting couples, and children?

13. What concrete things can community members, families, and churches do to promote healthy dating and relationships?

14. Which organizations, groups, or individuals should take the leadership for moving this issue forward?

2

CHURCHES
A CRISIS OF MISSION

IN 1996, the Reverend Henry Lyons became the president of the National Baptist Convention, the nation's largest denomination. Lyons took pride in cultivating large corporations for gifts and investments and counted many successes by allegedly falsifying member rolls to suggest a Convention of "potential customers" considerably larger than its actual size. While Lyons was on a trip to Africa, his wife discovered evidence of his having an extramarital relationship, including the deed to a lavish mansion co-owned with another woman, not far from his own home. Lyons's wife allegedly set fires in the mansion and was arrested for arson, calling national attention to the story. As the story unraveled, allegations of grand theft, racketeering, and other charges emerged; Lyons in turn was sentenced to prison, divorced, and lost his congregation. Although Lyons served a modest-sized congregation rather than a megachurch, his drive for personal wealth accumulation as president of the National Baptist Convention symbolized a new threat to the integrity of black clergy culture. Indeed, the theme of prosperity rather than the biblical mission of love, service, and justice, better describes the chief aim of many churches.

Black churches have earned a noble place in the complicated history of American democracy and American Christianity. Even before the republic was founded, there were black congregations.[1]

And there is something awe-inspiring about the fact that congregations founded by African slaves and free blacks were the only places where they could experience some semblance of the freedom about which America's Founding Fathers spoke. Nearly two hundred years later, those same churches initiated the modern civil rights movement and helped to transform America from a society based on racial apartheid to one where ethnic and religious diversity flourish. Black churches showed the rest of American religious communities that faith could be a force for serving the common good. Their numerous cultural gifts of music, preaching, and spirituality have become global exports that have enriched many cultures across the globe.

Unfortunately, I've discovered that many educated people do not know basic information about America's black churches. Whenever I talk about the history, mission, culture, and achievements of the black church, audiences, no matter what their age, class, or ethnic identity are amazed by the story and want to know more. They immediately appreciate the fact that black churches are *American institutions* with which they should be familiar. Indeed, black churches helped to define the terms in which American democracy and freedom would be discussed. So before discussing the problems that face the church, consider this short list of "need to know" facts about the black church. Far from trivia, this information is part of American religious history with which all educated people should be familiar.

WHAT EVERYONE SHOULD KNOW ABOUT BLACK CHURCHES

1. *The cultural roots of the black church extend back to Africa.* That makes them "quasi-African institutions." In order to understand the black church in America, it is important to understand the African roots of black church culture and spirituality. From 1619 (when the first Africans arrived in Jamestown, Virginia) until

the 1740s, most African slaves were not encouraged or permitted to join Christian churches out of fear that they would claim equality to white people and demand equal citizenship rights. Africans were permitted to continue practicing African traditional religion. After the Great Awakening revivals began to sweep across the South, tens of thousands of Africans converted to Christianity for the first time and soon thereafter independent black congregations emerged.

2. *The black church in America, despite its African heritage, is a profoundly "American" institution.* Indeed, the birth of the black church preceded the birth of America as a republic. There were African Baptist congregations in the South as early as 1773 (Silver Bluff, South Carolina), several years before the American Revolution. As such, the black church is another example of early American institutional inventiveness. The best and worst of American values, habits, and practices found their way into the "institutional DNA" of the black church.

3. *Slave religion was a complex fusion of at least four elements: African traditional religion, Catholic popular piety, Protestant evangelicalism, and Islam.*[2] The thought and practices of early black churches were a cultural gumbo of these and other elements that expressed both the creativity of the African population and the capacity of the American society first to tolerate, and later to celebrate, the complex character of black churches.

4. *Early American congregations were interracial.* As Africans became Christian in the United States, they worshiped in the same churches as their white masters and owners. But as their number grew to exceed the somewhat small white church-going public, both whites and blacks agreed that it would be better to establish separate black churches. In some cases, black people felt pushed out of the interracial churches and founded their own congregations in protest of religious racism.

5. *The black church also preceded the origins of the black family as a legally recognized institution.* At a time when marriage and family

life among slaves was illegal and often impossible, slave owners often supported the founding of black congregations hoping that a "servant-centered" gospel would instill traits of obedience, quiescence, nonviolence, and loyalty. Honoring marriage vows was more troublesome and disruptive to the slave economy, which thrived on breeding and the spontaneous sale and trade of Africans, practices that discouraged sustainable familial bonds.

6. *The black church has been and continues to function as the hub of civil society and remains the center of social life in many black communities.* It was the community's source of aid and philanthropy, a center for learning and literacy, a zone for political education and mobilization, an organizer of financial capital, and keeper of a collective cultural memory. During the relief efforts after Hurricanes Katrina and Rita, we saw the nation's local congregations engage in rapid-response life-saving activity that prevented an even greater tragedy.

7. *The black church is typically an asset-rich institution and generally one of the wealthiest institutions in the community.* It often owns its sanctuary and other property, manages a weekly cash flow, enjoys influence with, and access to, financial institutions, employs people, makes charitable donations to the community, and is a symbol of collective economics (saving, pooling resources, acquiring land and property, and so forth). Often the church itself is a financial institution or sponsors a credit union that holds savings and makes loans. Collectively, black churches control billions of dollars in assets that can be leveraged for the good of the community.

8. *Black churches were incubators for black colleges.* In some instances, the colleges were either founded in the church (Spelman College) or held classes in church buildings (Morehouse College). Churches supported the growth and vitality of institutions of higher education and were advocates for intellectual development and academic achievement. Black churches nurtured and satisfied the educational longings of a people that had been prevented from attending formal schools or learning to read. From their beginnings,

as a whole, black churches were not anti-intellectual institutions. But, over time, as many churches assimilated the parochialisms and cultural habits of their white neighbors, many black churches embraced an anti-Enlightenment posture suspicious of innovations in science and religion.

9. *Black churches have been and continue to be political power brokers in the village.* As one of the few places in which black people could gather on a regular basis, churches picked up the agenda of pursuing freedom and full participation in American society. The political culture of black churches was multidimensional and spanned the spectrum from nonpartisan voter education to endorsement of preferred candidates to supporting clergy and laity who sought elective office. Among their many political strategies, some sought to negotiate and cooperate with political power structures to produce change, while others emphasized the need for a more radical approach to change. Still others rejected politics and focused solely upon saving and rescuing souls from the corrosive nature of secular society.

10. *Black churches have been therapeutic institutions fostering a culture of psychological freedom, mental health, and self-esteem.* Churches promoted a sense of personal pride and value along with the ego strength necessary to face daily assaults on their self-worth and dignity. In black churches, everyone could attain status, hold office, wear a title, have responsibility, and be affirmed for their contribution. Insiders amusingly observe that there are often more titles than actual jobs to be done. But everyone feels important, and that goes a long way when you're trying to nurture personal responsibility, power, and moral agency.

11. *Black churches have functioned as extended family networks.* As surrogate families where members were referred to by family role titles such as "sister," "brother," and "mother," most people in the church could feel part of a larger social network of caring people. Although "church as extended family" was the ideal, often churches recapitulated the discriminatory practices and hierarchies

according to gender, race, class, and sexual orientation found in the larger society.

12. *Today, the vast majority of African American Christians are clustered in a dozen denominations.* We lack fully reliable figures on the total number of black congregations in the United States. Our best estimates place that number between fifty thousand to sixty-five thousand congregations that break into three large families: Baptist, Methodist, and Pentecostal-Holiness. Indeed, approximately eighteen million blacks belong to the eight largest historically black denominations (National Baptist Convention, USA; National Baptist Convention of America; Progressive National Baptist Convention; National Missionary Baptist Convention; African Methodist Episcopal Church; Christian Methodist Episcopal Church; African Methodist Episcopal Zion Church; and the Church of God in Christ [COGIC]). But there are significant numbers of black people in predominantly white denominations such as the Roman Catholic Church (3 million), the Episcopal Church (750,000), the Presbyterian Church (USA), and the United Methodist Church. This fact requires that caution be exercised when speaking of "the black church" as if it were a single, monolithic institution. I use the term *black church* with that caution and caveat in mind. Moreover, it is a useful and elegant form of sociological shorthand that facilitates helpful distinctions.[3]

13. *Black churches were the cultural incubators for several expressions of American genius.* Churches helped to encourage the flourishing of individual talent and innovation that gave rise to the spirituals, blues, jazz, gospel, Motown, hip hop, and a variety of other musical traditions. Some churches were antagonistic toward "secular" art forms, however, even those that were born within the church itself (gospel music).

14. *Today's megachurches are products of the traditional black church and are beginning to expand and redefine that tradition.* Congregations with thousands of members have social, political, and economic power that is unprecedented in black church history.

Unfortunately, a cleavage between the tradition and these innova-
tors has emerged. Black megachurches cluster in urban centers such
as Los Angeles, Dallas, New York, Atlanta, Chicago, Houston, and
Washington, D.C.[4]

15. *The historical influence of black churches appears to be in decline.*
Scholars have demonstrated that congregations in low-income communities have modest outreach to the surrounding community. Most
black churches are "commuter congregations" in which a majority of
members reside one or more miles from the sanctuary. Their members tend to lack profound knowledge of the local neighborhood and
do not offer a broad range of social services to their neighbors.[5]

Each of the above items could occupy an entire book; indeed,
several good books have been written on these topics, many of which
are listed in my endnotes for those who wish to pursue further reading. The purpose of this book is not simply to state facts but to raise
an urgent set of questions whose answers will put our feet in motion
to solve the crises. But in addition to raising questions for village
discussion, I'd like to propose a specific set of mission assignments
that, if taken seriously and revised appropriately, could become the
basis for an exciting community revitalization.

- How can churches avoid the dangers and distractions
  of the "prosperity gospel" movement?
- How can the church be challenged to take greater risks
  on behalf of the least-advantaged members of the
  community?
- Given the authority of clergy in the black church tradition, how can the village assist clergy to become more
  effective?
- How can clergy be encouraged to avoid the distractions and seductions of ego inflation?
- What can be done by all of us—churches, laypeople,
  clergy, and the public at large—to recover the church's
  declining moral authority?

- How may the church renew its own spiritual identity and practices?

WHAT'S WRONG?
The Prosperity Movement

I am convinced that the single greatest threat to the historical legacy and core values of the contemporary black church tradition is posed by what is known as the "prosperity gospel" movement. That movement, however, is only symptomatic of a larger mission crisis or "mission drift" that has placed the black church in the posture of assimilating into a culture that is hostile to people living on the margins of society, such as people living in poverty, people living with AIDS, homosexuals, and immigrants.

I regard this to be the fundamental challenge for the church. It is not a new challenge. Christians have grappled with their relationship to material goods and opportunities in this world since the first century. But in our era something new and different has emerged. Today, prominent, influential, and attractive preachers and representatives of the church now are advocates for prosperity. Perhaps this could only occur at a time and in a place where two conditions exist. First, Christianity is the dominant faith tradition; second, the nation permits and rewards extraordinary inequalities of wealth and power. This new face of an old problem constitutes the crux of the church's mission crisis.

The gospel of assimilation provides sacred sanction for personal greed, obsessive materialism, and unchecked narcissism. That distorted gospel dares not risk a critique of the culture and systems that thrive in the presence of a morally anemic church. This is more than a concern about the encroachment of the "prosperity gospel" movement that receives so much negative attention. Rather, this is a more thorough and comprehensive distortion of the religion of Jesus.

To be a successful (different from faithful) pastor in today's world is to confront the ever-present temptation to sell one's soul, compromising one's vocation and ethical responsibilities, in exchange for or access to wealth. One Houston-based minister observed that when the church gets a mortgage, "poor people" become just another church program. Poor people were central to Jesus' own self-definition but they are often relegated to one of many service programs of today's corporate church, simply another item on the services menu.

> The Spirit of the Lord is upon me for he has anointed me to preach good news to the poor. He has sent me to heal the broken-hearted, to proclaim release to the captives, recovering of sight to the blind, to deliver those who are crushed and to proclaim the acceptable year of the Lord. (Luke 4:18)

Most pastors are under pressure to become "large figures," people of importance. Many religious leaders are preoccupied with establishing a large footprint in the soil of history. They are expected to build great sanctuaries and establish great works that will outlive them. Biblical scholar Michael Joseph Brown observes, "We live in a society that evaluates success on the basis of numbers. Many denominations and congregations have adopted a corporate mind-set. I liken it to the fast food industry where the number of patrons served is the measure of success. In my more cynical moments, I expect to be driving down the street one day and pass a church sign that reads: 'Over 2,000 Members Served.' Congregation size, income, number of services are possible by-products of ministerial excellence. They do not constitute excellence in themselves."[6]

One can imagine the temptations that confronted the Reverend Mr. Lyons while president of the National Baptist Convention. As we reflect on his story and on the smaller challenges of most clergy and laity, consider the following testimony from an early biblical religious and political figure:

Biblical Portrait of a Large Leader

I made myself great works. I built myself houses. I planted myself vineyards. I made myself gardens and parks and I planted trees in them of all kinds of fruit. I made myself pools of water. . . . I also had great possessions of herds and flocks, above all who were before me. . . . So I was great, and increased more than all who were before me. . . . My wisdom also remained with me. Whatever my eyes desired, I didn't keep from them. I didn't withhold my heart from any joy . . . then I looked at all the works that my hands had worked and behold, all was vanity. (Ecclesiastes 1 & 2)

This testimony from the book of Ecclesiastes is often attributed to King Solomon but was probably the "composite" voice of many ancient figures. It sounds a lot like a hip-hop rap lyric waiting to be put to music. But, it also resembles the "guild talk" I hear at all kinds of clergy gatherings across the ethnic and denominational spectrum. Pastors like to brag about the kingdoms they have built and the monuments they will leave behind.

But the tragedy is that one fourth of the black community lives in poverty while many clergy and churches are distracted and seduced by the lure of material wealth. When churches devote more time to building their local kingdoms, something political scientist Michael Owens has called an "edifice complex," and less time to nurturing and uplifting poor people, they are struggling with a mission crisis.

My understanding of the religion of Jesus suggests that the church is God's gift to the world to express God's love for humanity and to implement God's vision of a renewed creation. If that is the case, then people in the church and in the community should hold churches accountable to their vocation and identity. Churches must retrieve their autonomy from the culture and work to transform social institutions and practices in ways that help rather than harm the most vulnerable members of the community. That is the mood and social profile of the religion of Jesus.

A Prosperity Field Trip

One Sunday, I visited the church of my Atlanta neighbor, the Reverend Creflo Dollar. I attended with an open mind, as I was anxious to learn more about this popular pastor's interpretation of the Christian message. For a few years I had heard about the burgeoning ministry of the World Changers Church and felt I should see for myself. I wondered, "Why are thousands upon thousands of people voting for this interpretation of Jesus?" In addition, several seminarians and friends whom I know and respect are active members of the church.

Arriving late (an incorrigible habit of mine!), I found a parking space "far from the peaceful shore," nearly three blocks from the sanctuary. The hike to the sanctuary was so far that I momentarily forgot where I was headed and began to window shop the stores en route to the church, perhaps unconsciously getting into prosperity mode. I gathered my wits and continued the pilgrimage. Slightly winded, I finally arrived and entered the enormous domed sanctuary, taking a seat near the front. I discovered that I wasn't late at all. Everything was neat and comfortable. The blue carpet and plush pew covers were welcoming. The huge rotating globe and other props on stage subtly reminded one that what happens here is intended for a global television audience.

I looked around, searching for a familiar face. Recognizing none of the eager and focused faces seated all around, I focused on the altar as the choir entered. After the choir sang a couple of numbers, the pastor entered the sanctuary dressed in a business "power" suit and took his seat. He took a moment to scan the entire congregation, perhaps ensuring that everything was in order, then he focused on his notes for the day.

Moments later, he was standing behind the pulpit. Most black preachers begin their sermons in a conversational way. They acknowledge the presence of special guests and familiar faces and invite people to relax and laugh before they begin the journey toward an encounter with the "holy." But this was a bit different, perhaps because the stage lights and television cameras were operating. Dispensing with all of the "old school" black church conventions, he went right to the text for the day. No mention of members who were sick and had returned to church appearing better. No mention of the awesome peach cobbler that Mother Williams delivered to the office. No time spent on connecting with individual members at all. It felt as if we were his audience, not his congregation.

The first fifteen minutes of his message were encouraging and impressive. I heard evidence of a critical thinker who had done his homework and given careful attention to various scholarly sources for the selected biblical text. I recall thinking that this sermon could be preached in the chapel of any of Atlanta's seminaries. Then, out of nowhere, he began to testify about a friend who had recently given him a second Rolls Royce. He continued, "Now, that's not the Rolls that you all gave me years ago. See, so don't get mad. This was a gift from a friend. It's good to have friends." I wonder if anyone else wondered, "Why does he need *one* Rolls Royce? But, *two*?"

More amazing was the affirming manner in which the congregation seemed to affirm this testimony of personal indulgence and excess. No one in the church seemed to have the power to hold the preacher accountable for exceeding his proper allowance as a representative of Jesus. I do not know Reverend Dollar personally and I will reserve judgment about his motives and character, but it does appear that he has followed the script for how a successful and affluent corporate executive behaves. He does not seem to have entertained the possibility of rewriting that script and offering to other ministers and followers a new paradigm of socially responsible affluence.

In 2006, I delivered a radio commentary on this topic on the National Public Radio program *All Things Considered*.[7] I was out of the country when it aired but received an urgent e-mail from my producer indicating that Rev. Dollar's staff had contacted the station. A letter to the producer was read the next week expressing their challenge to my "imbalanced" interpretation of the church's ministry.

If most black preachers—and other preachers for that matter—are preoccupied with pursuing the "bling-bling" life of conspicuous consumption, then poor people are in big trouble. Because it indicates the hearts of their chief advocates are "drunk with the wine of the world"[8] and incapable of speaking truth to power.

Given the distorting influence of the prosperity movement on authentic Christianity I should say more about the phenomenon and say what it is and is not. We should distinguish between the following three realities: (1) the "gospel of prosperity"; (2) the "prosperity gospel"; and (3) radical Christian stewardship that may include the ownership of material goods. Much confusion occurs today from the tendency to confuse or combine these distinct approaches to faith and money.

The Gospel of Prosperity: "Greed is Good"

The "gospel of prosperity" refers to the cultural ideology or message that suggests that the accumulation of material possessions, wealth, and prosperity are morally neutral goods that are necessary for human happiness. One popular expression of this ideology appeared in the movie *Wall Street*, where the central character declares that "greed is good." I characterize it as an ideology rather than merely an idea because it functions like a powerful, unconscious force that does not revise its position in the face of counterevidence. For instance, none of its advocates would admit that possessing material goods in excess may actually induce unhappiness. As an ideology, its believers insist upon its correctness, deny the legitimacy of other perspectives, and pursue wealth without concern for long-term consequences. Prosperity becomes an intrinsic good, and an end in itself.

Now, most of examples of this vulgar form of material worship do not pretend to be religious, certainly not Christian. Rather, they are elements of what might be called America's largest quasi-religious tradition, namely the religion of capitalism. If you look at our economy as a belief system, it makes sense to regard its sanctuaries as the local stores and its megachurches are malls. Its theology is the field of economics. Its bishops are the CEOs of the *Fortune* 500 companies. Its missionaries are the salespersons who take American business to the uttermost parts of the earth where you can find Coca-Cola signs amidst the most impoverished and wretched living conditions in the most distant villages of nonindustrial nations. Its evangelists are the marketing and advertising departments that create desire for products that we don't need, and its theological teachers are the faculties of America's business schools.

Financial enrichment seminars have become an industry unto themselves to advance this American "folk religion." For example, a company called "The Learning Annex" has advertised a seminar or program billed as a "real estate wealth expo," which invites people to pay $99 in order to "discover Donald Trump's real estate secrets all in just one weekend."[9] In addition, several other motivational speakers (including the former boxing champion George Foreman) are promised to be on hand to evangelize for wealth, as well as seventy-two additional "wealth counselors" to assist people in their financial planning.

In American history and culture, the gospel of prosperity has been a guiding ideology or myth embodied in the Horatio Alger story (among others), who acquired wealth through the heroic exercise of risk taking, ingenuity, high energy, inordinate self-confidence, and tireless effort. That's the gospel of prosperity that underwrites American capitalism. The gospel of prosperity is a competitor to authentic Christianity (and other faith traditions) and ruthlessly seeks to establish its preeminence in the culture.

In the African American community, one could argue that Booker T. Washington represented a version of the gospel of prosperity for the masses at a time when most black people had experienced slavery and were now aspiring to pursue the American dream without upsetting the social and racial status quo. He insisted that the newly freed black population invest its primary energy in economic self-reliance, hard work, and entrepreneurship rather than political empowerment. Washington often spoke of a "gospel of the head, hand, and heart." However, his social context did not make it feasible for many blacks to achieve extraordinary wealth. Those who did tended to be generous in their philanthropy, such as Madame C. J. Walker. Rather, Washington urged blacks and poor whites to abandon the distraction of racial conflict and adopt the virtues of the Protestant work ethic as they pursued material comfort and abundance.

The Prosperity Gospel of the Spiritual Entrepreneurs

Second, there is the "prosperity gospel" that asserts Christian faith is an investment that inexorably yields material abundance. I think that Rev. Dollar fits in this category, along with scores of other televangelists who live and instruct others on how to "think and grow rich." Wealth is outward proof of an inner grace and righteousness. Salvation is both spiritual and material. And although the "prosperity gospel" may not be as vulgar an expression of greed as the "gospel of prosperity," both are corrosive and threatening to American churches, which are constantly tempted to focus on their own institutional well-being at the expense of serving the vulnerable.

Indeed, the prosperity gospel may be even more insidious and dangerous because it subverts particular elements of the Jesus story and of classical, biblical Christianity in order to instill a new attitude toward capitalism and riches. That is, it often deliberately suppresses, ignores, and/or deletes language about radical sacrifice for the sake of God's kingdom. In other words, it excludes a core message of the Jesus story, namely that which is symbolized by the cross, or what I characterize as "cross talk." It does not linger on the cross because that symbol is an enemy to the underlying confidence people invest in material prosperity at the expense of trusting God. "Cross talk," central to the third tradition I shall discuss next, insists that believers share their material prosperity rather than horde it. And at times (not always or in every case) the call to share wealth may be so radical that a person is compelled to give it all away in order to serve and please God.

I refer to the clergy who operate from this "prosperity gospel" orientation as "spiritual entrepreneurs" who know how to produce, package, market, and distribute user-friendly spirituality for the masses. The spiritual product lines that they market rarely make stringent ethical demands upon their listeners. Instead, they proffer a gospel of health, wealth, and success designed to help others become more affluent. When these leaders serve as pastors of congregations, they function like "entrepreneurial ecclesiastical executives" at the helm of corporate organizations. From my experience, worshiping in such churches doesn't always feel like much of a religious experience—and that is by design. Ultimately, I would say such congregations and leaders may be changing who they are and are called to be, distorting the meaning of church as a community of holy awareness, care, interdependence, sharing, moral deliberation, and action. This is another development that must be monitored carefully.

Similar to the "real estate wealth expo" described above, a parallel program has developed within the prosperity gospel community. At the annual Megafest, a religious festival of worship, workshops, and family entertainment hosted by Bishop T. D. Jakes, attendees are exposed to a broad array of financial advisors and motivational speakers who urge people to improve their modest lifestyles. Although Bishop Jakes is not representative of the full-fledged prosperity gospel preachers, his ministry includes an uncommon emphasis on material wealth and he appears to be a person of considerable personal means who does not speak often about the dangers of concentrated wealth.

Indeed, it is important not to confuse or conflate clergy who teach financial literacy with those who promote prosperity as a religious right and entitlement, especially the extravagant wealth of the pastor. Financial literacy includes transmitting information about how to utilize mainstream financial institutions and products, avoid predatory lenders, repair bad credit, develop a rational savings plan, incubate small businesses, and proceed to home ownership. These are principles of effective stewardship that have their proper place in the ministry of every congregation. Indeed, they constitute the foundation of the third model we should consider.

Black Enterprise magazine has developed a "Black Wealth Initiative," which offers practical tools for managing assets. Developed by financial experts and economists, the plan is designed to assist people in managing money through a comprehensive savings, investment, and consumer strategy. The program identifies the stages of wealth accumulation along with "10 principles of wealth."[10]

I include their "Declaration of Financial Empowerment" here because it illustrates an approach to wealth acquisition that is inspired more by the values of our capitalist culture than the spirit of historic Christianity. To its credit, the declaration encourages many valuable elements of financial literacy and best practices (saving, budgeting, home ownership, and so forth) that any rational person might wish to observe. Many clergy teach these same values. But, with the exception of principle # 9—"using a portion of my wealth to strengthen my community"—the principles are exceedingly self-centered rather than communally oriented. One finds no mention of traditional Christian values such as sharing one's possessions (Acts 2) or sacrificial giving to uplift vulnerable people. Clergy who embrace this approach should at least be aware and honest about the fact that this ideology lives in tension with prophetic Christianity. It may not be worthy of total condemnation, as it contains many useful principles of good stewardship. On the other hand, it encourages loyalty to an economic system, to the logic of the market, which does harm to poor people in its very process of generating wealth for disciplined investors. Religious people should grapple with the moral ambiguity of benefiting personally from a system predicated on exploiting the working poor and other vulnerable people.

Declaration of Financial Empowerment

In order to attain a measure of success, power and wealth, I shall uphold the principles of saving and investing as well as controlled spending and disciplined consumerism. I vow to fully participate in the capital markets and make a solid commitment to a program of wealth accumulation. Determination and consistency will serve as my guides, and I shall not allow external or internal forces to keep me from reaching my goals. By adjusting my course and embracing a new mandate that stresses planning, education and fortitude, I lay a strong, unbreakable foundation for the preservation and enrichment of my family, children and children's children.

I, [NAME], from this day forward, declare my vigilant and life-long commitment to financial empowerment. I pledge the following:

1. To use homeownership to build wealth
2. To save and invest 10% to 15% of my after-tax income
3. To commit to a program of retirement planning and investing
4. To engage in sound budget, credit, and tax management
5. To measure my personal wealth by net worth, not income
6. To be proactive and knowledgeable about investing, money management, and consumer issues

7. To provide access to programs that will educate my children about business and finance

8. To support the creation and growth of profitable, competitive black-owned enterprises

9. To use a portion of my wealth to strengthen my community

10. To ensure that my wealth is passed on to future generations

I have committed to this unwavering, personal covenant as a means of bolstering myself, my family and my community. In adopting this resolution, I intend to use all available resources, wisdom and power to gain my share of the American Dream.[11]

This model and the financial messages promulgated by Reverend Dollar represent the slippery slope about which churches and clergy should be cautious as they play the capitalist game according to rules that Jesus did not create. For nothing in such plans contains the internal ethical corrective Jesus provided, "What shall it profit a person if he gain the whole world and lose his soul?"

Prophetic Stewardship

A third view of faith and money is one I call "prophetic stewardship." I use the word *prophetic* in order to emphasize that this model represents something of a negative judgment on its alternatives, the secular gospel of prosperity and the pseudo-religious prosperity gospel. It seeks to displace them with a more radical version of stewardship and "shared prosperity."[12] Here it is understood that the Christian gospel includes many goods—spiritual, social, psychological, physical, and material. But none of them, apart from the spiritual good of salvation, is promised without qualification. Again, the cross and a disciple's faithful embrace of it may require one to practice what theologian Jacquelyn Grant has called an "ethic of renunciation," in which we may have to sacrifice physical well-being, psychological comfort, social support, and material goods for the sake of saving our souls. Is this the meaning of Matthew 6:33, "But, seek ye first the kingdom of God and his righteousness and all these things shall be added to you"?

Prophetic stewardship invites reflection upon the meaning of the values found in passages such as Matthew 6:19. There, Jesus engages in "cross talk" as he declares "do not store up for yourselves treasures on earth where moth and rust destroy and where thieves break in and steal, but store up for yourselves treasures in heaven." And in Luke 12:15 we read, "Watch out. Be on your guard against all kinds of greed, a man's life does not consist in the abundance of his possessions." That passage precedes the wonderful passage or pericope regarding one person's explosive accumulation of wealth.

Luke 12:16 reads, "The ground of a certain rich man produced a good crop. He thought to himself, 'What shall I do? I have no place to store my crops.' Then he said, 'This is what I'll do. I will tear down my barns and build bigger ones, and there I will store all my grain and my goods. And I'll say to myself, 'You have plenty of good things laid up for many years. Take life easy; eat, drink and be merry.' But God said to him, 'You fool! This very night your life will be demanded from you. Then who will get what you have prepared for yourself?'" The image of building bigger barns (boxes) for increased inventory always reminds me of what someone has called the "Wal-Martization" of retail shopping.

And in the Evangelist Luke's writings, Acts 2:44 indicates that "All the believers were together and had everything in common, Selling their possessions and goods, they gave to anyone as he had need. . . ." Although scholarly opinion differs about the extent of this early form of Christian communalism, it is certain that when people had a life-changing encounter with Jesus Christ, it also reshaped their attitude toward their possessions.

There is a fourth noteworthy possibility that deserves mention. It is the vocation of Christian asceticism, which involves vows of poverty, chastity, obedience, life in monasteries, and so forth. Most Christians do not feel called to such a way of life and understand this to be a special vocation for a few special individuals. For centuries, the Roman Catholic tradition has preserved and encouraged discernment about this understanding of vocation and many courageous souls have devoted themselves to the ascetic life. For most Christians, what I am calling "prophetic stewardship" represents the highest and most strenuous form of economic sacrifice they are willing or able to embrace.

To put it clearly, first, *the gospel of prosperity (greed is good) is diametrically opposed to Christian faith and ethics and merits the church's vigilant opposition.* This is because it permits and rewards moral relativism in pursuit of wealth and invests ultimate confidence in the happiness that comes from possession. In the second instance, *the prosperity gospel is a distortion of authentic biblical Christianity and warrants the correction and monitoring of responsible church leaders and laity.* That distortion manifests itself in varying degrees in the ministries of various preachers who are labeled in this way. Since we have no consensus about the definition of the prosperity gospel, which clergy are included under this rubric is highly debatable. The important thing here is that this option or orientation is redeemable and reversible. And in the third case, *prophetic stewardship is the most adequate and authentic expression of a Christian orientation to money. Consequently, Christians should aspire to understand, accept, and practice prophetic stewardships.* Such stewardship both encourages Christians to live in a simple but comfortable manner (leaving a small footprint on the earth), and publicly work to change the culture's prevailing habits of greed. This public move is what makes it prophetic. That is, prosperity per se should never become a prominent theme or mark of the faithful Christian life. It should never compete with the cross for center stage. Material acquisition should always be incidental to one's vocation and one must always be prepared to make radical sacrifices for the sake of one's soul and/or the good of the reign of God. This final and most faithful option suggests, tentatively, that it is possible to have and enjoy possessions but never to the extent of outrageous greed and prosperity.

How the Community Can Change the Incentives for Prosperity

Although the ultimate goal of clergy leadership development programs (whether sponsored by theological seminaries, denominations, or other institutions) should be to promote a culture of prophetic stewardship, we know that some people will need more incentives than others to grow into that perspective. I propose that the community, laity, and clergy work together to help change the prevailing culture of compensation and material reward. The community should declare that if a clergyperson and/or church demonstrates good faith in collaborating with other churches and organizations engaged in renewing the village or, in the absence of collaboration, they are working heroically and strategically to make a positive impact on our most pressing problems, it will reward these clergy with financial support and personal encouragement. Similarly, if clergy are unresponsive to the village-renewal agenda, then the community should withdraw its support for superfluous, clueless, or greedy clergy. The message should be clear: "If you want to become a popular and prosperous preacher who is admired and loved by the community, serve the community in the ways that it needs most. Do the right thing and you will do well. Do otherwise, and we will ignore you into obscurity and bankruptcy."

This idea was inspired by the preacher and public theologian Dr. Jualynne Dodson. Speaking to an audience at Colgate Rochester Divinity School, she urged that pastors not be given or encouraged to drive luxury cars unless they have proven faithful to the community's needs. Indeed, speaking only half in jest, I would suggest that when the community observes pastors driving cars that they do not deserve (by fault of poor community service), then residents should offer the "thumbs down" sign when they drive by. And for those who are deserving (assuming that they wish to drive such cars), the community should render the gift of a "thumbs up" or an approving smile.

Leslie Callahan, professor at the University of Pennsylvania and pastor of a Pentecostal church, humorously suggests that there should be a "one cool car rule" for clergy who wish to serve the community and live well without losing their souls. Such a rule might have prevented Rev. Dollar's sermon from detouring onto the Rolls Royce parking lot.

Ministry and Missed Opportunities

Against the background of the prosperity gospel movement and the seductions of spiritual leaders is the more chilling report that many churches located in high poverty neighborhoods are not responding to local need very effectively. R. Drew Smith, a senior fellow at the Leadership Center of Morehouse College, undertook research in four cities (Camden, Denver, Hartford, and Indianapolis) on the relationship between churches and low income residents. His 2003 report, *Beyond the Boundaries: Low Income Residents, Faith Based Organizations and Neighborhood Coalition Building*, states the following conclusions:

- Two-thirds of the housing complex residents surveyed report having little or no contact with faith-based organizations in the previous year;
- Many congregations report having programs of potential value to neighborhood residents but indicate that church members take advantage of these programs more frequently than non-members; and,
- Roughly two-thirds of the congregations report that most of their members live more than one mile from their place of worship.[13]

These findings only confirm a reality about which sociologists have spoken for many years with respect to "commuter churches" that serve people who do not reside in the neighborhood. Smith and others underscore the social isolation of low-income, urban residents from the jobs, social services, and poverty-alleviating networks in their metro areas. And he points to the potential of churches to bridge that distance and help to connect people and their communities.

In 2006, the Joint Center for Political and Economic Studies released a report on the black church and the White House faith-based initiative.[14] Some of its data offered a more positive perspective on the extent of church involvement with local communities. One of its key findings was that 93 percent of clergy report that they have served people living in the local community and only a small percentage of churches had applied for or received funding from the government initiative. Even more interesting was the finding that a majority of pastors who sought and received funding could be characterized as "socially progressive," but they were also among the clergy who most disapproved of the initiative. I interpreted this as an example of "pastoral pragmatism," wherein pastors who were initially suspicious of government retreat from providing social-welfare services and opposed to partisan manipulation of the black churches also were concerned about the misery of people living in poverty and sought to address it with all available resources.

If there is a question about the disconnect between churches and their local neighborhoods, I hope that it will become an issue that evokes community conversation about how congregations that do little for local residents can revise their ministries to serve those people more effectively. And I hope that the same community which criticizes inactive churches will acknowledge and reward those that are active and faithful to their mission.

Based on my observations, many churches are engaged in high-energy ministry, but at the same time they are missing opportunities to help people in greatest need. Later in the chapter I offer a model of how churches could more systematically learn about and respond to the needs of their neighbors.

Why are churches so susceptible to misreading or misplacing their moral compasses? The work that Jesus left for the church is clearly set forth in the New Testament, and the people he wanted us to assist and empower are clearly identified. Moreover, Jesus provided the means for doing effective ministry before he departed. So what's the problem? I would submit that leadership, its quality, performance, and education are essential. Before turning to a proposal for making strategic assignments to our churches, I'd like to focus on the role of leadership.

Large Men, Little Dreams

The late preacher Dr. Charles Boddie used to relish telling the story of a Native American chief who visited his first black church revival. At the end of the service, a minister asked the chief what he thought of the sermon. He replied, "Big lightning, big thunder . . . no rain." This story brings into sharper focus the pretensions of preachers who enjoy presenting themselves as major power brokers ("big ballers and shot callers") but who fail to deliver much for people on the margins of society.

In an important and insightful essay titled "The Crisis of Black Leadership," Cornel West writes about a crisis in black leadership and suggests that today's leaders lack two qualities that were present among leaders in the civil rights movement era: anger and humility.[15] West is concerned about the lack of courageous public leadership by black clergy. This is what Tavis Smiley is pointing toward in his ten challenges (#9: "Encourage the Black Church to Do More").[16]

The irony is that many black preachers stylistically present themselves to the world as large, powerful, and accomplished individuals—large men with little dreams. They ignore the words of the great Chicago architect Robert Burnham, who said, "dream no small dreams." How many of today's denominational leaders, local pastors, or founders of the new megachurches have risked their access to important people or revenue streams in order to achieve "higher ground" goals in the arena of social justice, such as dismantling penalties against the working poor, expanding health-care coverage, or dramatically improving the well-being of children?

Indeed, the leadership performance of America's best-known and most visible black clergy should become more than the usual "gossip topic" in the village and instead become a cause for community action. We must invite and challenge leaders to do the right things, to do them more effectively, and in a collaborative manner. Further, we should reward generously institutions and leaders that meet our expectations and ignore those who are unresponsive or deliberately clueless. Moreover, we should actively isolate, stigmatize, and discourage those who are harmful to our communities. This must never be done in a mean-spirited way, but we must not permit leaders who exploit people to think that the community approves of such poor stewardship. The community deserves prophetic stewards.

Large clergy with little dreams should study the examples of risk-taking leadership and prophetic stewardship demonstrated by Dr. Martin Luther King Jr. and Pope John Paul II. Dr. King had an opportunity to accumulate riches and live a lavish lifestyle but he committed himself to a simple life. He did not berate the black middle class for its aspirations to accumulate wealth, but chose not to become a symbol of conspicuous consumption. When Pope John Paul II visited Jerusalem, he apologized to Jews and Muslims for Roman Catholic complicity with the Nazis and the Crusades. When he visited Africa, he bowed to the earth and kissed the ground. Although theologically conservative on many issues, he was a prophet on behalf of the social outcasts. For instance, the Catholic Bishops' "Pastoral Letter on the Economy" offers a model of the kind of moral analysis, argument, and suggested activism that black churches could easily engage if there was sufficient vision and will to do so.

Many clergy remain "small" in their dreams and sense of moral responsibility because they have not yet risked large things. Recall that the young Reverend Martin Luther King Jr. was very comfortable as the pastor of a small, middle-class congregation. His job was to provide pastoral care, administer the affairs of the church, and deliver brief, intellectual sermons. But, when the freedom movement accelerated, when the *zeitgeist* (the spirit of the times) stalked and found him, he was compelled to risk much—his job, his reputation, his family, his life. He became a great soul in the process.

But for too many pastors and religious leaders today, small dreams are comfortable and manageable. Bishop Charles Blake of Los Angeles once said that small leaders shrink grand projects down to the dimensions of their own capacity to control them. Imagine that, reducing a big dream to the size of one's comfort level! Have we considered acquiring the skills necessary to lead and manage large projects? The question is, Can the village assist the black church in playing a larger role in its revitalization? And in the process of serving the community in more effective ways, might the church itself be renewed?

The Misallocation of Titles and Honor

One of the symptoms of the mission crisis we face is manifest in the contemporary preoccupation with titles and status. Today, the title that a clergyperson bears may be a marker of his or her attitude toward the traditions that the elders created and handed down, and of her or his personal self-assessment. One should grow suspicious whenever a clergyperson disposes of the title conferred during an official licensing or ordination in favor of one that better expresses a personalized sense of significance. Rarely do such leaders choose a more humble, self-effacing title. For instance, many who were ordained "Reverend," "Elder," or "Pastor," have replaced those conventional titles with self-appointed replacements such as "Bishop," "Archbishop," "Apostle," "Dr.," and so on. Let me emphasize that I am not referring to leaders who have earned those titles from legitimate ecclesiastical organizations. My focus and concern is with how "self-appointed saviors" are cheapening the value of valued honors and status.

Here again, the example of Dr. King provides an important contrast and challenge to such contemporary market practices. King did the hard work and earned a doctor of philosophy degree from an acclaimed university, and he received a Nobel Peace Prize. But he never adjusted his title upward.

A short lesson on church titles might be useful for those who are not familiar with "clergy culture." The titles "minister" and "reverend" are generic terms used in church and in secular society to designate a person who is an official representative of a religious tradition. Most churches have a set of procedures, required learning, and evaluation prior to conferring an official license or ordination. After ordination, a minister is entitled to wear the title that her or his church designates as appropriate, such as "elder" or "deacon," both biblical terms. When a minister (usually an ordained person) is appointed to serve a particular congregation or sphere of ministry (such as chaplaincy), that person is generally recognized as a pastor (a word derived from the Hebrew word *ro-eh*, meaning "shepherd." The pastor is the shepherd of the flock and responsible for their spiritual nurture, care, and discipline. In the New Testament, many church leaders or pastors were appointed to manage large collections of congregations. They came to be known as "bishops" (in Greek, *episcopos*). The bishop is a pastor of other pastors. Some churches permit and expect a bishop to continue as the pastor of a local church (or more than one). This is the case in the Church of God in Christ, Pentecostal Assemblies of the World, and the Full Gospel Baptist Fellowship. Others do not permit their bishops to serve as both a local pastor and a pastor of other pastors. These include the AME, CME, AME Zion, United Methodist, Episcopal, and Roman Catholic churches.

Some church leaders today claim the vocation of "evangelist" or a minister who travels about and preaches full time without serving as pastor of a local congregation. Two other biblical titles have begun to appear with greater frequency and confusion: "prophet" and "apostle." According to most Christian traditions, a prophet is one who possesses a supernatural gift to see what others do not see, sometimes seeing forward into the future and foretelling it. And an apostle is one who possesses the supernatural gift to establish (or plant) new churches and ministries wherever he or she travels. These terms are generally not used as official designations by contemporary Christian churches. Generally, as a gesture of respect for the unique vocation they held in history, the title of prophet has been reserved for the Old Testament preachers who spoke on behalf of Jehovah. Similarly, "apostle" has been reserved for the first disciples who lived and worked with Jesus and helped to establish the churches following his earthly departure.

Today, more church leaders in black church culture are claiming and appropriating the titles of "prophet," "prophetess," and "apostle." Out of respect for what an individual may understand to be his or her God-given vocation, it is difficult to make a judgment about this practice. However, I do take offense from those who seem to appropriate the title as a marketing strategy or a way to distinguish their ministries from all the others in the religious marketplace. In the history of the church, it was never appropriate for a leader to simply claim a title, as if selecting a favorite hat to wear. Titles are symbols of the authority a recognized tradition vests in a faithful individual. They should not be treated with such disdain. And church leaders should not confuse other church members, especially younger people, who are unaware of the structure and history of the Christian churches. I would urge the churches in the village to resist the invasion of market culture and entrepreneurial ethic of individualism. We should discourage young leaders from such aspirations and should isolate and stigmatize those who insist on making a mockery of sacred and valuable assets.

What we are witnessing is the misallocation of status and authority in the black church community. This is a disturbing development. The highest term of admiration and affection within the black preacher fraternity and sorority is "Doc." That is the nickname his friends attributed to Dr. King and the one most often used for the community's most admired public theologians, such as Dr. Benjamin Mays, Dr. Gardner C. Taylor, and Dr. Samuel DeWitt Proctor.

Carter G. Woodson illustrated the problem in his time with a story.

> The degradation of the doctorate especially dawned upon the author the other day more clearly than ever when a friend of his rushed into his office saying, "I have been trying to see you for several days. I have just failed to get a job for which I had been working, and I am told that I cannot expect a promotion until I get my 'darkter's 'gree.'" That is what he called it. He could not even pronounce the words, but he is determined to have his "darkter's 'gree" to get the job in sight.
>
> This shameful status of higher education is due in large measure to low standards of institutions with a tendency toward the diploma-mill procedure.[17]

This phenomenon is duplicated by church leaders who appropriate for themselves titles from church history that have a definite, purposeful, and precise meaning.

The Shameful Silence of Clergy

Commenting on "the shameful silence of too many black ministers," journalist Earl Ofari Hutchinson writes in *The Disappearance of Black Leadership*, "Many black ministers and church members were stone silent on the rollback of affirmative action, the assault on civil liberties, the gutting of job and social programs, the slash in health care programs, the disparity in the criminal justice system, the rise in racially-motivated violence, the deterioration in public education, the draconian cuts in welfare, the surge in police abuse, and homelessness during the 1980s and 1990s."[18] Despite his generally accurate analysis of clergy neglect of the social-gospel agenda and his eloquent plea for increased clergy activism, Hutchinson fails to frame his case in a way that might evoke clergy action and community accountability. In other words, he delivers an indictment and makes the case for a change in clergy behavior but then fails to offer specific strategies that could be put into operation and monitored for progress. And like others who opine on clergy underperformance, he fails to direct his critique at specific apathetic leaders. In the village, this is known as "calling folks out."

It may be time to call people out, by position and office if not by name. And this should be done in the spirit of the "Woodson test," namely, "not intended as a broadside against any particular person or class, but . . . as a corrective for methods which have not produced satisfactory results."[19]

In order to mobilize a new level of accountability for clergy and other community leaders, a new culture of village accountability will be necessary. The community needs to "call out" their leaders and request a declaration of their vision for serving and transforming the community. Such leaders should be encouraged to explain what they are doing to ameliorate the problems or exorcise the demons that harm our children and communal well-being. Borrowing from the business and nonprofit sectors, clergy and community leaders should provide an annual report on their activities, accomplishments, and unfinished business.

Carter G. Woodson was also concerned about the state of clergy performance when he criticized the unnecessary dissension and cumbersome bureaucracies that plagued Negro churches that imitated their white counterparts.

> All of the Negro Methodists in the world, if united, would not need more than twelve bishops, and these would have time to direct the affairs of both Methodists and Baptists in a united church. There is no need for three or four bishops, each teaching the same faith and practice while duplicating the work of the other in the same area merely because a long time ago somebody committed the sin of dissension and strife. For all of this unnecessary expense impoverished Negroes have to pay.[20]

Woodson places the issue of the cost of church bureaucracy on the agenda for village discussion. Bureaucracy has a high price tag and poor people should not be coerced into expending their money for something that does not help them. If the topic of the "financial costs of church politics" has been seriously discussed in the past, I am not aware of it or of its conclusions. Woodson's idea first struck me as audacious and impossible. But, on second thought, I pondered, "Why shouldn't black church leaders rethink the styles of church governance they embrace and perpetuate? And why shouldn't the village pressure church leaders to be more efficient and faithful in their governance decisions?" Is it desirable that a new church appear in every vacant storefront or empty lot if those congregations exist only for the benefit of the pastor and his or her inner circle? Is it not time for the village to be more intentional about monitoring what its anchor institutions are doing?

Needless to say, black Methodists have not taken Dr. Woodson up on his challenge. Yes, there are still more than a dozen black Methodist bishops. But I think the most important question is not how many bishops there are or how much they cost. Rather, the question is, "What are those bishops doing to renew the village, and does that activity justify their cost?" Woodson was not an expert in the study of congregations and church life, known as ecclesiology, and may not have understood some of the theological reasons for the proliferation of bishops and stewards to care for an expanding church. But he placed an important idea on the village agenda for future consideration.

The Teaching Vocation of Public Elders

One of the great leadership challenges facing leaders today is the lack of accessible wisdom from the elders about how to respond to problems that emerge. There is no lack of information. We have computers and Web sites and books and conferences for getting more and more information. But we sorely lack elders who are willing and able to offer wisdom to leaders. Wisdom emerges from dialogue, and conversation, with wise people who know how to listen, to discern, and to offer guidance constructively as did Jesus and Socrates. There are many elders who reside in senior-care communities or homes who are never invited to share their wisdom in the church, community, or pastor's study. This could be changed without enormous effort or financial support. What if the local clergy council were to set aside two hours once every month to dialogue with a wise senior pastor or community leader?

The African American church tradition is blessed with a variety of extraordinary leaders who are approaching the end of fruitful careers. We need them to become resources for the next generation of public theologians and public pastors. Among them are Dr. Gardner C. Taylor, Reverend Andrew Young, Drs. Henry and Ella Mitchell, Dr. Gayraud Wilmore, Reverend Benjamin Hooks, and each church tradition's other revered elders. It would seem that, with the institutions, technology, and resources available to us, we would find a way to engage the wisdom of these leaders on a more regular basis.

Calling and Recommissioning Jesse

Without question, the most remarkable black church leader alive today is the Reverend Jesse Louis Jackson. His deliberate efforts over the years to preserve his "country preacher" credentials express his desire to remain connected to a southern tradition and style of leadership carriage and communication. He has done many things well, but perhaps his greatest achievement has been to construct an extraordinary life out of the stuff of unpromising material. Born to an unwed mother, he later became the quarterback at North Carolina A&T University, student-body president, and a protégé to Dr. Martin Luther King Jr. and Dr. Samuel DeWitt Proctor, his college president. He became a formidable civil rights protest leader and preacher who sometimes upstaged Dr. King. He founded his own civil rights organization, which he promptly outgrew. He was a kingmaker for the Chicago's first black mayor and other elected officials around the country. In search of a larger parish and pulpit, he ran for president twice and became a liaison to the continent of Africa for President Clinton. He won international praise and scorn for a series of risky but successful ambassadorial interventions on behalf of captive U.S. soldiers, and for a Cuban child, Elián González, held in Miami against the protests of his father in

Havana. All those who know the Jackson family know that he and his wife have reared an extraordinary group of children, including Congressman Jesse L. Jackson Jr.

That said, in view of all that he knows and all of the support that he has called upon from the national village, I believe that Jesse owes the African American community something that he is currently not providing in sufficient measure. With very few peers, he possesses a unique treasure trove of information and experience that would be of benefit to younger leaders but who do not currently have regular access to him. With the technology that now exists, this situation could be easily remedied. Even a quarterly telephone or video conference between Jackson and younger leaders would create a new mode of learning and mentoring in which Jackson could teach and inspire others while being held accountable for his activities. For instance, both Howard University School of Divinity and the Interdenominational Theological Center have state-of-the-art technology facilities that could broadcast conversations and seminars to countless other institutions and individuals. Yet, rather than the occasional teleconference call to mobilize clergy or the occasional visit to a campus, I think that Reverend Jackson and leaders of his stature should become regular and accessible resources of the black clergy community.

Some of Jesse's critics may read this and argue that the community doesn't need him or any other charismatic leader to transmit that style of leadership. They are rightly suspicious of the underside of charisma. Charisma often creates *dependence* upon the great leader. People are disempowered from acting or innovating while awaiting the "messiah's" arrival. And charisma can foster codependence between the leader and followers as they need the messiah and the messiah needs to be needed by them. Charisma tends to *concentrate power* in a single leader who becomes vulnerable to attack by outsiders and susceptible to the usual human frailties that compromise so many leaders (money, sex, power, or drugs). Even more dangerous, charisma often undermines and *devalues other styles* of leadership such as more bureaucratic, grassroots, and collaborative styles. One of the best discussions of cooperative and complementary leadership during the civil rights movement can be found in sociologist Aldon Morris's book *The Origins of the Civil Rights Movement*.[21] Using the conceptual framework inspired by the great sociologist Max Weber, Morris reminds us that during the 1950s and '60s all types of leadership cooperated for the common good and success of the movement.

Jesse's much-publicized moral failing has not sidelined him as it might have done a mere mortal. But I fear that rumors of his "headline-grabbing" habits and aggressive fund-raising tactics may leave his final legacy tottering in the balance. It would be tragic to see Jackson move into his mature years without the moral authority that he has earned through a lifetime of service.

Preparing the Next Generation of Public Pastors and Theologians

One of the challenges ahead is the preparation of thoughtful leaders for the church and society. Following Max Stackhouse, I have referred to them as public theologians.

It is understandable that denominations have not required formal graduate theological education, but it is not acceptable that they are not moving in that direction. If the churches are not going forward and serving the community effectively it may be because their leaders are not sufficiently educated to essential knowledge for negotiating our complex social environment.

One of the influential bishops in the A.M.E. church was Daniel Alexander Payne, in whose honor the Ohio-based seminary is named. Payne was committed to raising the intellectual bar for black clergy. As one of the most influential bishops in the A.M.E. Church and president of one the first institutions of African American higher education in this country, Payne challenged religious and private black institutions to develop higher standards of academic excellence. He advocated the establishment of ministerial reading classes and denominational schools aimed at strengthening the capacity of clergy to provide informed leadership. Payne regarded education as a prerequisite for the difficult work of institution building and raising the intellectual bar in the leadership community.

Public Preaching and Poetic Idiom

Dr. Irwin Trotter, a professor of homiletics (the study of preaching), has divided the history of preaching in North America into three dominant traditions, each with its own distinctive purposes:

1. The Puritan tradition is exemplified by Cotton Mather and Jonathan Edwards. Puritan preaching appealed to the *intellect* with the goal of *enlightenment*.
2. The *Evangelical tradition* of preaching is embodied by Rev. Billy Graham and appeals to the *soul* for the purpose of *convicting a person of their sin*.
3. The *Pentecostal tradition* appeals to the *spirit* of a person for the purpose of *evoking praise* and is today represented by Bishop T.D. Jakes.[22]

I believe that the finest black preaching has combined the best of each of these traditions. Dr. King's corpus of sermons perhaps best illustrates this. In my own book, *Another Day's Journey*, I provide an interpretation of black church culture and its core traits and note that prophetic preaching is rooted in, and emanates from, a rich congregational culture with the following features: emotionally expressive, sensory engaging worship; cathartic shouting; triumphal song; therapeutic congregational prayer; and politically empowering religious education.[23]

So much of what passes for preaching today is little more than moralizing about a particular issue. Some of the moralizing takes the shape of repeating what a particular and favored Bible verse says without providing the context or critical interpretation of what these words might mean, including the alternative interpretations of what they could mean. Other species of moralizing take the form of personal opinion brokering without even the benefit of specific biblical guidance. Usually, these issues are ones that have emerged in the context of modernity, that is, a world dominated by modern science, technology, religious pluralism, biblical criticism, and individualism. These "new questions" challenge churches (and all communities) to puzzle out how they should think, speak, and behave in moral terms.

For instance, should stem cells from embryos be used in research aimed at discovering therapies and cures to various diseases? If one is a strict biblical literalist, one faces a real challenge in responding to such questions. For if Jesus didn't say anything about medical research in the Sermon on the Mount, how can churches answer the question that they must ask, "What would Jesus do?"? Indeed, the very posing of the question sets in motion an important intellectual and spiritual discernment process that I believe is healthy and productive, even when clear answers are elusive and slow to come.

The worst of such preaching assumes the form of motivational speaking (usually about wealth acquisition) and the annoying habit of insisting that people repeat some phrase repeatedly, such as "Touch your neighbor and tell them . . ." I don't mind this once or twice during a service but some pastors abuse the practice until it comes to resemble a crude game of "Simon says." Preachers who abuse this rhetorical device should be concerned about diminishing the dignity and majesty of sacred worship.

Preachers should not simply proclaim their moral conclusions in such matters as closed and final judgments. Rather, they should teach people how to reason and to reach conclusions in light of their discernment of the witness or message of at least four sources.

- The witness of sacred Scripture and revelation
- The witness of tradition, church history and the testimony of elders
- The message of contemporary culture and science
- The witness of reason and personal experience

After all, when the church and the pastor are not present, each believer should be equipped to begin thinking through the basics of Christian ethics. Moral instruction involves research, testing the fidelity of a moral claim against Scripture, tradition, reason, and cultural information, as well as teaching the congregation to engage in moral discernment and deliberation before making bold, absolutist statements of "God's will."

And while we're on the topic of moral instruction, I hope that black churches and preachers will not lose the gift of *poetic voice* (idiom) that has been part of the genius of black preaching. Too much contemporary preaching employs flattened rhetoric that does not persuade the intellect, does not touch the emotions, and does not ignite the imagination in the way King's best preaching did. Poetic voice is the black preacher's skill for speaking to the imagination and ear of the listener. Poetry is different from prose. It transgresses the usual rules of straightforward, logical, discursive language. It paints pictures for the mind to savor. You can use a thousand words to describe the strange smile on a simple woman's face, or you can show them Leonardo da Vinci's 1506 masterpiece *Mona Lisa*. You can try to convey with words what happens when the fury of orchestra and choir are united or you can let them hear Handel's "Hallelujah Chorus" and they will stand to their feet in awe and tears. You can describe democracy's unrealized possibilities now awaiting our realization, or you can listen to Dr. Martin Luther King Jr.'s, "I Have a Dream" speech. Indeed, I hope that seminaries and college departments of English will somehow help to recover the tradition of fusing *prophetic vision with poetic voice.*

Resolving Gender Tensions

There is another dimension to the leadership challenge in the black church: the gender dimension or fault line. With respect to women in ministry, a long-standing divide continues to separate black churches: some churches fully acknowledge the gifts, promise, and rights of women to ordination and equal access to ministry leadership while others do not. The Reverend Suzanne Johnson Cook notes that black churches as a whole are making progress on the issue of gender justice. She points to two significant developments: first, the African Methodist Episcopal (AME) Church in recent years has elected two female bishops; and, second, the fact that she herself has been elected president of the Hampton University Minister's Conference, a traditional male, Baptist stronghold that meets each year for leadership development, worship, and fellowship.

Reverend Johnson speaks of the slow process of acceptance that she has witnessed over many years and how both the testimony of reason and of experience confirmed those portions of sacred Scripture that affirm women in ministry (Joel 2: "In the last days I will pour out my spirit on all flesh. Your sons and daughters shall prophesy. . . ."

She also believes that the contemporary black church is not sufficiently strategic about healing and rebuilding the village. "We have no specific mission and no movement. Leaders are shooting at problems but not aiming at them." Also, she notes, "We lack collegiality and tend to be more competitive, more lonely, and insecure than is necessary."[24]

It would be wonderful if black churches would use these early years of a new century to embrace the presence of women in ministry. Churches that are not prepared to leap from the status quo of nonordination to the ideal of equal opportunity and rights should consider a number of developmental, incremental steps toward the end of fulfilling God's desire for God's "sons and daughters to prophesy."

• Churches should invite existing female clergy to become consultants who reflect about their experience and provide advice to congregations and denominations in transition. All churches could learn, for instance, from the experience of Bishop Vashti McKenzie of the AME Church. She was ordained, served as local pastor (and a very effective one, at that), and later elected bishop. In the process, neither her local congregations nor the AME denomination faltered, lost members, or reaped divine judgment. Is it possible that her experience was a message from God to all other churches?

• Churches should reform their credentialing practices to ensure that all men and women who seek ordination for specialized ministries undergo a standard leadership formation curriculum. This should include taking required courses, working as apprentice ministers with a seasoned veteran, and practicing various arts of ministry (counseling, preaching, teaching, administration, leading worship, and so forth) under the supervision of a committee. This would improve the quality of all ministers in our village.

- Churches that are interested in entering a period of discernment about ordaining women could also establish a probationary ordination during which a careful review of each candidate would be undertaken. Following the probation, ordination would be conferred or denied.

Yet, generally speaking, many black denominations, such as the Church of God in Christ and the National Baptist Conventions, do not ordain women or appoint them as pastors, although a steady number of women from these traditions feel called to ministry and pursue theological education. Many of them arrive at seminaries and have difficult choices to make. I have counseled with many who have struggled with departing their home denomination to affiliate with one that not only would ordain and appoint them to a church, but also provide adequate compensation for their ministries and retirement.

When I served as dean of black church studies at Colgate Rochester Divinity School, I managed the nation's first program intended for women in such predicaments. Established by my predecessors, Drs. Henry Mitchell and Gayraud Wilmore, the program provided theological education for people seeking to refine their skills for ministry while earning a certificate during a three-year period of evening courses. One third of the students were women. One of the women, who belonged to a church known for its strong anti-women's ordination stance, came to me secretly to tell me that she was going to pursue the program because she felt God had called her to do so. But she pointed out that she would be pursuing this education secretly and did not want her pastor to know she was in the program. For three years, she faithfully attended and earned the certificate, which was presented during the regular commencement for degree candidates. Watching her accept that certificate a tear crept into my eye as she evoked the memory of black people who had to "steal away" in order to learn. Her education had a different value from that of all the other students who were openly encouraged by their pastors and congregations.

My hope is to encourage the churches that need to reckon with this issue to trust the Holy Spirit to do what is best for the church and not to deprive the churches of gifts that may enrich it at a time of mission crisis. In addition, a subtle demographic factor may have an impact on this issue in the future. I have spoken to many young people reared by single mothers who have spent their lives observing a woman provide leadership, manage money, govern a household, negotiate with the public sector, and so on. These young people, especially men, have no trouble viewing women as capable and accomplished pastors, bishops, and church executives. This is an issue that merits empirical research.

Leading Village Renewal

Thus far, I've tried to indicate that the greatest threat to the mission integrity of the churches is the prosperity gospel movement in all of its forms. One outgrowth of that threat is the recent preoccupation with titles and personal status of the clergyperson/CEO. This entire cultural phenomenon has ushered in a new cult of expansion and inflation. Church sanctuaries grow ever larger whether or not there is a corresponding growth in their service to the community. The stature of the pastor grows larger although the church members rarely benefit from the pastor's growing celebrity. His or her title changes, theirs do not. And I've tried to call attention to the missed opportunities for helping those who need it most.

Here, I'd like to take a larger risk (jumping into the deep end of the pool) and be a bit more prescriptive about how churches and denominations could lead in village renewal. I suggest that *the major families of the black church should divide the labor of unfinished business and tackle their respective agendas with spiritual restlessness and hope.* I do not feel altogether presumptuous in this exercise because I have tried to enter into the culture of each of these traditions. I had the privilege of becoming a "black ecumenist" while serving as dean of Black Church Studies at Colgate Rochester Divinity School and as president of the Interdenominational Theological Center. In those capacities, I have preached and worshiped in a broad spectrum of churches, become familiar with their leaders, developed working relationships with many of them, and supervised the leadership formation of their seminarians. Hence, I pray that I will be given some allowance to speak in the following way.

Renewing a Culture of Educational Excellence: A Call for Methodist Leadership

Let me state this boldly and clearly: *The black community needs African American Methodists, all of them, to step up and take responsibility for leading the educational renewal of the entire village.* Given their admirable track record of achievement in education, is it not reasonable for the village to expect our sisters and brothers to play a more vigorous role in reversing the negative trend-lines on black education? What if they were to stun the nonprofit sector by announcing an initiative to ensure educational mentors for each and every child in their local neighborhoods (something that many secular nonprofits groups have attempted with limited impact)? They could overwhelm mentoring organizations that seek assistance with at-risk youth. What if they were to challenge hundreds of black men who now work in the corporate, political, and nonprofit sectors to become public schoolteachers for three years? Would that not have a direct impact on hundreds, perhaps thousands, of young lives?

Black Methodists in America have a long history of leadership in promoting a culture of educational excellence and literacy. The African Methodist Episcopal (AME) tradition was founded in 1787 in Philadelphia by Richard and Sarah Allen and others. In 1862, the AME Church purchased Wilberforce University, "making it the first U.S. university controlled by African Americans." According to denominational historian Dennis Dickerson, several AME congregations have established innovative church-based alternatives to the public schools. Local congregations have brought hope to impoverished neighborhoods that want to see their children excel in school. Moreover, the AME Church has an impressive number of schools on the African continent.

In gross terms, the three major black Methodist traditions (the AME Church, the African Methodist Episcopal Zion Church [AMEZ], and the Christian Methodist Episcopal Church [CME], combined with the African American presence in the United Methodist Church (UMC), represent approximately twenty thousand black Methodist churches and eight million members.[25] Twenty thousand churches that could become community centers focused on educational excellence and after-school programs and ministries. Twenty thousand centers of hope and empowerment that are desperately needed at this time.

It would be extraordinary and inspiring to see the bishops of these churches mobilize to assert the need for urgent action on behalf of the nation's poorest children and families. These three black Methodist denominations, along with black United Methodists, should commit themselves to some focused and well-coordinated educational initiative that grabs the attention of the entire village and of the public.

On a practical level this would mean that every community with Methodist congregations could count on them as community centers of educational support, mentoring, tutoring, computer resources, and assistance in taking standardized tests. Methodist churches would have information about colleges and technical schools and resources for students and families that are having difficulty in school. Obviously, such an initiative would require cooperation between church leaders and school officials and teachers. But many teachers have long waited for the time when the community would offer itself as a supportive agent for their educational mission.

If Methodists undertake this challenge, organized philanthropy in America should rush forward to ensure that they have adequate resources to sustain this effort over several years until it can become self-sustaining. Even acting by themselves, however, African American Methodists have the capacity and the potential to make a positive impact on the educational challenges that haunt many black communities and smother the will to learn in many black youth. They have the track record of success. They have the potential army of volunteers. And if they take up this challenge, they will have earned the right to expect financial support from foundations, government, corporations, and private donations. Further, they will have earned the right to expect that community members who are serious about the educational renaissance of the community will attend and join those congregations.

But imagine what could happen if most churches were inspired by this Methodist witness to incorporate educational excellence into their ministries. What if all churches were serious in implementing after-school tutorials, spelling bees, and educational Olympic Games, increasing their presence and financial support for urban schools, and holding public officials accountable for better performance?

I saw the potential of a new attitude toward educational excellence in the church where I was reared. When I was a child, my pastor instituted something called "The Breakfast Club." The Club met every Sunday morning prior to Sunday school and morning worship. Scores of children gathered for academic contests, Scripture memorization tests, debate, and commentary on topics in black history and current events. We enjoyed milk, orange juice, and "tea cakes" baked by the Mississippi transplants to Chicago. Today, the young people who were nurtured in the Breakfast Club, including Craig Marberry, author of the popular book *Crowns*, and the Las Vegas eye surgeon Dr. Tyree Carr, have completed college, are employed and rearing bright children. These success stories emerged from one congregation led by a caring and committed pastor. It was a life-changing ministry sponsored by a medium-sized church (four hundred members) that did not cost lots of money, drew upon the voluntary love and support of lots of adults, and engaged hundreds of kids per year. Why can this not be duplicated by hundreds or thousands of others?

This is precisely what former National Urban League president Hugh B. Price urges in his book *Achievement Matters: Getting Your Child the Best Education Possible.*[26] In a provocative chapter titled "Spreading the Gospel of Achievement," Price recounts his efforts to launch a "Campaign for African American Achievement" in 1996. The Urban League enlisted organizations that were "fixtures in the black community for generations and that would be there generations from now." I'm calling these organizations our "anchor institutions." He notes that the Campaign included the Congress of National Black Churches (CNBC), a coalition of eight major black denominations (an organization about which I'll say more later).

The Urban League focused on the problem of negative peer pressure applied to children who want to achieve but are "ignored by adults or intimidated by schoolmates." Declaring war on this "anti-achievement peer culture" he noted the need to "create a vibrant new atmosphere in our community that values and celebrates academic achievement."[27] In a multipronged initiative, they began with high-profile events aimed at celebrating academic achievers, mobilizing adults to support the messages, and encouraging news media to cover positive activities of youth for a change. Through local "Achievement Campaigns" that included block parties, street festivals, and parades each year, these events have drawn fifty to sixty thousand young participants since 1996. The other major approach included creating National Achievers Societies that were "community-based honor societies for students who have earned B averages or better in school." This idea was created by the now-deceased but brilliant educator, Dr. Israel Tribble, former president of the Florida Education Fund, which provides scholarships to minority college students to pursue doctorate degrees in math and science.[28]

Since that time, Price notes that the initiative succeeded in catalyzing community ownership of the educational achievements of their children and that has had a positive impact for the kids involved. However, it has not yet achieved the impact that he had intended. In an interview, Price indicated that it takes "time, volunteers and repetition to get traction" but the potential is exhilarating. Price also observes that unlike police brutality, education is a more difficult issue around which to organize and mobilize people.

I was present when this Campaign was launched at a CNBC conference and think that its impact was limited because no group of influential clergy (a dedicated circle of change agents) claimed it as their rallying issue which might have included vigorously promoting it in the public square, making assignments to other leaders, and creating a culture of accountability for it. Nevertheless, I think that its basic elements hold promise today for the renewal work ahead.

I submit this proposal to my Methodist family, especially to the senior leadership who have the capacity to organize and commission people for action. Also, I write to the dedicated grassroots activists who always do the heavy lifting and get things done. I submit this with humility and hope that they will accept the ethical obligation, contextualize it according to their wisdom, and launch bold action. If they do not, I hope that these key leaders will offer an explanation of what they found to be more important than leading this dimension of village renewal.

Prisoner Reentry and Redemption: A Call for Baptist Leadership

The black community needs African American Baptists to answer the call for leadership in assisting people that have been incarcerated to reenter the village with integrity and support.

Consider the power of the Baptist witness in black church history. There would have been no civil rights movement without the freedom accorded clergy by the Baptist tradition (back before there were Baptist bishops). The only African American clergyperson to run for president twice in the twentieth century was a well-known Baptist preacher, Rev. Jesse Jackson. Reverend Al Sharpton, who was a presidential primary candidate in 2004 is a hybrid Bapto-Pentecostal minister and founder of the National Religious Action Network.

Based on their reported numbers, the four major black Baptist denominations (the National Baptist Convention-U.S.A., the National Baptist Convention of America, the National Missionary Baptist Convention, and the Progressive National Baptist Convention) represent an approximate total of thirty-five to forty thousand Baptist congregations with an estimated ten million members.[29] What may the village expect from the presidents and leaders of these Baptist communions? Wouldn't it be redemptive if America's black Baptists were to take the lead on the issue of prisoner reentry into our communities? They would not work alone, for others would be inspired to take their places alongside and in partnership with them. But someone has to take the lead and to sustain community awareness, participation, and investment in making measurable difference in the lives of our neighbors who have transgressed and been punished.

In the future, experts report that over 650,000 inmates will be released each year into local communities. Congregations have an important and unique role to play in welcoming and reintegrating them into the community. Unlike secular service providers, they bring to the table the powerful religious capital of forgiveness, redemption, and the promise of reconciliation. These resources cannot be simulated in a secular framework. They are works of grace and mystery that reach deep into the core of a person. And we have seen that they can be transformative. Currently, faith-based reentry ministries differ widely in their capacity, resources, and mission. There is a need for a more systematic and comprehensive approach to providing support and guidance to these prodigal sons and daughters.

Prison chaplain A. J. Sabree says that congregations need to move beyond thinking of prison ministry as an occasional visit to the local jail to convene a worship service and deliver basic goods. They need to become sponsors of what he calls "prisoner aftercare." He notes that the women and men who enter prison are transformed by that experience and thus congregations on the outside need to know what to anticipate when these prisoners are released. Fortunately, there are numerous exciting programs around the country engaged in such religious aftercare.

Let me offer an illustration of how reentry themes can emerge spontaneously. Not long ago, while attending worship services at a southwest Atlanta church, something extraordinary happened. Near the end of an extended service that celebrated the pastor's tenth anniversary, he invited a vocal group comprised of five young women to sing a concluding song. I was aware of the restlessness of many fellow worshipers who had been there for almost three hours. No one seemed thrilled to have another song rendered at that particular moment. But as the five young, attractive, African American women confidently gathered with microphones in front of the congregation, some anticipation began to stir. One of the group members began to "testify," or tell her personal story:

> I used to be a streetwalker. The men called me "baby," "sweet child," "pretty lady." Then I was arrested and the judge called me a hooker and a criminal. But, now I've been saved and redeemed and God calls me a "child of God." My name has changed.

A wave of surprise and excitement suddenly permeated the air. Then the next singer shared her testimony. One after the other, they all admitted to crimes of theft, murder, and so on. Then, just before they sang, they asked if any other former offenders in the congregation might wish to come and stand with them.

It was a moment of high anxiety. Finally, a young woman from the congregation, then a young man, began to walk down the aisle. The young lady mentioned that she had been released just that week. The moment was so overwhelming that the pastor jumped into the middle of the developing scene and declared, "Some of you are ashamed to own up to your past life, but look at these ladies. Aren't they showing you courage?" Suddenly others began to come to the altar. The pastor embraced the newly released young woman and said, "God knows and God forgives, and we forgive too."

There was not a single dry eye in the church. All of this happened within five minutes. We were all transfixed and, I think, transformed. For we had all just experienced an unrehearsed ritual of redemption and forgiveness that conveyed a new sense of the gospel as a force for change.

What if churches, mosques, synagogues, and temples were to practice similar and more intentional forms of redemptive ritual action? Of course, the ritual would have to be culturally and situationally appropriate to the congregation and community. But the somewhat spontaneous process of confession, pardon, forgiveness, and redemption that occurred at that one congregation should give all congregational leaders reason to pause and consider, "Are there perhaps members of my congregation or community who are waiting for the declaration, 'You are redeemed, welcome home'?"

I am suggesting that black Baptist churches could and should take the lead, working in collaboration with other congregations and traditions to lead the redemptive work that is necessary on this issue. Of course, not every Baptist church would need to host a reentry ministry. But they could take responsibility for assessing the community need and delegating primary responsibility for various components of an effective reentry effort in every community. Also, given their strong track record in the area of political activism and civil rights, Baptist churches could provide leadership on the issue of reenfranchising previously incarcerated people who are unable to vote in many states.

We should also bear in mind that making an impact on reentry could have a positive impact on increasing the number of marriageable men, increasing the numbers of fathers and mothers who are willing and able to return to their parental responsibilities, thus becoming productive members of the community and bringing to the children and community their stories of redemption and renewal.

I offer this proposal to my Baptist family with hope and humility that they will take up this challenge or explain why they cannot.

Positive Youth Development: A Call for Pentecostal Leadership

The black community needs African American Pentecostal and Holiness traditions to step up and answer the call for leadership with positive youth development, especially with the most at-risk youth in the village.

Black Pentecostals are not a monolithic group, although they share many family resemblances, not the least of which is tracing their roots to the famous Azusa Street Revival that began in Los Angeles in 1906.[30] As a teenager growing up in a large Pentecostal church on the southside of Chicago, I became keenly aware of the ability of some churches to attract and retain young people. From my unscientific observations, more of them were either Pentecostal or Baptist and Methodist churches with strong Pentecostal tendencies. Part of the genius of Pentecostal youth ministry is its awareness that young people have high energy, seek to be part of something larger and important, have a need to be cool, and to feel safe and protected.

How would our villages be different if the elders and bishops of the Church of God in Christ and the Pentecostal Assemblies of the World joined together to publicly commit to a concrete initiative?[31] What would happen if they were to devote their enormous intellectual, political, economic, and spiritual capital to working with at-risk urban youth? The moral vision and authority of the Pentecostal church would be a tremendous help to village renewal.

Of course, these churches could not and should not jump into casting a wider net to provide youth services by themselves. They would receive valuable support from the vast secular youth-service sector. And with respect to the more difficult challenge of reaching at-risk adolescents and children, those who are gang involved, substance addicted, and/or involved in the juvenile justice system, one promising model has emerged in Boston that deserves study and imitation.

Known as the "Ten Point Coalition," this ministry established by Pentecostal pastor Eugene Rivers, AME pastor Ray Hammond, and

Baptist pastor Jeffrey Brown has developed an innovative approach to youth ministry. The following are components of their approach.

1. Establish four- or five-church cluster collaborations to sponsor "Adopt a Gang" programs that organize and evangelize youth gangs. Inner-city churches would serve as drop-in centers and provide sanctuary for troubled youth.

2. Commission missionaries to serve as advocates and ombudsmen for black and Latino juveniles in the courts. Such missionaries would work closely with probation officers, law enforcement officials, and youth street workers to assist at-risk youth and their families. They would also convene summit meetings between school superintendents, principals of public middle and high schools, and black and Latino pastors to develop partnerships that will focus on the youth most at-risk. We propose to do pastoral work with the most violent and troubled young people and their families. In our judgment, this is a rational alternative to ill-conceived proposals to substitute incarceration for education.

3. Commission youth evangelists to do street-level, one-on-one evangelism with youth involved in drug trafficking. These evangelists would also work to prepare these youth for participation in the economic life of the nation. Such work might include preparation for college, the development of legal revenue-generating enterprises, and acquisition of trade skills and union membership.

4. Establish accountable, community-based economic development projects that go beyond "market and state" visions of revenue generation. Such an economic development initiative will include community and trusts, micro-enterprise projects, worker cooperatives, and democratically run community development corporations.

5. Establish links between suburban and downtown churches and front-line ministries to provide spiritual, human resource, and material support.

6. Initiate and support neighborhood crime-watch programs within local church neighborhoods. If, for example, 200 churches covered the four corners surrounding their sites, 800 blocks would be safer.

7. Establish working relationships between local churches and community-based health centers to provide pastoral counseling for families during times of crisis. We also propose the initiation of drug abuse prevention programs and abstinence-oriented educational programs focusing on the prevention of AIDS and sexually transmitted diseases.

8. Convene a working summit meeting for Christian black and Latino men and women in order to discuss the development of Christian brotherhoods and sisterhoods that would provide rational alternatives to violent gang life. Such groups would also be charged with fostering responsibility to family and protecting houses of worship.

9. Establish rape crisis drop-in centers and services for battered women in churches. Counseling programs must be established for abusive men, particularly teenagers and young adults.

10. Develop an aggressive black and Latino curriculum, with an additional focus on the struggles of women and poor people as a means of increasing literacy and enhancing self esteem in young people.[32]

As I develop the case for Pentecostal promise in youth ministry, I would underscore the fact that a huge part of their effectiveness is rooted in their willingness and skill in transgressing the conventional interpersonal boundaries that are the defining marks of bourgeois Christianity and citizenship. That is, they are willing not to "mind their own business" in deference to our culture of individual liberty. Pentecostals have been more inclined to acknowledge that when others are sinking fast in a lifestyle that promises only misery and death, love requires that urgent intervention be undertaken. Love requires the church to "get in your face" with hope of rescuing those who appear to be doomed.[33]

Let me illustrate another way in which a local church could initiate a ministry that had great impact on young people's lives. During my years as a graduate student at the University of Chicago Divinity School, I attended the church where I had been reared from childhood. One Sunday morning, while seated in the class designated for ministers, listening to school and minding my own business, the pastor appeared and called me out of class. He told me to follow him to the junior class area. He stopped at the first classroom and asked the teacher, "Which boys have been fighting in here?" With a look of surprise and relief, she pointed out the two about whom she had been complaining for weeks. He told these young teenagers to follow us. He went to the next class and asked of the young female teacher, "Do you have any boys that are acting up in here?" She identified one or two also. As he went from class to class, a pattern began to emerge.

First, each class was taught by a woman. There were very few men teaching Sunday school. Second, each class had one or two boys that found the class unsatisfactory and had begun to act out their frustrations and restlessness. Third, when the boys were asked to depart the class, both they and the teacher were relieved. I reflected on this as we continued to make our rounds, resembling the pied piper followed by a growing crowd of curious young brothers.

Finally, Bishop Ford led us to an isolated area of the church, literally underneath the altar of the church, where communion materials and choir robes were stored. He declared, "You all sit down, this is your new teacher. I don't want any more trouble out of any of you." As he departed, leaving me with this group of a dozen young men, we all looked at each other with a sense of "Now what?" I asked, "How do you want to use this time together?" One young guy looked at me earnestly and asked, "Are we in trouble?" I replied, "I don't think so. But, this is our chance to prove that you are more than troublemakers. So, let's have fun with this and let's learn from each other."

There were nine classes in the entire Sunday school and so our new class came to be known as "Big 10." The boys branded the class with that name and began to take pride in their uniqueness. Each week, we gathered and spent a few minutes reviewing the designated Bible lesson and theme for the Sunday. But we quickly turned to a different agenda. I asked, "How has the week gone for you and what have you been thinking about?" That simple question led to some profound soul searching and sharing. Sometimes the boys shared hair-raising tales of seeing a gang-style shooting that week. Some spoke of violence in their own households as their mothers fought with boyfriends. We talked about those issues and I tried to relate the Gospel lesson to their life experiences.

One Sunday during Black History Month, I suggested that they memorize the words of "Lift Every Voice and Sing." They looked at me incredulously as if to declare, "We can't learn all that." But we began singing it each week. One week, we were pressed for time and needed to get back to the assembly, so I skipped the song. They protested vehemently. "No, we want to sing the song." I immediately recognized how important ritual had become in the lives of these young men whose daily lives were filled with unpredictability. The therapy of our discussions and the coherence provided by the weekly ritual had become an important part of their lives.

When summer arrived and I knew that they would have more time on their hands, I had an idea. I asked them, "How many of you have ever been on the campus of the University of Chicago?" Not a single one had. Then I asked, "How many have visited the DuSable Museum of African American History?" A couple of them had. I asked the pastor if I could borrow the church van to take them out once a week on field trips. So, we began to explore parts of Chicago they didn't know existed. We visited some of Chicago's extraordinary museums, college campuses, parks, beaches, famous homes, and great deep-dish pizza shops. As word got out in the Sunday school about how we had augmented our Sunday class, other kids became jealous and wanted to join Big 10. I recall visiting the University of Chicago one Saturday afternoon with my class and running into my thesis advisor, Don Browning, who was headed to his office. I felt defensive about the fact that I should have been studying for exams and here I was, an apparent scout leader with a dozen young black boys, touring the location where the experiments that contributed to the first atomic bomb had been performed. But Browning surveyed the situation and my discomfort, and even offered a word of encouragement to the young men about staying in school and coming to the university to follow in my footsteps.

Now, years later, I occasionally run into these young men. I regret that I've lost touch with some. Most of them are doing well. One of them recently called from Chicago and asked me to perform his wedding. I am proud of them. I am amazed by the vision and courage of Bishop Ford. And I am restless to see more churches engage in such innovative ministries with young people, especially young men.

Let me also mention the potential for developing a global dimension to this approach to urban ministry. Even as I focus on the potential of such congregations to have an impact on youth in African American villages, I think that such potential extends much further abroad. In an address at Harvard Divinity School, I tried to develop this point with respect to several global demographic trends that should be monitored.

In his book *Globalization and Survival in the Black Diaspora: The New Urban Challenge*, Hunter College sociologist Charles Green has compiled an important collection of essays from scholars throughout Africa, Europe, North America, South America, and the Caribbean. Green focuses on an interesting demographic development that is largely taken for granted—namely, that the "majority of the world's population is urbanized and resides in mega cities, mid-size cities, and suburban areas."[34] Green also notes that as people are attracted to the cities, largely in search of jobs and a better standard of living, they abandon their land and many of their land-based rituals and traditions. And they arrive at a time when the global economy is rapidly becoming an information economy that has little need for uneducated, low-skilled labor. We are witnessing the emergence of an international underclass residing in overcrowded slums throughout major urban centers of the world. To be blunt about it, the oppressed, poor masses of these vast urban villages constitute a traditional Pentecostal demographic.

When I travel internationally, I often collect religious, folk, and secular music from local cultures. Interestingly, the hip-hop genre has become a compelling vehicle for commentary on the phenomenon of globalization (the compression of the world's populations and the dominance of certain cultures) and the presence or absence of the holy therein. In my casual survey of global hip-hop music, it would appear to have engaged the imagination of youth in a way that much sacred music has not. Much of the sacred music is less responsive to developing social facts and, consequently, perceived to be less creative and helpful for negotiating postmodern realities.

Without risking overgeneralizations, much of this music expresses an underlying anger and suspicion toward adults and the adult institutions and traditions that have placed youth in these awful circumstances. The youth I met in Hanoi, Bangkok, Beijing, Casablanca, Cape Town, Nairobi, and Port of Spain were sampling Marvin Gaye as they observed a world defined by war, genocide and concentrated wealth: "What's going on?"

In light of the track record of Pentecostal efficacy in urban ministry, my hope is that the churches will embrace a more vigorous and strategic engagement with the masses, especially the youth of the world who are looking for better answers to their existential questions. What is the message of American Christians to the street children of Rio de Janeiro who are the victims of violent attacks by police as well as armed citizens, or to the marginalized and self-conscious Afro-British youth in London's Brixton neighborhood, or to teens in San Juan, Puerto Rico and Kingston, Jamaica? They all are utilizing a common rhetoric of rebellion in their search for meaning and authenticity. These are the young people who will not be hired by McDonalds, the largest first employer of young people. They know that they are expendable: unemployed and unemployable.

Tragically, these kids they may be vulnerable to terrible vocational options in what South African scholar Ann Bernstein calls a growing international criminal culture. This culture includes the new "Nigerian drug dealers" and the "Russian Mafia."[35] It engages in international money laundering, weapons sales, kidnapping, and expanding the sex tourism market. It offers a fast, intense life in which one can score big money and live like a great American gangster who dies young and in a blaze of glory.

How can American churches aid in the healing of this global population of angry and alienated youth, a virtual "rhythm nation"? I would propose that a pan-Pentecostal group of leaders consider convening an international youth summit to include the most influential and dynamic youth leaders throughout the developing world, and include both Christian and non-Christian youth. These talented youth are well known by most nongovernmental organizations (NGOs) in these communities.

The summit or "youth congress" might serve two purposes. First, church leaders could listen and learn from these young people as they present their pain, aspirations, and struggles. Second, church leaders could present current and proposed programs, strategies, and activities in the area of foreign mission and youth ministry, and allow these leaders to respond to them in an honest manner. Such youth might benefit from exposure to the urban ministry of Boston's Ten Point Coalition, or international youth leaders might be inspired to know of Bishop Charles Blake's track record of healing the villages and saving many AIDS orphans in Africa.

This is my proposal for my Pentecostal and Holiness church family. I hope they will consider and embrace and revise it appropriately or explain why they cannot.

As I talk about the potential good that could be accomplished by dividing the village renewal agenda among these three large segments of the black church family, I certainly do not intend to ignore the important role of other segments of the black Christian or non-Christian community. My goal is to provide an agenda for the village to deliberate and debate and contextualize it for each community. Also, as we assess the potential of this vast black church family, we should consider the good that could come from greater coalition building and cooperation among the traditions.

Restoring the Collective Power of Black Churches

In 1978, black church leaders accomplished something that would have pleased Carter G. Woodson and defied those critiques that doubt the churches' ability to unite and collaborate (if not merge). A group of senior black pastors, seminary deans, scholars, and foundation executives met to create an ecumenical organization comprised of the eight largest historically black denominations, known as the Congress of National Black Churches (CNBC), headquartered in Washington, D.C. It was the latest manifestation of a long line of black ecumenical organizations that spanned the twentieth century. In its heyday, CNBC operated several programs and convened a series of memorable meetings of black church leaders. Interestingly, almost no black scholars or seminary professors were present at these meetings, which underscores the lack of dialogue between the church's thinkers and its leaders. Just to give some sense of the importance of the conversations, one year two ministers, Dr. James Forbes and Dr. H. Beecher Hicks Jr., debated the morality of Christian approaches to sexuality. On another occasion, I heard two New York City ministers, Rev. Calvin Butts and Rev. Floyd Flake, debate the virtues of school vouchers and increasing support for public education. At other convenings, Senator Bill Bradley, Rev. Michael Eric Dyson, and Dr. Cornel West challenged participants to keep alive the social gospel, and pastors such as Rev. Eugene Rivers of Boston directly criticized these senior church leaders for their ineffectiveness in reaching the "boys in the hood." Rivers was especially caustic as he urged them to relinquish their own hypocrisy in matters related to wealth acquisition and loose sexual morals in order to serve young people more effectively. Unfortunately, in the late 1990s, CNBC experienced serious funding and other organizational difficulties that led to its demise and the dismantling of an impressive staff of lay and clergy leaders. I miss these extraordinary meetings and believe that the richness of black church theology and ethics have been impoverished in their absence. The dormancy of this important organization represents one of the great tragedies of our time and should be reversed at once.

In the absence of the CNBC, another clergy organization emerged in 2004 to revive and sustain the focus on social justice. Founded by Dr. Jeremiah A. Wright Jr. and managed by Dr. Iva Carruthers of Chicago, the Samuel DeWitt Proctor Conference now hosts an annual meeting in February to gather hundreds of social-gospel leaders for a week of leadership-development seminars, worship, fellowship, and renewal. (I serve on the board of the Proctor Conference.) Its constituency, however, is quite different from the Congress structure. Whereas the Congress sought to engage official representatives of eight black denominations, the Proctor Conference seeks to convene and mobilize all black (and other) clergy who are committed to the social gospel and public theology. The tent is bigger and more focused and strategic in its mission.

Unfortunately, the Proctor Conference's impact has been challenged by some of its potential members for its courage in providing venues to discuss the issue of same-gender marriage and the public stance of some of its leaders who support marriage for and the ordination of homosexuals. It remains to be seen whether or not the Congress will return to the public fray, and whether or not the Proctor Conference will continue to grow and sustain itself for the long haul. If both are able to live and move forward, it will be necessary to achieve collaboration and reconciliation among clergy groups with differing cultures and theological-ethical positions.

WHAT'S RIGHT?

As we turn to consider the sources of promise for renewing the church's mission, rather than providing an inventory of existing best faith-based practices (there are many books that do that well), I'd like to sketch two models that offer a vision of how churches can be more faithful and effective in their ministries. The first model provides a picture of five different ways of engaging in community-service ministry or, as I prefer to call it, public ministry. The second model is adapted from the work of a brilliant African American Catholic theologian and bishop.

Franklin Framework

I'd like to suggest that there are five distinct but overlapping phases of faith-based public ministry. Each phase rests upon a body of theoretical knowledge. Each possesses its own learning agenda and classic texts. Each possesses an appropriate training agenda and skill set. And each includes best implementation practices. The model can be employed in a variety of ways. Three are central for me. First, it could be organized as a *developmental* stairway of learning and implementation that prescribes and invites those operating at the early or lower levels to progress or ascend to higher levels of religious practice. Second, the model could have a simple *diagnostic* function in which one would seek to identify the primary or dominant tendency present in a congregation or clergyperson's *modus operandi*. And third, the model could be used as a *discernment* tool in which congregations or leaders are assigned specific tasks based upon their gifts and excellences in ministry. Recall the wonderful image of 1 Corinthians 12, which suggests that every disciple has been given a particular gift or set of gifts, and they should use them in a complementary manner to edify the church and glorify God. Finally, as a person or group moves beyond the first phase, each subsequent phase makes greater demands and involves a larger investment.

PHASES OF PUBLIC MINISTRY

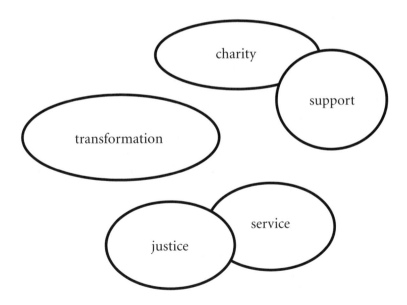

Chart 2-1

Phase One: The Ministry of Charity

In charity, the focus is upon direct, immediate relief of pain and suffering. At this most basic level, no theoretical knowledge or insight is needed. One simply needs to be a healthy, functional person (not necessarily adult) capable of experiencing empathy.[36]

Phase Two: The Ministry of Transitional Support

In the ministry of support, the focus is upon longer-term but not permanent counseling and assistance that facilitates the journey from dependence to self-sufficiency and self-determination. People who are moving from welfare to work or moving away from substance addiction to independence and health may not primarily need charity but, rather, six months of counseling and hand holding and coaching. At this level, people can provide counseling in an informal and well-intentioned way. But they can probably deliver a better quality of counseling if they understand the principles and foundational theories in the disciplines of psychology, sociology, and public health.

The training agenda would seek to inculcate basic and general counseling skills as well as more specialized counseling skills for people with specific challenges.[37] For instance, people who survived Hurricane Katrina and the subsequent levee floods may need counseling that understands the dynamics of trauma and resilience. People who do not possess this advanced knowledge and skill base may do good work. But they could do even more with the additional insight that comes from acquiring training. And in practicing their counseling skills, the counselors should have someone who can supervise their work and serve as an advisor for the complex and challenging issues that emerge for the counselor while she or he provides counseling to clients in need.

Phase Three: The Ministry of Social Service

Here churches move beyond providing counseling to providing regular social services to a community, perhaps on a fee basis. Eileen Lindner has reported that houses of worship provide more than one third of the child-care services in America.[38] Ministries of support often involve complying with regulations and laws that govern the delivery of services to citizens as consumers. Houses of worship are often called upon to provide after-school services of various kinds. Among the most popular have been academic tutorial services, recreation and food, health screening and treatment, violence prevention, and teenage pregnancy prevention. Often congregations have sought and received grants from the government and foundations to support their ministries of social-service delivery. Depending upon the type of social service, a different body of theoretical knowledge may be required, such as sociology, juvenile justice, human biology and sexuality, and so on. Also, knowledge of the law, organizational management principles, and best practices are essential.[39]

Phase Four: The Ministry of Justice

When congregations move from providing services, support, and charity to people and focus upon representing the needs of people to the public systems and structures of power, they have moved into the ministry of justice or advocacy. Congregations have an opportunity to speak truth to power and to amplify the voice of the voiceless in the corridors of wealth and decision making.

Generally, the knowledge required here pertains to the nature of larger social systems, economics, politics, theology and ethics. One should know something about the interrelationships between what Paul Tillich framed in his book title, "love, power, and justice." One might benefit from knowing what Reinhold Niebuhr meant as he reflected on what happened in Nazi Germany and emphasized that we pay attention to the ways that humans behave differently as individuals from when they are in large groups.[40]

Phase Five: The Ministry of Transformation

In the ministry of comprehensive community transformation and development, the congregation becomes a leader or a co-leader in crafting a vision of the beloved community and then organizing the capital, mobilizing the people, negotiating the systems, and hammering out the details in order to develop new and better communities. With respect to the knowledge required, I would suggest that it would help to become a "Renaissance person," that is, someone who knows a fair amount about everything. This is where the value of that undergraduate liberal arts education really proves its value.[41]

But, as all of these levels are developed, I would suggest that the guiding criterion must be, What is in the best interest of the children? As we seek to be faithful to the Jesus who loved children and always sought their well-being, our decisions about when, where, why, and how we deliver charity, support, social services, justice and advocacy, and community development and transformation should be guided by how they foster better outcomes for kids. This is where I think that the public ministry and advocacy of Marian Wright Edelman and the Children's Defense Fund offer useful guidance for constructing a matrix of effective ministries that provide a "healthy start, a head start, a fair start, a safe start, and a moral start" for young people.[42]

A Framework for the Spiritual Renewal of the Village

Spiritual renewal of the village will require resources that might help us to conceptualize how we are all traveling along the same road toward truth, justice, goodness, and beauty. As noted earlier, the model I present here Bishop Edward Braxton developed in his book *The Wisdom Community*.[43] The model sketches six phases or moments that represent distinct but overlapping manifestations of the conversion and transformation journey.

> religious —> theocentric —> christocentric —> ecclesial —>
> intellectual —> moral

Religious Conversion

In the religious conversion, one moves from indifference toward the mysteries in the universe and life to curiosity. When we are curious about such questions as, "What happens to the soul at death?" "What lies beyond the farthest galaxy as I peer out into the dark?"

or "What is the purpose of human existence?" we need to know that such questions are religious questions. Further, one doesn't have to attend church or mosque to ask them. Indeed, we all know that folks in barber shops, taverns, street corners, and beauty salons ask these questions all the time. Whether they realize it or not, they are engaged in religious discourse and speculation, and they have had already a religious conversion. The theologian David Tracy suggests that religious questions are also "limit questions," as we realize and reflect on the fact that life has certain limits.

Theocentric Conversion

Theo is the Greek word for God (adapted in the Latin, *deo*). *Theocentric* refers to a "God-centered" conversion. Here one moves from curiosity about the mysteries of life to using God language to frame the discussion. People who are comfortable using the word or concept of "God" may be said to have had a "theocentric conversion." In other words, they accept that God had something to do with the origins of the universe and human existence. They may not know or be able to explain what role God played, as there are many different religious and theological answers to that issue. But they are comfortable asserting that God, whatever we mean by that word, exists. Theologian Rebecca Chopp is fond of invoking the work of theologian Langdon Gilkey, who used to suggest that theology and preaching are fundamentally engaged in trying to "name God" in human experience.

Christocentric Conversion

The Christ-centered conversion refers to people who have moved from a comfort with "God language" to a personal embrace of the historical and metaphysical Jesus Christ. This may be characterized as the traditional "Christian conversion" or moment of accepting Christ as a personal savior. This is the "moment of decision" for which so much Protestant evangelical preaching aims. This builds upon their previous acceptance of God-talk and curiosity about religious questions.

Ecclesial Conversion

The word *ecclesia* refers to the church. When Jesus declares, "You are Peter and upon this rock I will build my church [*ecclesia*]," *ecclesia* refers to the "called-out ones," the people who are set apart by their faith in Jesus. This is the move from an individual faith in Christ to a communal experience of the faith. Here, people move from "my faith" to "our faith" as the "body of Christ." This move is especially important at a time when more people are worshiping at home alone in front of the television set or radio. Although media ministries are a blessing for people who may be shut in, these may become a cop-out for those who do not want to deal with the challenge of relating to other human beings in all of their flaws and foibles. The ecclesial conversion challenges such individualism and compels us to join the church and be part of the collective community of faith.

Intellectual Conversion

In the intellectual conversation, people move from a random set of beliefs to a coherent belief system. Many people who join the church bring with them a variety of beliefs that may or may not be considered orthodox ("straight" or correct belief). People may cobble together a homegrown theology that is pragmatic and functional. Such a theology may draw from a variety of faith traditions and blend it with popular myths and superstitions that are incompatible with Christian faith. Hence, believers must be properly taught to understand the logic of their faith traditions. They should be exposed to the history of doctrine or teaching about the nature of God, Christ, the Holy Spirit, the church, sacraments, salvation, ministry, and so on.

Moral Conversion

In the moral conversion, we move from orthodoxy to orthopraxis, a fancy word for "straight" or correct practice, practice with a critical, reflective component always aimed at improvement and ongoing correction. This is the move from believing correctly to behaving correctly. Often people are not prepared to respond to the "call to action" because they have not had a moral conversion. Rather than growing angry or impatient with them, leaders are behooved to back up, assess the area of deficiency, and rebuild the foundations of their faith.

Here again, this model may be used for diagnostic purposes to assess when and where people were left behind or where they "got stuck." I often urge preachers to go back and consider developing a series of sermons on the religious moment or conversion. Rather than assuming that everyone is prepared to hear a sermon about Jesus (leading to a christocentric conversion), why not consider getting back to what people may believe about God or about the nature of reality and truth?

Perhaps the most remarkable development in black church culture during the post-civil rights era has been its spiritual renewal through the expanding influence of the least familiar forms of black church tradition, namely, Afro-Pentecostal churches and leaders. This is all the more remarkable because this segment of the black church community has not simply been ignored by most church scholars and leaders but has long been a source of scorn and suspicion by mainline American churches and by the assimilated black affluent class. Indeed, during the 1970s and '80s, there were significant denominational culture wars over how contemporary Christians should regard this segment of the church and its claims about the person and work of the Holy Spirit. Riverside Church pastor Dr. James Forbes regarded this skirmish as the American church's opportunity to rediscover and redeem the Third Person of the Trinity in their theologies and liturgical lives.

But today we are in a different place. Nearly all African American churches have tapped into the liturgical energy, joy, power, and excitement of doing ministry that has been especially nurtured in black Pentecostal traditions. In view of the mission crisis I am attempting to address, it may be time for churches at large to give increased attention to underutilized resources that may be able to reverse the mission crisis. In other words, African American Pentecostals have opened the door to spiritual renewal for other black churches and for the Christian church at large. Our *mission crisis will be reversed first and foremost by spiritual renewal and revitalization.* Beyond that primary commitment and process, there are several additional components of a comprehensive renewal agenda. They include the learning agenda that addresses what clergy need to know as they go forward (something my model addresses in part). There is an ethical agenda that pertains to including female leaders as I have discussed above. There is an ecclesiastical reform agenda that includes carefully and critically changing how the church organizes itself to accomplish its mission. This is what Carter G. Woodson addressed with searing clarity and candor. And there is an economic justice agenda that must involve churches exerting their leverage to insist that financial institutions, corporations, and political structures direct capital into ethnic minority communities. I have no doubt that churches will continue to advance the economic justice agenda.

But back to the spiritual, internal reorienting and reenergizing that we need. *If all contemporary churches embrace the spiritual earnestness and energies that animated black Pentecostal congregations during their early years, then we may witness the spiritual renaissance of American churches.* This doesn't mean that all churches need to become Pentecostal. Nor do I believe that Pentecostal denominations per se are the key to this spiritual rebirth. Frankly, many of them have been compromised by their loyalties to the prosperity gospel and right-wing politics. Rather, those who have been nurtured, blessed, and enriched by Pentecostal traditions now have access to the radical and life-giving energies that are unleashed by the Holy Spirit who is available to all believers and all churches.

Perhaps Dr. King has advice to church leaders who struggle to renew their missions and reclaim their prophetic voices. He faced a similar challenge as he reckoned with the Vietnam War in light of his faith commitments. The day was April 4, 1967, one year before his assassination. The venue was the Riverside Church in New York City. King said:

> A time comes when silence is betrayal. That time has come for us in relation to Vietnam. The truth of these words is beyond doubt, but the mission to which they call us is a most difficult one. Even when pressed by the demands of inner truth, men do not easily assume the task of opposing their government's policy, especially in time of war. Nor does the human spirit move without great

difficulty against all the apathy of conformist thought within one's own bosom, and in the surrounding world.

Over the past two years, as I have moved to break the betrayal of my own silences and to speak from the burnings of my own heart, as I have called for radical departures from the destruction of Vietnam, many persons have questioned me about the wisdom of my path.[44]

Just as Dr. King had to reckon with the call of history and the call of conscience, contemporary black church leaders must reckon with the dilemmas, the compromises, and the nonnegotiable conscience points that accompany their visibility and potential influence.

Recall these words from theologian Reinhold Niebuhr:

Nothing that is worth doing can be achieved in our lifetime. Therefore, we must be saved by hope. Nothing which is true or beautiful or good makes complete sense in any immediate context of history. Therefore, we must be saved by faith. Nothing we do, however virtuous, can be accomplished alone. Therefore we are saved by love. No virtuous act is quite as virtuous from the standpoint of our friend or foe as it is from our own standpoint. Therefore, we must be saved by the final form of love, which is forgiveness.[45]

QUESTIONS FOR DISCUSSION

1. How can churches avoid the dangers and distractions of the "prosperity gospel" movement?

2. How can the church be challenged to take greater risks on behalf of the least-advantaged members of the community?

3. Given the authority of clergy in the black church tradition, how can the village assist clergy to become more effective?

4. How can clergy be encouraged to avoid the distractions and seductions of ego inflation?

5. What can be done by all of us—churches, laypeople, clergy, the public at large—to recover the church's declining moral authority?

6. How may the church renew its own spiritual identity and practices?

3
COLLEGES
A CRISIS OF MORAL PURPOSE

MORRIS Brown College is one of the six institutions that comprise the historic Atlanta University Center (AUC). Founded by the African Methodist Episcopal Church in 1881 and named in honor of one of its bishops, Morris Brown is the only of the AUC schools founded by African Americans. In 2003, the Southern Association of Schools and Colleges, the accreditation agency of higher education in the region, did not reaffirm the school's accreditation. News began to emerge that the school was over $20 million in debt and would have to release most of its faculty and staff. Within the span of a year, the school enrollment plummeted from 2,500 to seventy-five students and the campus resembled a ghost town. A series of interim presidents maintained life support and sought ways to reduce the debt. Most students transferred to other schools while its senior leaders were released, some of them under the shadow of allegations of financial improprieties with federal student loan funds. The larger community looked on in disbelief and anger as a beloved institution, part of whose mission was to offer some academically marginal students a chance to enter and excel in college, prepared to close its doors. This was not a small, obscure school in a rural area, but a major institution in the capital of the New South. Ironically, as this drama unfolded, the school was featured in the hit film

film *Drumline* as the school of choice for budding musicians. While the school's celebrated marching band lent its brand-name value to the movie, and the film's director and stars collected royalties, according to former administrators, no fundraising campaign was launched linking the movie's success to the school's survival.

Communities of the African diaspora have a long and noble history as "learning communities." That history has many roots, some of which date back to creative, adaptive responses to slavery and systematic oppression. Some reach back to indigenous educational and socializing customs of Africa, never completely annihilated because memory, story, and ritual are elastic. And some perhaps reach back farther still into the ancient human past, as old as mothers singing their babies to sleep, stimulating neurons and transmitting a love and yearning for sound and language. Booker T. Washington framed the quest of the newly freed black population as "an entire race trying to go to school." The words haunt me and linger in the air even now . . ." trying to go to school."

Today, the vitality of far too many African American communities is threatened by the rapid erosion of old, hard-won habits and cultures of learning and excellence. The question that looms now is, How resilient are those traditions? That erosion is dramatically manifested in the vast number of urban schools where kids are not learning, where learning itself has been devalued and ridiculed, and the public will and resources to reverse this situation are lacking. Reversing this will require a major outpouring of public and private investment, faith, and effort. But I'd like to make the case for community leadership that helps to lead and inspire that renaissance.

Specifically, I'd like to suggest that high school graduates and especially those who have the privilege of attending college are the village's greatest assets. As a group, they are young, energetic, idealistic, accomplished, smart, have high earning potential and (most of them) have relatively few major responsibilities that limit their freedom. During the civil rights movement, these same characteristics enabled students to make a significant impact on the future direction of American democracy. Now students, both as individuals and as a group, could play a major role in renewing practices of intellectual development, healthy relationships, and civic responsibility. Perhaps, they are waiting for the village elders and anchor institutions to call and commission them.

Communities that do not have a black college nearby certainly do have college graduates and current students who could and should be equipped to assume a leading role in community renewal, particularly with respect to promoting education, healthy relationships, and a culture of integrity, excellence, and community service. I do not mean to limit this appeal to HBCU (Historic Black Colleges and Universities) students and graduates as they represent a fraction of the college-educated black community. I am simply trying to retrieve the expressed hopes and expectations of the village ancestors that these young people would play a leading role in village renewal. In view of the urgency of our situation, the village must now call upon the best and brightest members of the village to exercise their will, reason, resources, and conscience to produce better results in the community. Already successful education renewal initiatives have been launched and may offer guidance for others. Hence, I offer the following moral imperative: *The indigenous traditions and values of community learning and individual academic excellence can and should be retrieved immediately by each village member. A person's intellectual maturity and social status should be measured by her or his service to people with fewer opportunities and supports. Every college-educated adult who has benefited from the public's investment in them should accept the moral obligation to provide leadership and service.* If we do this effectively, future generations will cherish our sacrifices and honor our names.

WHAT EVERYONE SHOULD KNOW ABOUT COMMUNITY EDUCATION AND BLACK COLLEGES

1. *The West African societies from which people were coerced into slavery were culturally accomplished and prosperous.* During Europe's medieval period, much of West Africa was experiencing prosperity, political stability, and intellectual achievement. Scholars from all over the Islamic world came to the empire of Mali to study in the libraries at Timbuktu. Today, several of the city's private libraries survive and the largest features over seven hundred volumes.[1]

2. *Many of the Africans who became slaves in America were educated and many were of royal African ancestry.* A large number of the Africans who were captured and enslaved came from the territory encompassed by the Mali Empire (current-day Mali, Senegal, Gambia [novelist Alex Haley's home country], southern Mauritania, eastern Guinea-Bissau, and eastern Guinea).[2]

3. *African Americans were excluded from formal education despite the fact that they constituted a significant percentage of most southern states' children.* For instance, in 1787, Thomas Jefferson "proposed a popular educational system that would offer three years of public schooling to every white child of the Virginia commonwealth and then send the brightest male youngsters on to grammar school and college at public expense."[3] Although enslaved children constituted 40 percent of Virginia's children and their enslaved parents' labor was the foundation for Jefferson's (and Virginia's) wealth, he declared that blacks should be excluded from learning and literate culture. This reprehensible decision reminds us that intelligent people may be blinded by self-interest and prejudice rather than be guided by right reason and the common good.[4]

4. *For many decades, black literacy was a crime.* Between 1800 and 1835, most of the southern states enacted legislation making it a crime to teach enslaved children to read or write.[5] This exclusion only heightened black people's desire for a good that was so coveted by their masters. They understood that education was essential to the experience of freedom and the exercise of power.

5. *Black churches played a leading role in establishing and maintaining schools for black youth at all levels.* Against the strong opposition of southern states and citizens that sought to exclude or not provide public support for black education, black churches and clergy became advocates for, providers and supporters of, elementary, high school, industrial, agricultural, and college education.[6]

6. *Black taxpayers subsidized the education of white children at a time when their own children were excluded from formal learning.*

During the first two decades of the twentieth century in the South, black taxpayers subsidized the education of white students and school buildings. In effect, blacks paid a double tax for education as they paid tax appropriations that did not benefit their children and they made contributions for privately financed schools for their own children.[7]

7. *The first historically black colleges and universities (HBCUs) were founded in the mid-1800s. Today, there are approximately 110 HBCUs.* There are more than three thousand colleges and universities in the nation. HBCUs represent less than 5 percent of the total but provide a disproportionate share of opportunity and access to higher education for minority citizens.

8. *HBCUs enrich the marketplace of American higher education through their distinctive historical mission and contemporary contributions to a diverse workforce and leadership class.* 45 percent of HBCU freshmen are the first in their families to attend college.[8] "While black colleges and universities make up just 4 percent of U.S. institutions of higher learning, they graduate 28 percent of all students who earn their undergraduate degrees. Seventy-five percent of African Americans with Ph.D.s earn them from HBCUs, as do 46 percent of black business executives, 50 percent of black engineers, 80 percent of black federal judges, and 85 percent of black doctors." This small group of schools is doing disproportionately more than its fair share to educate a workforce and leadership base that will contribute positively to America's global competitiveness.[9] That should be reason enough to compel national support.

9. *Many HBCU graduates have served the common good and enhanced America's global reputation as a nation of inclusivity and opportunity.* These include Dr. Martin Luther King Jr. (Nobel Peace Prize-winning minister), Andrew Young (minister, former U.N. Ambassador, congressman, and mayor), Julian Bond (NAACP chair, former Georgia state senator), Marian Wright Edelman (Children's Defense Fund founder and president), Louis Sullivan (former U.S. Secretary of Health and Human Services), David Satcher (former

U.S. Surgeon General), Ruth Simmons (Brown University president), Spike Lee (filmmaker), Lionel Ritchie (singer), Samuel L. Jackson (Oscar-nominated actor), and Tom Joyner (radio D.J.).

10. *Two national organizations serve as advocates for HBCUs: the United Negro College Fund (UNCF, aka The College Fund) and the National Association for Equal Opportunity in Higher Education (NAFEO).* In 1944, Dr. Frederick D. Patterson, president of Tuskegee Institute (now Tuskegee University), founded the United Negro College Fund. The previous year Patterson had published an open letter in the *Pittsburgh Courier* to the presidents of other private black colleges urging them to "pool their small monies and make a united appeal to the national conscience." Today, the College Fund has thirty-nine member colleges.[10] Its well-known motto is "A mind is a terrible thing to waste."

In 1969, a group of HBCU presidents founded the National Association for Equal Opportunity in Higher Education (NAFEO) as the professional association of the presidents and chancellors of all HBCUs. More inclusive than the UNCF, its member institutions are public and private, two- and four-year, community, regional, national and international comprehensive research institutions, located in twenty-five states, the District of Columbia, the Virgin Islands, and Brazil.[11] All UNCF schools are also members of NAFEO.

11. *Contemporary trends in higher education may threaten or inspire HBCU vitality.* For instance, between 1976 and 1994, predominantly white colleges experienced a 40 percent increase in black enrollment while HBCU rosters increased by only half that amount.[12] Since 1990, eighty-five HBCU presidents have resigned or left their posts. Forty-four black colleges have installed a new president in just the past four years.[13] Recall that there are less than one hundred and twenty HBCUs.

12. *In recent years, many HBCUs have closed their doors.* Due to financial, governance, and other problems, at least twenty HBCUs are now defunct. They include: Bishop College, Saints Junior Col-

lege, Mississippi Industrial College, Morristown College, Natchez Junior College, Shaw College at Detroit, Avery College, and Daniel Payne College.

WHAT'S WRONG

Perhaps the single most extraordinary fact about the history of black intellectual and moral advancement is that achievements were made and progress occurred against the resistance of monumental odds—odds that no other American immigrants faced in seeking to improve their lot. Before focusing on the challenges and strengths of black colleges and what the village needs from all of its graduates, it may be useful and illuminating to briefly revisit and introduce many readers to the history, values, and practices of black communities as learning communities. Although the focus of this chapter is on how to get more from the anchor institutions known as HBCUs and especially their graduates, we must first address what is happening in early childhood development, public schools, and their alternatives. Consequently, in order to ensure a common baseline of information, I will provide a bit more historical background here than I did in the previous chapters.

Historians of West Africa have documented the strong traditions of teaching and learning that were present in African empires that thrived, such as Mali, between the fourteenth and eighteenth centuries. During those years a famed university developed at Timbuktu. The city was home to approximately 150 Qu'ranic schools that offered formal instruction at multiple levels from elementary to advanced higher education. "Students and scholars came from all over the Islamic world to study and teach in Timbuktu."[14] Scholars note that some of the Africans who were caught in the net of the Atlantic slave trade and delivered to American shores would have been well-educated persons, probably including students and graduates of the schools in Timbuktu.

After the first twenty Africans were brought to Jamestown, Virginia in 1619, their usefulness as a cheap labor supply was rapidly established. By contrast, many of the European peasants who were also employed as indentured servants (who worked for a specified period and then were permitted to go free) and thought to be a potential labor supply soon showed vulnerability to the diseases (yellow fever) that fatally threatened the white planters. Then efforts were made to use Native Americans as a chief source of cheap mass labor. But there was one big problem with that plan: the Native people knew the land and routes of escape that made white planters vulnerable to ambush when trying to chase and capture Indians. Following the invention of the cotton gin in 1734, there was a demand for a massive supply of laborers. Africans had proven their strength, capacity to transplant knowledge from Africa, to learn new agricultural practices, and to innovate and invent new approaches to agriculture and industry.

But as their numbers grew, so also grew the fears of white planters who believed that if blacks were educated or baptized, they would begin to assert their equality to whites and demand the equal treatment about which the founding fathers spoke so eloquently. "In 1740, South Carolina made it illegal to teach blacks to write, though they still were allowed to read. Georgia passed its own law forbidding the education of black Americans in 1755."[15] In matters pertaining to education as with the formation of black families, American public policy lined up against the noble aspirations of blacks who were simply "trying to go to school" and to form strong families.

Education historian James D. Anderson notes that "between 1760 and 1835, most of the southern states enacted legislation making it a crime to teach enslaved children to read or write." That amounts to three generations of formal state opposition to educating black people. Just as the door was being shut on state-supported education for blacks, the state began to invest in education for white citizens. Anderson notes that "a massive campaign to achieve popular schooling for free Americans developed between 1830 and 1860, and out of this campaign emanated designs for state systems of public education."[16] We should note that this thirty-year period is significant not only because the infrastructure for today's education system was being developed during that period but also because it frames the two significant events that signaled a new and more dramatic level of urgency about abolishing slavery in America. Those events were Nat Turner's organized rebellion in 1831, and the start of the Civil War (1861).

Throughout slave communities, literacy and learning were treasured skills. People understood that these abilities were critical to freedom, self-improvement, and citizenship. Charity Bowery, an ex-slave, indicated that "On Sundays, I have seen the negroes up in the country going away under large oaks, and in secret places, sitting in the woods with spelling books." Some slaves also organized secret schools in clear violation of an unjust, inhumane law. Anderson cites this testimony of an ex-slave: "every window and door was carefully closed to prevent discovery. In that little school hundreds of slaves learned to read and write a legible hand. After toiling all day for their masters they crept stealthily into this back alley, each with a bundle of pitch-pine splinters for lights." But the opportunity to attend such a school was rare. Indeed, for the typical slave the following testimony is heartbreaking: "Why, we were no more than dogs! If they caught us with a piece of paper in our pockets, they'd whip us. They were afraid we'd learn to read and write, but I never got a chance." The more slave masters sought to repress and prevent black learning, the more the slaves understood its importance for freedom and they strove even harder to attain both learning and liberty.

Due to the criminalization of African American learning, people who sought literacy by surreptitious means also risked extreme torture and threat. One of the most heart-rending stories I have heard comes from the extraordinary testimonies of slaves recorded by the Federal Writers' Project in the early 1930s.[17] This is the testimony of Tonea Stewart:

> When I was a little girl about five or six years old, I used to sit on the garret, the front porch. In the Mississippi Delta the front porch is called the garret. I listened to my Papa Dallas. He was blind and had these ugly scars around his eyes. One day, I asked Papa Dallas what happened to his eyes.
>
> "Well daughter," he answered, "when I was mighty young, just about your age. I used to steal away under a big oak tree and I tried to learn my alphabets so that I could learn to read my Bible. But one day the overseer caught me and he drug me out on the

plantation and he called out for all the field hands. And he turned to 'em and said, 'Let this be a lesson to all of you darkies. You ain't got no right to learn to read!' And then daughter, he whooped me, and he whooped me, and he whooped me. And daughter, as if that wasn't enough, he turned around and he burned my eyes out!"

At that instant, I began to cry. The tears were streaming down my cheeks, meeting under my chin. But he cautioned, "Don't you cry for me now, daughter. Now you listen to me. I want you to promise me one thing. *Promise me that you gonna pick up every book you can and you gonna read it from cover to cover.* You see, today daughter, ain't nobody gonna whip you or burn your eyes out because you want to learn to read. Promise me that you gonna go all the way through school, as far as you can. And one more thing, I want you to promise me that you gonna tell all the children my story."

Papa Dallas survived slavery and I, I kept my promise. I'm now a university professor, a Ph.D., and an actress. He and many others deserve to have their story told.[18] (My emphasis)

Papa Dallas's harrowing testimony should be read to young and old people today who are indifferent to learning. Too much blood was shed and too much pain endured not to view learning as a moral enterprise.

During the twelve-year period (1865–1877) that followed the Civil War, known as Reconstruction, ex-slaves briefly enjoyed the benefits of citizenship, Republican government, and wage labor. Several blacks were elected to Congress, state legislatures, and governor's houses. Moreover, a new era of black education emerged with the founding of schools such as Morehouse and Fisk. But that period came to a sudden end with the election of a new president, Rutherford B. Hayes, who cooperated with a plan to roll back black progress. Once again, blacks faced hostility, state-supported exclusion, and citizen-sponsored terror to keep them in their "place." Anderson says, "Black education developed within this context of political and economic oppression. . . . Although black southerners were formally free during the time when American popular education was transformed into a highly formal and critical social institution, their schooling took a different path."[19]

Still, despite these state-supported obstacles to black progress, the hunger for education and literacy grew all the stronger within black communities. Anderson quotes an ex-slave who declared, "There is one sin that slavery committed against me which I will never forgive. It robbed me of my education."[20] In 1879, Harriet Beecher Stowe reported of newly freed blacks that "They rushed not to the grog-shop [tavern] but to the schoolroom—they cried for the spelling book as bread, and pleaded for teachers as a necessity of life."[21] Booker T. Washington, himself a former slave, noted in a widely quoted statement, "Few people who were not right in the midst of the scenes can form any exact idea of the intense desire which the people of my race showed for education. It was a whole race trying to go to school. Few were too young, and none too old, to make the attempt to learn."[22]

Washington's provocative words stick in the mind and serve to underscore the tragedy of the weakened and eroded intellectual culture in many contemporary villages. But he also reminds us of a foundation that can be recovered and renewed: ". . . *a whole race trying to go to school*." Anderson summarizes,

> Before northern benevolent societies entered the South in 1862, before President Abraham Lincoln issued the Emancipation Proclamation in 1863, and before Congress created the Bureau of Refugees, Freedmen and Abandoned Lands (Freedmen's Bureau) in 1865, slaves and free persons of color had already begun to make plans for the systematic instruction of their illiterates. Early black schools were established and supported largely through the Afro-Americans' own efforts.[23]

Churches played a major role in sponsoring schools for ex-slaves. One Freedmen's Bureau superintendent of education in Kentucky said in 1867, "The places of worship owned by the colored people are almost the only available school houses in the State."[24] Indeed, the churches were often the incubators for black schools and provided the space, volunteers, and value of learning.

In 1862, African Methodist Episcopal Bishop Daniel Alexander Payne exhorted the village to value education in a manner that reminds us of Bill Cosby's exhortations and introduces the idea of the moral purposes of education:

But of the children take special care. Heaven has entrusted them
to you for a *special purpose*. What is that purpose? Not merely
to eat and to drink, still less to gormandize. Not merely to dress
finely in broadcloths, silks, satins, jewelry, nor to dance to the
sound of the tambourine and fiddle; but *to learn them how to live
and how to die—to train them for great usefulness on earth—to
prepare them for greater glory in heaven.* [His emphasis.]

   *Keep your children in the schools, even if you have to eat less,
drink less and wear coarser raiments; though you eat but two meals
a day, purchase but one change of garment during the year, and
relinquish all the luxuries of which we are so fond,* but which are as
injurious to health and long life as they are pleasing to the taste.
Let the education of your children penetrate the heart."[25]

Again, we are reminded of the depth of commitment earlier
village leaders had to shaping both the intellect and character of
the next generation. Bishop Payne's exhortation has implications
for the kind of personal sacrifice that both village members and our
allies should embrace in the service of educating our kids.

Despite the educational aspirations and accomplishments of
black churches, the control of the curriculum, scope, structure, and
financing of most black schools was rarely in the hands of African
Americans. With the rise of ex-slave Booker T. Washington, a model of
how blacks could be educated while remaining subordinate to whites
seized the public imagination. His famous 1895 speech in Atlanta at
the Cotton Exposition declared that industrial and agricultural education for blacks was essential for the economic prosperity of the South.
Rather than permit northern whites to feel superior to the South and
its distinctive cultural mores, whites and blacks in the South should
work together to show the world its potential for prosperity and progress while respecting the color line. Wealthy philanthropists lined up to
support Washington's vision, which was simply the "Hampton Idea"
he had learned from Hampton founder General Samuel Armstrong.

By the end of the Civil War (1865), the idea of universal public
education for children had still not taken hold in the South. Many
planters felt that classical or liberal arts learning would distract
white peasants and black slaves from their lives of hard labor. Even
more frightening was the possibility that "educated Negroes" would

seek the right to vote, run for office, equal wages, union member-ship, and so on. They were determined not to revisit Reconstruc-tion, and denial of learning was the key to extinguishing those aspirations. Note that Georgia didn't require compulsory public school attendance until 1916. By then, thousands of black college graduates, including graduates of Morris Brown College, were vig-orously organizing and agitating for equal rights and had founded the NAACP (1910), the Urban League (1914), sororities, fraterni-ties, lodges, the major black church denominations and an impres-sive array of other commercial and nonprofit organizations.

Due to a "convergence of circumstances," Anderson notes that "the lack of federal and state support for the development of black higher education, the opposition of industrial philanthropy, and the impoverishment of missionary and black religious philanthropy—combined to retard the development of black higher education dur-ing the first two decades of the twentieth century." "Most important," he continues, "the key promoters of black higher education, mis-sionary and black religious societies, could not accumulate the large amounts of capital required to place black colleges on solid financial grounds. Though they plodded on persistently, preserving a mod-est system of black collegiate education, their nineteenth-century momentum declined sharply after 1900." He continues, "By any standard, the material and financial status of black higher education was bad. Black colleges were understaffed, meagerly equipped, and poorly financed. The combined efforts of the missionary and black organizations could not raise sufficient funds to meet annual oper-ating expenses, increase teachers' salaries, expand the physical plant, improve libraries, or purchase new scientific and technical equipment. Indeed, almost all of the missionary black colleges lacked sufficient endowments to ensure their survival." "In 1926, the total endowment of ninety-nine black college and normal schools had risen to $20.3 million, and more than $14 million of this belonged to Hampton and Tuskegee Institutes; the ninety-seven remaining institutions had a combined total of $6.1 million. As late as 1932, seventy-five black colleges had either a negligible endowment or none at all."[26]

Now, one hundred years later, in the early years of a new cen-tury and millennium, the scene is dramatically different. Due once again to the successful partnership of creative and dedicated school and community leaders, corporate and philanthropic investment, donations from affluent blacks and religious communities, and gifts from the public, most of the remaining black colleges stand on relatively firm ground, although many have closed their doors during the post–civil rights movement period.

In view of the foregoing, several questions should be posed. Given the critical importance of education for the uplift of disadvantaged people and the strength of a nation, why has the nation not found the will to allocate adequate resources (not just money) to educating its neediest citizens? Given their historical role in establishing and advocating for black education, have churches and clergy done their part to advance this agenda by making an urgent and unrelenting case for public, corporate, individual, and village support? And as for the schools themselves, have these anchoring institutions become what so many hoped and prayed that they would? Should the mere survival of many of these schools be counted as success? Are they engaged in producing the kinds of graduates who will lead village renewal? How can boards of trustees, faculty and administrators in our schools refocus and implement their mission of preparing excellent and ethical students who contribute to the common good as well as their own wealth accumulation? And can the village contribute to their renaissance as they contribute to its renewal? I'll restate the questions at the end of the chapter for helping to frame a village discussion.

As I shift from the financial constraints to the crisis of moral purpose these institutions face, I'd like to note that there is a virtual army of scholar-activists and a vast literature on promoting education excellence among African American children. Among them are James P. Comer, Asa G. Hilliard III, Janice E. Hale, Beverly Tatum, and many others. They will be invaluable for guiding and evaluating the academic renewal work ahead. I defer to their wisdom about implementing strategies that work. My focus here is to highlight the distinctive role that all high school graduates, especially black college students and graduates should play in the academic renaissance of African American communities. They constitute an army of potential mentors, volunteers, and financial supporters for reviving a culture of learning and excellence in black communities. For some young people, these graduates will have value merely for being academic "survivors" who completed twelve years of schooling, are capable of earning higher incomes, and living more fulfilling lives because of it.

The Crisis of Moral Purpose in Public and Private Education

By any measure, it would appear that the primary institutions on which Americans rely for the wholistic development of our children are failing far too many of them. Although America's system of publicly supported education, especially higher education, is admired throughout the world, we can only feel embarrassment about what happens in many of our schools, both in poor inner city and affluent suburban districts. On a regular basis we are reminded of the culture of violence, drug use, sexual experimentation, and moral relativism that seem to plague many schools.

In a report to the nation titled, "Smart and Good High Schools," Thomas Lickona and Matthew Davidson observe that "for America's 13 million high school adolescents there is both good news and bad news. Some trends are positive (adolescent drug use, sexual intercourse, and most forms of violence are down); some are negative (cheating is up, preparedness for college-level work upon high school graduation is down); and some (dropout rates, the achievement gap, our poor ranking in international test comparisons) are stubbornly stable."[27]

They also note that "in the Center for Academic Integrity's survey of 18,000 students at 61 U.S. high schools, 76% of the over 6,000 participating public school students admitted to cheating on exams."[28] In his book, *The Cheating Culture: Why More Americans Are Doing Wrong to Get Ahead*, David Callahan notes other expressions of our cheating culture: "resume fraud by job-seekers at every level soared over the past decade, tax evasion has gotten worse in recent years, computer technology has facilitated the large-scale theft of copyrighted material (especially music), and an unprecedented number of plagiarism cases have rocked the publishing world, including best-selling authors and star reporters."[29]

In a 2006 *New York Times* article titled "Colleges Chase as Cheats Shift to Higher Tech," Jonathan D. Glater called attention to a rising crisis of character among the nation's best and brightest, noting:

> Students at UCLA who were loading class notes into a handheld e-mail device and reading them during an exam; San Jose State University students who were "caught using spell check on their laptops when part of the exam was designed to test their ability to spell"; and Students at the University of Nevada, Las Vegas who photographed test questions with their cellphone cameras, transmitted them to classmates outside the exam room, and got the answers back in text messages.[30]

An exasperated professor observed, "If they'd spend as much time studying, they'd all be 'A' students."

Lickona and Davidson also cite Neil Postman's observation that *"because of television, 5 year olds now know things that only adults used to know"* (my emphasis).[31] All of this reminds us that children need to be surrounded and supported by messages and models of moral goodness. And adults must take special care to provide the media literacy to help kids understand and critique what they are viewing and hearing.

Let me drill down a bit deeper into a dimension of this moral crisis that has important implications for the future of families and congregations in the village. As I have traveled around the country and asked questions about how communities can support the renewal of schools, I have heard people repeatedly express their worries about why boys are not doing as well as girls in school, the devaluation of academic excellence by the most admired and popular members of the youth peer group, and the lack of respect for traditional moral codes and values. These are among the areas where the village could do more to improve educational outcomes for our kids.

The Educational Gap between Males and Females

Various scholars and activists have called attention to the challenges that many black boys experience in urban public schools. Afrocentric educator Jawanza Kunjufu was among the first popular voices to call attention to a disturbing pattern. He argued that black boys who have been good students during the early school years seem to "hit a wall" when they arrive at fourth and fifth grades.[32] That "wall" usually manifests itself in the form of female teachers (especially middle aged, middle class white females) who have internalized stereotypes, attitudes and fears that inhibit their ability to understand and relate well to these boys. As the boys repeatedly encounter the teacher's frustration, suspicion and lack of empathy, they tend to react by increasingly more inappropriate behavior that they know will irritate the teacher. It is a small power game that they know they can win. But, such victories are hollow and shortlived. Before long, the boys are labeled as problem kids that cannot be taught. Many end up on a special ed track that leads to expulsion, drop out and entry into the juvenile justice system.

Professor Kunjufu does have some good news. He reports that these same boys who do not respond well to teachers who could not be more different from them, do respond to very well to their school coaches. In fact, he notes that athletic coaches are able to discipline these guys and get them to do things requiring discipline, patience, listening, respect and teamwork that the teachers cannot imagine possible for them. Hence, he argues that these boys need fewer teachers and more coaches for their academic progress.

Kunjufu's decision to frame this issue as a "conspiracy to destroy black boys" has been construed to be unnecessarily provocative and sensational. However, the reality behind the frame has been confirmed by many scholars and practitioners. While many policy and opinion makers postulate the influence of inappropriate role models and broken homes, "the answers from education experts start with bad school experiences. Thousands of young black males, for example, get sidetracked by special-education referrals that, in truth, are failures on the part of schools to teach basic literacy skills."[33]

In a study titled Project 2000, researchers were curious about the impact on boys' academic and general behavior of having a male teaching assistant in classrooms with female teachers.[34] Rhonda Wells-Wilborn and Spencer Holland found that the boys tended to do better academically and their behavior improved when these male volunteers were present and showed an interest in their future.

The race of the teaching assistant did not seem to matter as some of the volunteers where white. But, the surprise came when they found that the presence of the men also improved the academic and behavioral performance of girls.

In the context where large numbers of urban youth are reared in households and neighborhoods where there are fewer positive male role models present, a small amount of exposure seemed to go a long way.

But the gender gap that emerges early on seems to persist into the high school years and beyond. In a February 2005 *USA Today* editorial titled, "Black Men Fall Behind," the following good news appeared, "The number of African American, Hispanic, Asian-American and Native American students enrolled in college doubled during the past decade."[35] Citing a recently released study from the American Council on Education, the editors went on to note that "for African American men, an alarming gender gap is widening."[36] Also, they report that "currently, 56% of black women graduate from high school, compared with 43% of black men."[37]

When it comes to college, the piece notes that "from 2000 to 2001, the number of black men in higher education rose by 30,000 . . . but during the same period the number of black women in college rose by 73,000, and twice as many black women as black men now attend college."[38]

According to a 2000 Census report titled, "We the People: Blacks in the United States," "The educational attainment levels among blacks varied by sex. About 15 percent of black women had earned at least a bachelor's degree, higher than the 13 percent of black men. . . . the proportion of black men (13 percent) with a bachelor's degree was one-half that of men in the total population (26 percent). The proportion of black women (15 percent) with a bachelor's degree was two-thirds that of women in the total population (23 percent)."[39] And "in 2000, 31 percent of African Americans ages 18 to 24 were enrolled in colleges and universities; nearly two thirds of them were female."[40]

An often-cited and sobering statistic is the number of black men in prison exceeds those in college. Recent reports have highlighted the growing proportion of women to men graduating from high school and enrolled in HBCUs. Some schools are beginning to see 75 percent female student bodies and note that when the numbers in a coed school become so imbalanced, it discourages prospective students, male and female, from attending that school.

Clearly, this demographic phenomenon has implications for the future of healthy relationships, marriages, family formation, and family economics. The entire village should be aware of, indignant about, and determined to take action with respect to how and why we lose so many young black men in the pipeline of success.

I'd like to call attention to another dimension of the challenges young men may be facing in our schools, namely, the problem of anonymity.

The Danger of Detachment and Anonymity

Related to the concern about what is happening to boys along the education journey is the phenomenon of kids who "fall through the net" of accountability and are not discovered until it is too late to redeem their elementary and secondary education. Sometimes, as in the Columbine school murders and in violent crimes on HBCU campuses, the troubled youth are not detected before they commit irreversible crimes and ruin many lives.

Commenting on the "challenges facing high schools," a veteran reformer offered these insights:

> Anonymity is the first curse of the typical American high school. Too-much-crammed-into-too-little-time-and-space is the second curse. Concerning the first curse. If the student-teacher ratio is 120:1, with the 120 shuffled repeatedly throughout the year, kids realize that few teachers know them well. Students conclude from this that knowing each student well is a low priority for the school. And when a teacher does not know a student well, it is easy for that student to cheat, cut corners, and "fake it." The lesson the student learns from anonymity is, 'I must not count for much here because the school does not know me, and so I have to take care of myself."[41]

A similar phenomenon is occurring around the nation as children who are experiencing obvious difficulties in school are likely to be detected before anyone in the community knows how serious things have become. The village needs to be alerted as early as possible in order to intervene in redemptive, supportive ways. We need to be alerted that our love and discipline are needed in abundant supply for particular individuals. I have heard numerous teachers, guidance counselors, coaches, and school staff report that they see the early warning signs of academic distress but often report this to parents who do not know what to do with the information. Also, we need to pay greater attention (and money) to those who are in the trenches with our children every day.

The challenges that I have discussed here do not go away when students go on to college. Indeed, students carry the challenges with them. Here, I 'd like to return to my primary interest in the vitality of HBCUs.

Acknowledging Crisis Requires Moral Courage

One of the most extraordinary and influential black college presidents of the twentieth century was Benjamin Elijah Mays. He occupies a seat at a small and distinguished table with similar leaders, including Mary McLeod Bethune, founder of the National Council of Negro Women, who purchased land that had been a garbage dump and in 1904 founded the Daytona Educational and Industrial Training School (that later became Bethune Cookman College); and Mordecai Wyatt Johnson, who presided at Howard University from 1926 to 1960, where he gathered and inspired a faculty that included some of black America's greatest minds. During Johnson's tenure, Howard faculty and students were among the leading black activists who dismantled the legal and constitutional foundations of Jim Crow, inspired the black masses to pursue full participation in America society, and also prepared a generation of African intellectuals who went on to lead national independence movements across the African continent.

Mays, Bethune, and Johnson were college presidents who led and managed effectively. But they were also public intellectuals and, in some cases, public theologians. That is, they were thinkers who brought research-based, analytic, historical, comparative, critical, and constructive cognitive powers to practical problems facing their people. They were advisors and confidants to U.S. presidents. Because of their strong advocacy for equal rights, social justice, and liberal arts education, they did not have the fundraising successes that marked the tenure of Booker T. Washington at Tuskegee Institute (now University). They were not celebrities nor did they seek such superficial measures of their effectiveness. Yet they became household names in most black working and middle-class households. They were "thought leaders" and opinion shapers operating on behalf of, but also beyond, the African American village. They grasped the big picture, often the global arena and significance of U.S. policy, presence, and action. And they led their institutions with strategic sophistication.

I'd like to focus on Dr. Mays, who served as president of my alma mater, Morehouse College, from 1940 to 1967. During those years, he had a direct impact on students such as Martin Luther King Jr., Julian Bond, Maynard Jackson, and many others, including leaders who did not attend Morehouse. For instance, many Spelman College graduates, such as Marian Wright Edelman and Dr. Audrey Manley, speak passionately of Mays's influence on the female students studying across the street from the Morehouse campus. Indeed, Dr. Mays's protégés were many, and I am among them.[42]

Dr. Mays's last opportunity to deliver the commencement address as its president came in 1967, the year of the school's centennial. I will draw on that speech extensively in order to illustrate how an exceptional HBCU president understood part of his responsibility was to offer a moral vision to graduates and the larger village.

If you have ever attended a black college commencement, you know that it is quite distinctive and different from commencements in majority institutions. In a commentary for National Public Radio, I characterized the black college commencement as a fusion of the culture of the academy and the culture of the black church.[43] Proud mothers and grandmothers wear their "church hats" or crowns, and people expect to celebrate. The standard announcement made at majority institutions, namely that the audience should hold its applause until all of the graduates have been awarded diplomas, is an exercise in futility at black colleges. For when that graduate is the first member of her or his family to experience this achievement, the extended family intends to celebrate.

By several measures, this would surely be a monumental and memorable occasion for everyone present. Those who gathered in Samuel Archer Hall for the ceremony would have expected spirit-lifting music from the famed glee club, sparkling smiles on the faces of the handsome and confident graduates, and an inspiring oration from the retiring president. And on this special occasion, they would have expected him to recount a century of achievement, share a few choice memories, and boost the brand-name of the school even higher. But President Mays's comments that day must have come as a shock to many, for, quite apart from leading the cheers for "dear old Morehouse," he engaged in a sobering bit of moral reckoning and institutional truth telling. Mays began:

> Since 1967 is Morehouse's one hundredth year, you will under-stand why I introduce this address with a bit of history, lest we forget the thought patterns out of which Morehouse was molded. When Morehouse was founded in 1867, virtually all of science, religion, and statesmanship were speaking with a unanimous voice, declaring that the newly emancipated people were little less than human.[44]

After providing several examples of such racist scholarship and public practice, he continued:

> This was the matrix out of which Morehouse was born. This was the prevailing notion up to and throughout the first quarter of the twentieth century. Though Morehouse did wonders to prove the falsehood of these prejudiced minds prior to 1940, I speak to the subject: "Twenty-Seven Years of Success and Failure at Morehouse."[45]

The announcement of a commencement address topic that contained the word *failure* must surely have heightened the attention and raised the anxiety of many. What was "Buck Benny" (as he was affectionately known) about to say?

I have no regrets in retiring from the presidency of Morehouse at this juncture in history. I regret, however, that what has been accomplished in these twenty-seven years trails so far behind my dreams for the college and so far behind what I aspired for More-house to be that I feel a sense of failure. I wish I could tell you today that the future of Morehouse was guaranteed in the stars. ... From this friends, alumni, trustees, faculty, and students—all share in the success of the college. Likewise, we all share in the college's failure.[46]

Mays's self-disclosure, institutional honesty, and moral courage are obvious and stunning. Reading these words alongside the commencement address delivered by W. E. B. Du Bois in 1939 at Howard University (excerpted at the beginning of chapter four), one readily sees that an earlier generation of black public intellectuals regarded commencement addresses as opportunities to engage in truth telling rather than the pieties, happy talk, and superficial inspiration that now dominates those occasions. But he then reminded them that success and failure are collective realities, not the track record of a single "star" president. Then he elaborated in practical and specific terms that establish baselines for individual and communal account-ability, a mark of a strategic public theologian:

If an alumnus could have given to support the college and did not, he must accept blame for not doing his share. If I were der-elict in my duty, I too, must be cited as one responsible for not doing what I ought have done.[47]

Whereas in recent years Morehouse has been voted the "best black college" in America by *U.S. News and World Report*, it will surprise many to discover that in 1940 Mays declared that Morehouse was the "weakest link" in the Atlanta University consortium of schools.[48] Next, in words reminiscent of the recent challenges of Morris Brown College, he noted,

We believed when we came, and we believe as we leave, that affiliation is the strength of all and that the weakness of one is the weakness of all. While we seek to cooperate fully, each institution must strive to be strong enough to add strength to the entire center.[49]

Then, he shares a litany of areas where failure was noted.

> We believed that if you could produce a quality faculty, show that the alumni were making their mark in the world, and that the college's able students did well in graduate and professionals schools, it would make fund-raising relatively easy. It isn't necessarily so.
>
> We believed that in ten years we could create a scholarly atmosphere at the college so that the majority of the students would pursue excellence and that the *purposeless could not survive* [my emphasis]. We did not fully succeed. We believed in 1940 that if we moved the college forward and made it better year by year, with some cultivation, we could raise the percentage of alumni givers by 50 percent. It wasn't true. That dream has not been fulfilled. If we can maintain the impetus of the Centennial, the dream will come true.
>
> We believed that Morehouse, a Georgia institution for one hundred years and an Atlanta institution for eighty-eight years, would be able to get someone to head a campaign for at least a million dollars in recognition of one hundred years of valuable service to the city, state, and nation. We were sadly mistaken.
>
> [The Atlanta community] has not accepted responsibility for the financial health and development of these colleges, despite the fact that we spend millions here each year and provide leadership for the South and for the nation.[50]

Here, in his final commencement address, Mays named the issue of "purpose" as a virtue that students should either already possess or develop while in college. The failure to do so was an indictment of both the individual student (and his or her family and community) as well as the college. Dr. Mays attempted to create a campus ecology of learning, service, and purpose, and an environment that should filter out students who were not sincere about the college enterprise, people he called "purposeless." Clearly, he regarded an expensive and extended liberal-arts education in a black institution as a moral enterprise infused with moral purpose. Such an education should be regarded as a treasure and an investment not to be wasted on those who could not discern its value.

Village and Public Neglect of Schools

Mays's disappointment did not stop with the lack of purpose displayed by some of his students, or with Atlanta's lack of generosity and support. He also attacked the lingering paternalism and racism in organized philanthropy and challenged liberal white citizens to critically examine their motives and avoid becoming obstacles to black progress.

> Discrimination in the future will not be administered by poor whites and the people who believe in segregation, but by the "liberals" who believe in a desegregated society. If this battle can be won, Morehouse will have an equal chance to develop like any other good college in America. . . . The Negro's battle for justice and equality in the future will be against the subtlety of our "liberal friends" who will wine and dine with us in the swankiest hotels, work with us, and still discriminate against us when it comes to money and power. The battle must be won because, for a long time, the wealth of this nation will be in the hands of white Americans and not Negroes. The abolition of economic, political, and philanthropic discrimination is the first order of the day, not for the good of Negroes alone but for the nation as a whole.[51]

Mays highlighted the underlying issues of "money and power" as the levers to authentic racial justice in America. A few black people might be permitted to desegregate previously exclusive institutions, but, in the matter of economic goods and the communal goods of self-determination and autonomy, they would be opposed, sabotaged, and unaided by their apparent allies.

Then, in a final rhetorical flourish, a flourish suggestive of his influence on the pulpit rhetoric of Dr. King, Mays's set forth his expectations of how these leaders would behave as they launched out into the world.

Now my dear seniors let me say to you what I said to the class of 1964.

Will you please rise? The curtain has fallen forever on the activities of your years at Morehouse. What you should have done and neglected to do cannot be done. Not even an Omnipotent God can blot out the deeds of history. It has been beautifully said:

> *The Moving Finger writes; and having writ,*
> *Moves on; nor all your Piety nor wit*
> *Shall lure it back to cancel half a Line,*
> *Nor all your Tears wash out a Word of it.*

Wherever I may be twenty-five years from today—on earth, beneath the earth, or above it—you will make my spirit glad if you are known in life by the quality of your work and the integrity of your character, rather than by the quality of your possessions.

If your work is government, I hope you do your work so well that you will be diligently sought after and widely acclaimed in government. If your work be that of a chemist, a physicist, a mathematician in industry, I hope you perform so excellently that when promotions are in order, your record will be so impressive that those in power will be compelled to examine your credentials.

If you make business a career, I hope the people will say in discussing you that you are both competent and honest.

If you choose the ministry, I pray that you will be so eloquent in speech, so profound in thought, so honest in performance, and so understanding in the knowledge of the strength and frailties of man that the people will say of you, "He must be a man of God."[52]

We should recall that 1967 was the final full year of Dr. King's life and ministry and the period when he was focused on the stopping the war in Southeast Asia and elevating the plight of poor people. Mays closes with these words:

My dear young friends, I do not know what happiness is, and I do not think it is important to be happy. But it is important that you find your work and do it as if you were sent in the world at this precise moment in history to do your job. If happiness can be achieved, it will be found in a job well done and in giving and not in receiving. May the years ahead be motivating, challenging, and inspiring years, and may they be gracious and kind to you and bring success in all the good things you do. Leben Sie Wohl![53]

W. E. B. Du Bois, writing in his 1903 essay, "The Talented Tenth," observed:

> The main question so far as the Southern Negro is concerned, is: What, under the present circumstance, must a system of education do in order to raise the Negro as quickly as possible in the scale of civilization? The answer to this question seems to me clear: It must strengthen the Negro's character, increase his knowledge and teach him to earn a living.[54]

But there were many students who did not embrace their responsibility as "missionaries of culture." In an earlier commencement address at Howard University (1930), Du Bois "chastised black college male students for their nihilistic behavior":

> Our college man today is, on the average, a man untouched by real culture. He deliberately surrenders to selfish and even silly ideals, swarming into semiprofessional athletics and Greek letter societies, and affecting to despise scholarship and the hard grind of study and research. The greatest meetings of the Negro college year like those of the white college year have become vulgar exhibitions of liquor, extravagance, and fur coats. We have in our colleges a growing mass of stupidity and indifference.[55]

In a similar vein, in 1937, Lafayette Harris, president of Philander Smith College in Little Rock, Arkansas, castigated black students for their general apathy and particular estrangement from common black folk: "Probably nothing gives one more concern than the frequently apparent fatalistic and nonchalant attitude of many a Negro college student and educated Negro. With him, very little seems to matter except meals, sleep, and folly. They know nothing of their less fortunate fellowmen and care less."[56]

Addressing the Crisis

Mays, Du Bois, Harris, and Bethune all highlighted a potentially embarrassing feature of black college life, namely, the presence of "purposeless" campus residents who appeared to waste the gift of college time with frivolities and negative behavior.

During my freshman year at Morehouse, I was shocked to discover more than a few brothers who were not serious about learning and community service. Weren't we all here, after all, to take up and continue Dr. King's unfinished mission? It did not take long to identify the smaller percentage of the student body, that seemed to appreciate the privilege of this experience. At a time when many young men our age were being drafted into the military and shipped to Vietnam, and with the echo of the tumultuous decade of the '60s still ringing in our ears, here were Morehouse men behaving like the stereotypical frat boys of the leisure class. They partied all night, smuggled women into the dormitories, consumed drugs, and engaged in fights against rival schools as well as young men in the surrounding neighborhood. After uproarious weekends, these same young men would sleep late into Sunday afternoon. The small number of us who were up for Sunday worship services walked through the dorm halls that resembled deathly quiet catacombs, tombs of the purposeless.

But, it would not be fair to simply indict these students as purposeless without noting that their previous schools, the larger society, and its most visible leaders share in the failure to inspire and challenge young people to discover and embrace higher purposes. At a time when the "culture of narcissism" was and is corrupting and destroying a culture of civic virtue and public service, students may be up against much larger cultural forces than they can oppose without support. This is where the entire culture of black colleges must be mobilized to instill virtues like personal sacrifice for the greater good. This is precisely what Bishop Daniel Alexander Payne, W.E.B. Du Bois, Mary McLeod Bethune, Mordecai Wyatt Johnson, and Benjamin Mays sought to promote.

As Mays noted, there have always been some college students who were "not with the program." And it seems naïve and unrealistic to suggest that college students should not enjoy their time in school. On weekends, I partied with the best of them on campus and had a great time. Party culture and frivolity are and always will be a part of the college experience of testing the limits of increased freedom and autonomy from parents. But in recent years, I have become profoundly disturbed by what appears to be a deeper crisis of moral purpose among contemporary black college students. Two events underscore my growing sense that the common culture of student indulgence and expressive individualism have taken a tragic turn. With the possible exception of explicitly religious colleges, campus cultures of indulgence are a fact of life, but I think that we are witnessing a lowering of the threshold of appropriate behavior that is contrary to the liberating purposes of education.

Consider these examples. First, during the 1990s and for several years thereafter, black college and high school students gathered in Atlanta each spring break for a rolling street festival known as "Freaknik." The event involved cruising along the city's busiest streets and highways in amazing vehicles that no student should have been able to afford. I wondered, "Where'd they get the money? Did they also receive financial aid?" Often, the cars stopped and people jumped out to dance in the street to the thunderous tones of the car stereo or play musical chairs as they jumped into a different vehicle to make new friends and who knows what else? As the practice grew, it began to alienate Atlanta's white and black middle classes who demanded that the mayor halt the practice. I recall discussing the issue with other Atlanta University Center presidents at our monthly Presidents Council. In our wisdom, we thought that if our schools sponsored official concerts, we could get the students off the streets, out of the cars and onto our campuses. Wrong!

We failed to understand that part of the power of the Freaknik phenomenon and hip hop culture in general was that it was student generated, semi-spontaneous, and resistant to being packaged for adult control and satisfaction. We have seen a similar phenomenon in the growing popularity of blogging, instant message word-of-mouth advertising, and virus marketing. This may be an important lesson for the village as it seeks to mobilize these same young people to serve village renewal purposes.

Eventually, Atlanta's mayor (Bill Campbell) came down on Freaknik and the official event migrated to Daytona Beach. But much of the wild party culture of violence and aggressive sexuality remained lodged in Atlanta campuses and elsewhere.

The second event was the tragic and much-publicized violent attack by a Morehouse College student toward another student whom he accused of staring at him in the shower. This case received national attention as the issue of black homophobia, the extent of Morehouse's black gay culture, and the school's commitment to protecting the rights of all students came under intense scrutiny. During the same period, Morehouse's Center for Ethical Leadership, led by theologian Walter Fluker, convened a meeting to promote the idea of ethical leaders. In his presentation, Morehouse alumnus John Wilson, a senior administrator at George Washington University, suggested that the college was not sufficiently intentional and aggressive about its mission to inculcate values in students and that it might be losing its esteem in the eye of the larger village.

Following the crisis surrounding the campus attack, Morehouse president Walter Massey convened a "blue ribbon committee" that included Harvard University minister Peter Gomes and diversity expert Dr. Roosevelt Thomas. The group studied and discussed the examples of other institutions that have grappled with the issues of respecting sexual diversity on campus, and issued a report that has led to a new emphasis on tolerance during the new student orientation. The attacker continues to serve his sentence and, in 2006, he and his victim met in court for a hearing to reduce the sentence. Despite the school's many constructive steps to prevent future student and sexual violence, the fact that one student could beat a fellow student with a baseball bat suggests that a new culture of violence has seeped into the hallowed halls of learning.

Subsequently, additional incidents of violence, murder, and rape surfaced in the Atlanta University Center that underscored the presence of a new "thug" and "gangsta" subculture on many campuses. This subculture must be challenged and rooted out lest the public lose good will and confidence in black schools. These negative behaviors must not be excused or tolerated. They threaten the very future of the institutions that the village needs for its health.

Decades ago, Dr. Mays expressed anxiety about the negative effects of materialism and personal indulgence on character development, and challenged graduates to hold each other accountable for service and authentic achievement even years after they had graduated. Speaking at commencement ceremonies for Albany State College in Georgia in 1967, Mays said:

> When you return in 2001 to celebrate your 25th Anniversary, if your profession be medicine, I hope your classmates will seek you out—not to know what your fine house, your yacht, and your car are, but they will want to know about your recent discovery in medicine, how many lives you have saved by your skill in surgery. If it be law, you will be sought after in 2001 to find out how you secured justice for the poor and the unlettered.
>
> Shakespeare is not known by his wealth but by Othello and MacBeth, Hamlet and Julius Caesar. Nobody stops to ask how much wealth Socrates had when he died; Socrates is known by dying as the first martyr for freedom of speech. Nobody cares how much wealth Booker T. Washington had when he died in 1915. Tuskegee gave Washington immortality. Martin Luther King, Jr. will not be known by his wealth but as one of the greatest prophets of the 20th century, bringing hope and liberation to millions of peoples across the world. Carter G. Woodson is known as one possessed with a dream, a Harvard Ph.D., who left his comfortable job at Howard University and founded the Association of Negro Life and History. Charles Drew is known by the Blood Bank. Mordecai Johnson is known by building a great university. Nehru was wealthy and high caste, but history knows him as one who turned his back on wealth and caste, suffered with his people, and became the first Prime Minister of independent India. Gandhi is known as the 98 pound man who lifted the British empire off its hinges through nonviolent activities.
>
> And it is to this task that the colleges and universities of the world and the men and women who teach in them should dedicate their lives. In no other way can we justify that toil and sacrifices we endure to maintain them.[57]

The challenge both to the colleges and to the village is how we can transform the culture of purposelessness and redirect those energies into village renewal? The key to repairing the problems inside HBCUs lies in reaching and nurturing children long before they graduate from high school. Purposeless college students probably didn't acquire the bad habits when they arrived on campus, they brought them along. Therefore schools, every school, must become centers for both intellectual and character development.

The College President as Chief Ethical Officer

Given the moral challenges in society and on campuses, perhaps we should think of presidents and deans increasingly as "chief ethical officers." As chief ethical officers, presidents and deans would lead more explicitly from the foundation of their institution's core values. They would articulate the moral vision of the kind of people that every graduate should become, embodying a commitment to excellence and ethics. Also, they could ensure that the institution's entire culture reflect and communicate those values. This should affect the required courses for new students, forms of community service, types of guest speakers brought to campus, and so on. Earlier generations of HBCU presidents embodied this ideal and served as public intellectuals and public moralists for the village and the nation.

This is a far cry from what college presidents have become since their time. It is not that society has less need to hear the insight and wisdom of its leading thinkers and those who administer the institutions that shape future leaders and citizens. When the burden of serving as the chief executive officer, chief academic officer, and chief development officer are piled onto one person, the probability of muffling the public voice of the president is very high. And although these three very different jobs have been divided in the modern university (thereby saving the lives of many presidents), in the public square, people expect that the president will represent her or his institution on at least these three fronts. That is, the president must be one who leads as a manager, leads as a thinker, and leads as a fundraiser.

Years ago, *The New Republic* magazine observed that since the resignation of Harvard University president Derek Bok, America has not seen university presidents emerge as leading voices in American public life. I believe that one of the chief reasons for this silence and absence is the rapid expansion of the administrative and managerial tasks for modern presidents. That is shorthand for saying that presidents have become full-time fundraisers who engage in the kind of calculation and institutional promotion that raises big bucks. While this may be a benefit for schools with tiny development staffs, unfortunately it robs the larger society of the public voices and minds that can serve as counterweights, even countercultural counterweights, to myopic elected officials, business leaders, and well-intentioned grassroots leaders.

This is a challenge for HBCU presidents. African American communities need to hear from these leaders but most do not have the time and many may not have the inclination or aptitude to function as public intellectuals. Of course, all HBCUs have a few faculty who do this, or certainly could do so. But professors are very different from those who manage and administer an institution. Professors are the primary talent for leading the campus conversation (teaching) and engaging in the production of new knowledge (research), and occasionally engaging the larger community or public (community service). But they are not often party to the deliberations that occur with board members who focus (when functioning properly) on the general and strategic mission of the school. Those deliberations are important for how an institution defines itself in the world and for how it goes about raising the funds to pay for its long-term sustenance.

One hope is that as trustees and university stakeholders load more responsibility onto the shoulders of the president, they will remember the need to support presidents who wish to inspire and cultivate moral purpose in students and alumni.

WHAT'S RIGHT
The Home as an Ethical Learning Center

The ancient Greek philosophers believed that ethical and philosophical instruction should begin when children are young. Gareth Matthews, professor of philosophy at the University of Massachusettes, says that "Socratic questioning, we could almost say, began as philosophy for children."[58] But it was Aristotle who taught that the "ethical formation of the child in the *oikos*" (household) should consist of "right nurture and discipline undertaken by the child's parents."[59] In African culture, children were taught their identity and moral obligations within both the family household and in extended family/village schools. Today, we must all be more intentional about what happens in our homes as centers of character formation.

The chapter on education in *The Covenant with Black America* offers important insights along these lines."[60]

Under the heading, "What Every Individual Can Do Now," they recommend:

- Read to your children or grandchildren everyday;
- Create clean, quiet spaces for your children to do homework; check to make sure that assignments are completed;
- Get library cards for each member of your family;
- Arrange enriching family and neighborhood activities for children of all ages: museums, educational games, spelling bees, and science fairs;
- Become involved in your children's school: PTA, school committees; attend back-to-school events; if you do not have children in the school, consider becoming a volunteer. And again, they urge us to:
- Hold all leaders and elected officials responsible and demand that they change current policy.[61]

It would be tremendous if every parent and adult in the village were to practice these sound measures. But the authors do not address explicitly the need and methodology for cultivating ethical values and character. Every home in the village must become an ethical learning center, a place where moral values are taught, discussed, rewarded, and modeled by the adults.

As children move from homes that are ethical learning centers into the schools, we must insist that schools also engage in nurturing moral character.

Smart and Good Schools

There is a growing industry concerned with teaching and promoting good character among elementary and secondary students. It is called the character education movement. Most states now require their schools to offer instruction about character. For a brief period, I served on the board of the Character Education Partnership (CEP), an organization dedicated to increasing formal character education through partnerships between leaders in business and the school system. One of the gurus in the field, Dr. Thomas Lickona (cited earlier) and his Center for the Study of the 4th and 5th Rs (Respect & Responsibility) provide accessible vision and theoretical foundation for the character education movement.

Building on Aristotle's ethics paradigm, Lickona suggests that at least three components are essential for character education: knowledge, desire, and practice. People must know what is right and good. This is something that can and must be taught. But people (especially children) also must have the desire or will to do the right thing. They should be encouraged to develop such a will. And third, they must practice doing what is good and right. They will make mistakes but they can learn from their mistakes. And over time, as knowledge, desire, and practice come together, they produce the habit of doing good. We call this habit character. I believe that it is time for colleges—indeed, all schools—to take this agenda more seriously than ever before.

Perhaps a greater focus on character education could help us to retrieve the love of learning that animated the village following the era of slavery. Perhaps they can help us to again become an entire village "trying to go to school."

Black Colleges and Character Development

Attending a four-year college, especially away from home, is one of the great adventures of youth (or adulthood, in some cases). My wife, a Stanford alumna, is one of the few people whom I know whose eyes still glaze over with tears as she speaks of her college years (even thirty-plus years later). There is nothing quite like the joy, excitement, anxiety, self-doubt, and lure of a college campus with its many opportunities, accomplished faculty, staff, and senior students, and the expectation that you are an adult who is in charge of your educational destiny.

For me, one of the great experiences was the opportunity to study with great teachers and extraordinary minds. I was exposed to towering intellectuals who kept our eyes on the prize of more than material fulfillment. Among the faculty luminaries at Morehouse in my days was Professor E. B. Williams, a Columbia University-educated economist whose lectures on the fundamentals of capitalism and global markets were sprinkled with how to impress employers in business interviews, including dress, what to order on a menu, appropriate table conversation, and how to ask probing questions. Professor Edward A. Jones, our renaissance gentleman, taught French and wrote a history of the college. Ever bedecked in his trademark vest with dangling Phi Beta Kappa key and exquisite silk bowtie, Jones regaled us with stories of African and Caribbean intellectuals active in the Harlem Renaissance and the Negritude literary movement. He also offered to teach us to tie our own bowties and expressed strong disapproval of those who chose to wear clip-on ties, something he believed appropriate only for young boys and service clerks. My closest advisor and friend was Professor Robert Brisbane, chair of the Political Science department. Brisbane was a Harvard-educated political philosopher and a Fulbright scholar to India as well as faculty sponsor of the debate team. I have great memories of traveling to what were for me obscure places for debate tournaments such as the Mississippi State College for Women and Valdosta State University. The captain of the team was Earl Shinhoster, who later became a brilliant lawyer, civil rights activist, and interim president of the NAACP. It was during those years that I paid my first visit to the campus of Emory University, where I now teach. Emory had been desegregated for only a decade at that point. My favorite Professor Brisbane memory occurred in preparation for the historic Morehouse-Harvard debate. Since we were a bit intimidated as we prepared for the big day, Dr. Brisbane urged my partner, Sherman Anderson, and me to read and study intensely, to relax the day before, and to use every argument in the book. And because we needed a laugh to reduce stress, he urged,

"If all else fails pick up a piece of the g--damned linoleum and throw it at them." Not the best ethical advice, but I think that he was joking.

Commenting on the exceptional pedagogical skills of most HBCU faculty, Dr. John H. Jackson, chief policy officer for the NAACP, observed that when he graduated from his Chicago high school with a 2.25 grade point average, he needed a college and a faculty that possessed the intellectual agility and wisdom to teach both the best and brightest as well as the academically marginal. He says that Harvard (where he later matriculated for graduate study) didn't have a faculty with such savvy. However, the faculty at Xavier University, the New Orleans HBCU he attended, did possess that bi-cultural competence.[62]

I should note that the faculty who taught and today teach at HBCUs are generally under-compensated (when compared with market standards) for their exceptional contributions to the education of the next generation. Most of these talented scholar-teachers could transfer to other institutions and receive handsome rewards, but they serve the community by remaining where they are most needed.

Having attended an HBCU and having led one as president, my admiration for the faculty in these institutions is as high as ever. But, if these educational leaders are to be as effective as possible, they must receive greater support from the administration, boards of trustees and the larger community. In order to remain on the leading edge, faculty need periodic sabbaticals, yes. But they need and deserve additional supports for their own excellence as teachers. Institutions should have professional development funds that are available on a competitive basis to support travel, reading, IT training, etc.

Earlier in this chapter, I quoted Dr. Mays extensively on the problem of purpose and his strategy to make such students uncomfortable with their underachievement. Curious about how some HBCUs are responding to the crisis of moral purpose, I sent a questionnaire to over seventy-five college presidents (almost three fourths of the total). Assisted by a student research assistant, Greg Jackson, I asked two basic questions:

1. What does your school do to promote what might be called "character education" or a sense of personal responsibility, efficacy, morality and community service?
2. What does your school do to promote African American identity and the norms, values, memories, loyalties, and commitments that accompany "proud black identity"?

Less than one third of the institutions responded. I was disappointed by the response and know that there are likely many good reasons for it. Assuming that they received our written and phone inquiries, I know that college administrators are incredibly busy and often find it difficult to justify the investment of time involved in answering questions, especially ones that require probing thought. But I am also disturbed by the possibility that some chose not to respond because they are aware of institutional shortcomings in the area of character development and community service. Recall Dr. Mays's courageous example of institutional truthtelling. And in fairness, let's admit that he spoke those truths as he was departing the institution, always an easier time to bear one's soul than having to come back and live with the consequences of one's words, (something I learned the hard way as a president).

Since the better-known HBCUs receive their fair share of the positive public attention, I'd like to call attention to what we heard from some of the less well known schools.

Langston University is located in Langston, Oklahoma, and is that state's only historically black university. In 2006, the school inaugurated its first female president, Dr. JoAnn W. Haysbert. Dr. Haysbert responded to my request by noting that the university embraces eleven character-building benchmarks, including: (1) Attend classes and university functions; (2) have respect for the rights and personal property of others; (3) refrain from the use of profanity and obscene language; (4) maintain appropriate dress and standards of cleanliness; (5) exhibit moral character; (6) exhibit courteous behavior; (7) obey rules, regulations and laws; (8) assist in keeping the university property clean; (9) be an advocate in academic integrity; (10) be an advocate of social integrity; and (11) demonstrate leadership qualities. She notes that with additional resources the school could extend its mission beyond the campus into the community with local young people. These elements remind me of the kind of advice that Booker T. Washington and many other presidents and faculties promoted until the emergence of the civil rights movement.

In response to the question about promoting proud black identity, I was informed, perhaps scolded, in the following terms:

> By virtue of its heritage as a historically Black University, the faculty, staff and students at Langston University are very proud of their Black identity. One is readily able to detect this in the fact that we require that the "b" in black is always capitalized when referring to us as a race and not a color. The names of races are capitalized, colors are not. Can you imagine a sentence written like this? "In the United States, there are many Jews, Asians and black people." Our pride will not allow us to write the "b" in black in the lower case. This is taught to students throughout the campus.[63]

Florida Agricultural and Mechanical University (FAMU) responded that the institution's expectations of personal responsibility, morality, and community service are built into the two-day new student orientation program. They also noted that parents tend to "accompany their children during the initial phase of their higher education." They also noted that "in prior years, parents themselves, would participate in the New Student Orientation Program" but for the first time (2006), "students and parents will attend separate orientation sessions." FAMU's School of General Studies also offers a "two credit hour course titled "College Orientation" in which many of the elements of character education are taught and explored in a more formal, structured environment." The course is offered every semester and emphasizes the "specific skills, behaviors, attitudes, and, most importantly, values" that are important to a successful college experience.[64]

Atlanta's Spelman College is one of the best-known HBCUs and has an impressive roster of alumnae, including Marian Wright Edelman, writer Alice Walker, and its former president, Dr. Audrey

Manley. Thirty years ago Spelman established The Women's Center under the visionary leadership of acclaimed scholar Dr. Beverly Guy-Sheftall. She self-consciously sought to nurture and connect a new generation of college women to earlier black feminists like Anna Julia Cooper and Maria Stewart. The Center is committed to dismantling patriarchy along with class and race oppression and attempts to equip students to engage in this kind of analysis. Some of that work begins close to home as students are urged to challenge sexist comments, attitudes, and stereotypes reflected by some students, faculty, and staff at Morehouse College (the all-male school across the street).

More recently, the Wisdom Center was founded at Spelman to complement the Women's Center. It also seeks to raise the profile of religion on campus, and infuse a faith perspective into existing social justice programs. With support from the Lilly Endowment Inc., Wisdom Center director and chaplain Lisa Rhodes, along with the school's department of religion chair Dr. Rosetta Ross, have collaborated to raise the level of character development on campus. These leaders report that mentoring the college women and serving as "embodied exemplars" has convinced them that it was a mistake to allow such mentoring to falter during the post–civil rights movement years. They also note that all students are required to perform community service during their first two years.

Evidence of the hunger for religious and moral role models is found in the fact that the number of women majoring in religious studies has doubled in recent years. Some Spelman leaders also note that tensions between college men and women occasionally flare up and expose how the ugliest manifestations of contemporary popular culture have taken root on their elite campuses. One professor affirmed that there is a "thug subculture" on all campuses, both majority and HBCU schools. This is due to the influences students bring to the campus and not necessarily a lax campus environment. "We may be witnessing the death of conscience on the college campus," Reverend Rhodes observed, "something that Dr. Anna Freud observed in some of her patients decades ago." She went on to note, "We should not forget that we are educating the Columbine generation" (referring to the tragic shootings at Columbine High School in Littleton, Colorado several years ago).[65]

It is also noteworthy that Spelman College students mobilized to block the campus visit of rapper 'Nelly,' an artist who has produced a series of songs and videos that depict black women in offensive and degrading ways. This example of moral agency by college students offers great hope to those who worry about whether or not the current generation of college students will extend the movement for black dignity into the future.

Internal Renewal and Moral Purpose

Worried about the decline of character at Morehouse College, Dr. Otis Moss Jr., a prominent Baptist pastor and past chairman of the Morehouse board, observed that while many students in black colleges were accumulating impressive achievements in the scientific, mathematic, and technical fields, they did not seem to possess much in the way of spirituality. "I'd like to see faculty and administrators invest as much energy in seeking grants and designing programs to build the spiritual and moral fiber of students as is devoted to their professional and intellectual advancement." Moss also generated an interesting idea that would be relatively easy to establish if the will were present:

> During freshman orientation, why can't professors of music teach all the students ten songs that they would be singing throughout their college careers. These students don't even know "Lift Every Voice and Sing." Years later when they return to church, they would hear that hymn and recall that this is what the school was trying to teach me. . . . [And] what if black colleges were to use their commencement ceremonies for student retention purposes. All the entering freshman could be brought in early to witness the event and assist, maybe as hosts to the graduate's families or the like. They would see the path that they would travel in four years. I wonder what impact that would have on retention of students.[66]

All of these ideas and examples are encouraging and suggest possibilities both for renewing HBCUs and for their role in renewing the village.

Village Accreditation of Schools and Colleges

Colleges, universities, and schools in America must be periodically reviewed and given the coveted seal of approval: accreditation. Accreditation makes a school eligible for a variety of benefits, such as federal financial aid and the status that can be leveraged with private donors. The periodic accreditation review is one of the significant tests that Morris Brown College failed. Regional associations undertake the work of accrediting schools, drawing upon the labor of faculty and staff in other institutions. Most HBCUs are located in the southern states and are reviewed by the Southern Association for Colleges and Schools (SACS). But before these accrediting associations began to evaluate and accredit black schools, African American scholars were already engaged in assessing their quality and their needs.

In both 1900 and 1910, Du Bois made the first attempts to evaluate and classify black colleges. In his first effort, he listed thirty-four institutions as "colleges," with a total collegiate enrollment of 726 students. He concluded, however, that these 726 students could have been accommodated by the ten institutions that he rated as first-grade colleges. In the 1910 evaluation, he was even more rigorous and classified thirty-two black colleges (one third of those that exist today) as "First-Grade Colored Colleges" (including Howard, Fisk, Atlanta, Morehouse, and Virginia Union). Another group was classified as "Second-Grade Colored Colleges" (including Lincoln, Talladega, and Wilberforce) and a third group classified as "Other Colored Colleges" (including Lane, Bishop, and Miles Memorial). It should be noted that his evaluations at the turn of the last century reflect in no way upon the status and quality of those institutions today.

Anderson notes that Du Bois's "evaluations were, on balance, friendly ones designed to strengthen the black college system by concentrating college-level work in about thirty-two of the better black institutions."[67] But other evaluations of black colleges were undertaken that took a harsh stance and shed a negative light on the schools. Usually written by those who wanted black colleges to adopt the Washingtonian-Tuskegee industrial approach, they suggested that only two or three black colleges were capable of offering college-level work. These reports also put even greater pressure on black schools to conform in order to receive funds.

Anderson notes also, "Beginning in 1913, the North Central Association of Colleges and Secondary Schools issued the first list of regionally accredited colleges and universities. This signaled a movement to define institutions of higher learning by specific, factual, and uniform standards. This movement, financed by foundations like Carnegie, increased the pressures on black colleges to become full-fledged institutions of higher learning."[68] In 1928, the Southern Association of Colleges and Secondary Schools decided to rate black institutions separately.

As a former president, I still recall the high anxiety in the air during the final day of the Southern Association of Colleges and Schools conference when the "verdict" was read for schools that had been recently evaluated. Many presidents sat in disbelief and depression as they heard the name of their school publicly placed on a list indicating something less than a clean bill of health. They had invested so much work only to be told that the committee would have to return to monitor progress on some important matter of underperformance.

I can recall that this long process began with preparing a document known as a "self-study," which would be sent to the reviewers prior to their visit. Sitting at a laptop at 3:00 A.M. editing the hard work of my colleagues into a final document, I regarded the entire process as a "valuable burden" in that it diverted so much of our limited energy and resources not to delivering education or raising funds but to preparing for a three-day visit that could determine the school's future. It really felt like a burden amidst the business of running a school. But it was also a valuable gift in that we paused to engage in critical self-examination, to hear from every stakeholder group in the school, and to receive the candid feedback of outsiders.

I believe that it would be valuable to retrieve and innovate on the tradition of having black scholars render critical and appreciative evaluation of our institutions. We could innovate by inviting the community to participate in evaluating each college or school on its efficacy, and issue a regular report to the trustees and to the community. If that is too cumbersome, such evaluation and community feedback sessions could take the form of town hall meetings. In addition to SACS (and the other regional associations), something like a "Village Association of Colleges and Schools" (or VACS) might emerge. The village review process could include questions such as, "What does the village think of the performance and value of the college? What has the school done in the past year to enhance the community? What kind of neighbor is the institution? How could the school become a better citizen in its neighborhoods?"

I believe that it would help the institution immensely to receive feedback from the village on the issues it cares about most. Although colleges cannot be expected to solve most of the community's problems, they can and should be held accountable, at least for having a positive impact on the educational, economic, and cultural condition of the surrounding community. For instance, no community that resides in the shadow of an HBCU should have children who are not excelling in school. With the vast army of potential mentors and tutors, colleges and their villages need to develop the kind of mutually beneficial partnerships that offer opportunity and hope to our children.

I wonder whether or not such a village accreditation of the HBCU might have made a difference in the fate of Morris Brown College. During the gradual decline of the school, repeated fundraising calls went forth with modest success. On Atlanta's black format talk radio program, "Power Talk", host Rev. Dr. Lorraine Jacques-White fielded calls from irate village residents who upon hearing of a possible $20 million debt opined that the school had not provided sufficient accounting of its past stewardship and could not now expect charitable gifts in the midst of a severe crisis.

Since losing its accreditation, the school has taken several measures in preparation for applying for accreditation including: the election of its first corporate board chairperson (CEO of a local black bank), leasing of underutilized classrooms and campus space, reducing its short term debt to $4.8 million and long term debt to $11.5 million, and inviting the Reverend Jesse Jackson, Sr. to join its Institutional Advancement and Public Relations Committee. We can hope that these steps, together with the generosity and good will of a prosperous nation, will be sufficient to restore an important anchor institution to its proper place in society and history.

CONCLUSION

Thanks to the sacrifices and courage of college students during the civil rights movement, America is a better nation. I believe that it is time, once again, for the village to call college students to the important work of renewing our villages.

Recall theologian Howard Thurman's words about vocation and calling: "Do not ask what the world needs. Do what makes you come alive. What the world needs are people who have come alive."[69]

QUESTIONS FOR DISCUSSION

1. What can village volunteers do to revive the culture of learning in black communities?

2. How can adult men be motivated to mentor boys in school?

3. Are black schools and colleges doing what we need them to do in reversing the trend of dropping out before graduation?

4. Are HBCUs engaged in producing the kinds of graduates who can become leaders of village renewal and, thereby, contribute something more important to the common good than their individual achievement and wealth accumulation? Specifically, what do you expect from them?

5. How can the village contribute to the renewal of moral purpose in black colleges?

6. What are the implications of the growing gender gap between the number of college educated black females and males?

7. Given the critical importance of education for the uplift of disadvantaged people and the strength of a nation, why has the nation not found the will to allocate adequate resources (not just money) to educating its neediest citizens?

8. Given their historical role in establishing and advocating for black education, have churches and clergy done their part to

advance this agenda by making an urgent and unrelenting case for public, corporate, individual, and village support?

9. And as for the schools themselves, have these anchoring institutions become what so many hoped and prayed that they would? Should the mere survival of many of these schools be counted as success? Are they engaged in producing the kinds of graduates who will lead village renewal?

10. How can boards of trustees, faculty and administrators in our schools refocus and implement their missions in response to the present, urgent need to prepare excellent and ethical students who contribute to the common good as well as their own wealth accumulation?

4
STRATEGIES
RENEWING THE VILLAGE

THE year: 1939. The setting: the commencement exercises at Howard University. The speaker: professor, public intellectual, activist and NAACP co-founder W. E. B. Du Bois. On that day, nearly seventy years ago, Du Bois urged the "talented tenth" to heed the ennobling challenge of utilizing their talent to uplift others, even at the price of some personal sacrifice. Black college commencements are rituals of high dignity and drama. They synthesize the cultures of the academy and the church as they produce and present African American dignity and achievement. Such occasions are high holy moments for the black establishment. Consequently, one expects to hear polite words of commendation and genteel urgings to serve, give, and achieve more. But, in a surprise move prescient of Dr. Mays's 1967 address to Morehouse (which I discussed in chapter 3), Du Bois offered bitter medicine:

> To increase abiding satisfaction for the mass of our people and for all people, someone must sacrifice something of his own happiness. This is a duty only to those who recognize it as a duty. It is silly to tell intelligent human beings: Be good and you will be happy. The truth is today, be good, be decent, be honorable and self-sacrificing, and you will not always be happy. You will often be desperately unhappy. You may even be crucified,

dead, and buried. And the third day you will be just as dead as the first. But, with the death of your happiness may easily come increased happiness and satisfaction and fulfillment for other people—strangers, unborn babes, uncreated worlds. If this is not sufficient incentive, never try it—remain hogs."[1]

WHAT IS TO BE DONE?

In the previous chapters, I have attempted to provide some background and diagnosis of challenges to the future of three anchor institutions in African American villages. African American children face serious threats to their healthy growth and development. Their situation is complicated further due to the challenges confronting their families, churches, and schools. Improving the institutional health of these organizations is one strategic key to ensuring the well-being and development of all of our children. And if we're successful, our efforts will ensure the best prospects for sustaining our democracy.

There is a time for diagnosis and there is a time for prescription. But, what good is a prescription that doesn't get filled? And what good is a filled prescription that we won't faithfully take? So, it's time to fill the prescription, that is, to act in strategic ways, perhaps doing new things or simply old things in a new manner. And we must be certain to take our medicine, that is, to apply the good advice we give to ourselves and to those closest to us. That's the ethical imperative for all of us today: *fill the prescription, take the medicine.*

As I elaborate the following notes, proposals and suggestions for action, I'd like to revisit a compelling reminder of what is at stake in this village renewal imperative. These words, also included in my Introduction, were spoken by the "queen mother" (or community mother?) of the child advocacy movement in America, lawyer, child advocate, and public moralist, Marian Wright Edelman. In an essay titled "What We Can Do," Edelman offers a comprehensive and practical case statement for "saving our children." And in a compelling commencement addresses of her own, Edelman told graduates at Emory University in 2006:

We are at risk of letting our children drown in the bathwater of American materialism, greed, and violence. We must regain our spiritual bearings and roots and help America recover hers before millions more children—Black, Brown, and white, poor, middle-class, and rich—self-destruct or grow up thinking life is about acquiring rather than sharing, selfishness rather than sacrifice, and material rather than spiritual wealth. And even as so much progress has been made, for too many Black children and families, progress is not coming quickly enough or at all.

Consider these recent statistics about Black children living in the U.S.:

- Every five seconds during the school day, a Black public school student is suspended, and
- Every forty-six seconds during the school day, a Black high school student drops out.
- Every minute, a Black child is arrested and a Black baby is born to an unmarried mother.
- Every three minutes, a Black child is born into poverty.
- Every hour, a Black baby dies.
- Every four hours a Black child or youth under twenty dies from an accident, and
- Every five hours, one is a homicide victim, and
- Every day, a Black young person under twenty-five dies from HIV infection and a Black child or youth under twenty commits suicide.

We must learn to reweave the rich fabric of community for our children and to re-instill the values and sense of purpose our elders and mentors have always embraced. . . . A massive new movement must well up from every nook, cranny, and place in our community involving millions of parents; religious, civic, educational, business, and political leaders; and youths themselves. This movement must insist on treating all children fairly and making sure every child receives a Healthy Start, a Head Start, a Fair Start, a Safe Start, and a Moral Start in life and successful passage to adulthood with the help of caring families and communities. . . .[2]

This will be difficult, but like so many other difficult tasks worth doing, it is possible and necessary. This new movement will answer the question of what we as a community and we as Americans really value and believe in as a people. It will make Black America better, and save America's soul and future. After all, children are our future and every child is a sacred gift of a loving God. If the Black community and nation cannot agree on anything else, we must agree on saving our children right now—all of them.[3]

In view of our diagnosis of what ails the village, the question now is what will we do? Will we simply be *witnesses* or will we become *moral agents*? Will we become the kind of *people who act with integrity on behalf of the common good?* Will we become the kind of *adults who provide for the next generation?* The important thing to remember is that everyone has a contribution to make toward the renewal of the village. No gifts will be refused. You can make a difference!

I believe that a realistic and actionable plan must include the following elements:

1. Enlist specific institutions as catalysts;

2. Assign specific roles to them;

3. Identify points of entry for those who are mobilized by the catalysts;

4. Incorporate a developmental approach to action mobilization;

5. Present a realistic accountability framework;

6. Mobilize every willing and able person to tackle the problems that now threaten our families, our communities, and our democracy;

7. Appeal for broad public and philanthropic support; and

8. Challenge larger structures (government, business, and the independent sector) to help us sustain and reinforce progress.

Ground Zero

The single most important first step for village revitalization, in my view, is to invite and convoke village-wide, collective spiritual exercises that include prayer and personal sacrifice. More specifically, I would ask the "praying women and men of the church" to begin to invoke divine presence, guidance, power, and wisdom upon this bold venture. The "office" of the praying women of the church is a biblically inspired tradition that black church culture has taken seriously in the past. The "prayer warriors" of my church upbringing were the women (and occasionally some men) who understood their role and ministry to be that of interceding with God on behalf of the church and community. They fasted and prayed and thereby appeared to dip into deep wells of spiritual resource, power, and hope. This is how village renewal can and should begin.

Assignment

The elders of the village should pray for our renewal. The praying elders of the village covenant to pray for the prodigal sons and daughters to come home from the wastelands of their "psychic captivity": prison, drug stupor, or from wherever else they've drifted. But this assignment also includes praying that the parents in the homes (and other anchor institutions) and all the adults in the village will welcome the prodigals back into our midst and commit themselves to keeping everyone connected, loved, respected, and accountable.

I would recommend that this period of prayer, reflection, and preparation extend long enough to have an impact upon us—perhaps a symbolic period such as forty days to connect us to the period of preparation and temptation that Jesus experienced prior to his public ministry. Because of my own upbringing I cannot trust any plan to go far or to reach deeply unless it is "bathed" in prayer. The philosopher Pascal observed that, "God has instituted prayer to confer upon men the dignity of being causes."[4]

By beginning with prayer led by grassroots spiritual warriors (the praying women and men of the village) we set this revitalization movement on a radically different, radically transcendent, and subversive foundation. For by its very nature, prayer "de-centers" us, removes our agenda from the central place, and makes room for God to inhabit our lives and ethical wills.

Assignment

Every sympathetic person should join the elders in concrete rituals of personal renewal. The entire village (every responsible, caring individual) should commit daily or weekly time to prayer and reflection that connects us all to the collective process of spiritual renewal. Daily time would be great but, from a developmental perspective, one could start with once a week and strive to increase that time gradually. Perhaps each Wednesday as part of your lunch hour, you could set aside thirty minutes for reflection, reading, prayer, constructive dialogue, or some spiritual practice that brings us closer to our inner selves. This is what theologian Howard Thurman called "centering down":

How good it is to center down!
To sit quietly and see one's self pass by!
The streets of our minds seethe with endless traffic;
Our spirits resound with clashings, with noisy silences,
While something deep within hungers and thirsts for the still moment and
*   the resting lull.*
With full intensity we seek, ere the quiet passes, a fresh sense of order in our
*   living;*
A direction, a strong sure purpose that will structure our confusion and
bring meaning to our chaos.
We look at ourselves in this waiting moment—the kinds of people we are.
The questions persist: what are we doing with our lives?—what are the
*   motives that order our days?*
What is the end of our doings? Where are we trying to go?
Where do we put the emphasis and where are our values focused?
For what end do we make sacrifices? Where is my treasure and what do I
*   love most in life?*
What do I hate most in life and to what am I true?
Over and over the questions beat in upon the waiting moment.
As we listen, floating up through all the jangling echoes of our turbulence,
*   there is a sound of another kind—*

A deeper note which only the stillness of the heart makes clear.
It moves directly to the core of our being. Our questions are answered,
Our spirits refreshed, and we move back into the traffic of our daily round
With the peace of the Eternal in our step.
How good it is to center down![5]

In order to accomplish the work of village renewal, we must all strive to become better human beings, people who are more compassionate, more generous, and less arrogant and self-absorbed. The spiritual renewal we need should include *rituals of personal and village renewal*. This is the simple action available to all of us that could begin to make a difference.

On Wednesday for the first half of a lunch hour, wherever we are and no matter what we are doing, we would all know that the village-renewal project is moving forward. Wednesday is the middle of the work-week, and noon is the symbolic middle of the day. This concept of being in the middle can evoke a historical sense of the Middle Passage, the slave journey across the Atlantic Ocean to the New World. For many, half of their souls remain in Africa and the other half is here. Also, we are in the middle of a painful transition that has brought many distressing social statistics. We will not always be in this place. But we must exodus through this difficult time to a better place.

We will engage in a collective ritual of remembering our ancestors. A sacred half hour every Wednesday would be set aside, sanctified, in which we do not eat or engage in frivolous pursuits. We will engage in the audacious act of remembering the past and of imagining a better future. As we remember the tragedies of yesterday from the horrors of the Middle Passage, to the bodies that dangled from lynching trees, we should draw strength from the ancestors for the work that we have before us. We should pause to allow ourselves to connect with their pain, and, in the process, that suffering should open us to the pain of those throughout the world who suffer most today. We need to reconnect to the past for the sake of recovering our moral center and authority.

Wednesday noonday prayer would be "our time" to look forward with imagination and hope. My hope is that these collective rituals of centering might go a long way toward knitting the connective tissue we need to remind us of the grand and bold reasons for our small sacrifices, namely, the "happiness, satisfaction and fulfillment of strangers, unborn babes, and uncreated worlds."[6]

So, let us resolve that once a week, every week, we will focus on the future of the village and its needs.

- Every week, we will pray for the village.
- Every week, we will contribute time and/or money for village renewal:
- Every week, we will engage in some unseen act of healing, repair, and uplift that helps someone else.
- Every week, we will hold someone else accountable for renewal by asking them about their activity on behalf of the village.
- Every week, we will think about the connections between our struggle and other people's struggles including global struggles for justice and restoration.

I respect those who may regard this suggestion as naïve or pointless. And, of course, many will choose not to participate. But we have not tried this in the recent past, so those who would dismiss it should withhold judgment and respectfully observe or propose better alternatives.

I earnestly hope that this suggestion does not alienate village members who do not pray or believe in a deity, nor alienate potential allies outside African American villages whose renewal practices may differ. We can and must respect their alternative philosophical perspectives, especially if they are committed to a common set of outcomes. I only ask that they show patience and respect for the anchoring practices and traditions that have sustained "the souls of black folk." And, I must emphasize, those who believe and pray must show similar respect for perspectives they do not share.

Assignment

Every single man, woman, and child should engage in at least one risky act of reconciliation and forgiveness soon and whenever possible.

Reconciliation and forgiveness are concrete expressions of a deeper theological virtue—love. Love is more than a positive emotion; it is a force, a concrete manifestation or release of energy and power. It is a movement of the soul that attracts and affects others profoundly. This is the energy or "soul force" that motivated Dr. King and those who led the civil rights movement as well as those in South Africa who led the anti-apartheid movement. The radical love ethic of Jesus is at the core of the Christian way of being faithful.

Whenever love encounters fragmented relationships or broken lives, it engages in reconciliation, which is the art of *restoring right relationships* between those who are estranged. But it seeks more than the good feeling that comes from a good reconciliation. Indeed, good reconciliation must also include justice, the fair and equitable treatment of parties who have been harmed. Some prefer to call this "restorative justice." When class warfare occurs, as appears to be happening in America today, and affluent people feel no connection to, or responsibility for, improving opportunities for people living in poverty, then there is an urgent need for reconciliation. Similarly, the divides separating men and women, gay and straight people, the young and the old beg for love's response of concrete reconciliation. Republicans and Democrats need to be reconciled.

This means that wherever we encounter fragmented and conflicted relationships, we should allow love to "force" us, to empower us, to take risks to melt the frozen sea that keeps people locked in unhealthy emotional and social states for decades. Dr. King used to talk about the need for one of the parties in a tense relationship to be "grown enough" and "big enough" to overcome their pride, to relinquish the privilege of being right and taking the first steps towards forgiveness and healing.

I don't mean to be naïve here. There are situations where this is not possible. For instance, women who have been battered by the men in their lives do not have an obligation to take the first step in reconciling with those men for the sake of the children. The men must step up, "man up," and do the right thing. Moreover, the village should help those men to adopt the right attitude and to speak the right words in order to seek forgiveness and healing.

But in order for the lovely language of reconciliation to have an impact, it must move even beyond the level of interpersonal reconciliation. Reconciliation must be reconnected to its public dimensions. It is God's will for individuals and for human societies. It is a public act or process of faith. This is often referred to as restorative justice, love's public work. As social institutions are reformed to manifest concern for the least advantaged members of the community, they must devote financial resources and public will to that enterprise.

Here are six phases of reconciliation that I have observed in working with a variety of individuals and groups. Most recently, students at the Candler School of Theology embraced and practiced this model during the Lenten season following Hurricane Katrina. It is a model that we have tried with good results at Colgate-Rochester Divinity School, between black and white churches in Rochester, New York, and in a black-Jewish dialogue group in New York City. The steps of the restorative justice process described below are intended to be suggestive rather than prescriptive. In fact, the process is dynamic and the steps are not rigidly sequential:

Covenant: The people begin in worship or some venue in which our common, shared identity may be acknowledged and celebrated. A litany or reading that joins all voices is suggested. And a reminder of common ground (the covenant or deep bond that holds us together) and of the probable tensions that will emerge when they are discussed is provided.

Conversation: The people gather in small and diverse groups (when possible) for conversation. Guidelines should be stated, including these three: "everyone should speak," and "no interruptions" and "no judgments." The focal question might be, "Tell us about your first memory of realizing or recognizing difference (racial, gender, and the like)? What was your 'aha' or discovery of difference experience?" This is a moment to appreciate the power of story, especially personal story, in shaping our adult perceptions and behavior.

Confession: This is a time for acknowledging personal shortcomings in the area of the selected theme. This should not be coerced or preprogrammed. Usually a courageous person will begin this process. Again the guidelines—the ethic of hospitality—are important: no interruptions, no judgments, but, rather, careful and empathic listening is encouraged.

Cooperation: The people (as a whole or each group decides upon its "common work and witness") move from word to deed. They then engage in some common project (support for another organization or community, preparing a banner or art, bulletin board, a statement, a march, building a Habitat for Humanity house, and so forth) that turns the group outward to a challenge in the community or world needing attention.

Criticism: The people return to the circle (now a healing circle) of conversation that is candid but trustworthy. People are encouraged to speak of "How have I grown? What more do I need to learn? How and where do I continue to struggle with this issue? Why can't I go further now?" This is an opportunity for more candid conversation with respectful critique (judgment), and sharing of opinions that were held in silence earlier in the process. Presumably, after our conversations, confessions, and cooperative work, we have developed the trust to criticize constructively. This kind of talk demonstrates that we are strong despite our fragility.

Celebration: The people return to the venue of worship where the new, expanded common ground is celebrated. Growth, new commitments, new friendships, and some good work in the world are acknowledged and affirmed.

As African Americans engage in renewing the village by revitalizing its anchor institutions of marriage and family, congregation, and school, we must also place pressure on government structures to distribute resources, institute policies, and support the efforts of citizens to improve their lot. For instance, restorative justice should insist upon revisiting the 1960s "War on Poverty," learning from its shortcomings, admitting that we never fully prosecuted the initiative, and mobilizing the nation to take action to eradicate severe poverty once and for all. In this way, reconciliation and restorative justice become public manifestations of the love ethic.

I believe in the power and centrality of reconciliation. We have seen it in action in our lifetime. This work is the work of reconciliation. God declares in advance of any action that humans are one family, religiously speaking, one body of Christ, equal and united in our common relation to God. No matter what we do or get wrong, God's declaration of our oneness holds us accountable to a profound truth and higher reality that we may rarely perceive but is always there. We are being drawn toward that which we were meant to become. Christian theologians and psychologists have spoken of sin as the state of separation or estrangement from God, our neighbors, and our true selves.

God seems to possess a single strategy, love, to invite relationship with humans, but God does not appear to have a single avenue for reconciling the multiple branches of God's family. Who are we to presume to know what God is up to in another land, another language, another way of perceiving the Holy? This should prompt all Christians to recall Christ's words to his disciples: "I have other sheep that are not of this sheep pen. I must bring them also. They too will listen to my voice, and there shall be one flock and one shepherd" (John 10:16).

Thus, my theological perspective is rooted in an understanding of God as the One, the ultimate reality or force who is constantly, relentlessly reconciling humanity to God's self. Further, God reconciles humanity in ways that are above and beyond our comprehension; hence, we are wise to stand in patience with awe and humility with respect to how God is working in the lives of other people. Indeed, we should think twice before rushing to judge the spiritual status of our neighbors or disrespect their landmarks. But, we must move from ground zero to first steps.

Step One: Focused Conversation

In order to be strategic and make an impact on the well-being of our children, it is absolutely essential for all community stakeholders to have focused conversations about the work that is ahead. This must go beyond inspirational rhetoric or invoking lists of past achievements. It must involve bringing a new outlook to the table. Since we live in a time where "town hall meetings" have become popular venues for giving voice to people, it may be prudent to make better use of that vehicle.

Assignment

Leaders of anchor institutions, especially black churches, colleges, and nonprofit organizations should convene a village-wide conversation about the future of black families, churches and other religious institutions, colleges (all of them) and schools, and what we want and expect from each of these institutions. With the popularity of the annual "State of the Black Union" hosted by media personalities Tavis Smiley and Tom Joyner, we're all acquainted with one compelling model for how the conversation could be staged. But that is not the only model out there. Each community should decide how it wishes to organize and launch its village-wide dialogues and resourcing sessions.

The purpose of this call for a *village-wide conversation* is to create the democratic space in which the community can gain information and make decisions about what it needs and expects from its major anchor institution. Someone has to start the conversation and those leaders who feel and hear this call most acutely should step forward first. The initiative to convene the community may be taken by the usual community elders. But it could be taken by younger, impatient, and resourceful leaders and common people who are ready to see our village renewed and will not sit by idly while a generation of kids goes down the noisy spiral.

Educational activist Paulo Freire has also emphasized dialogue as a necessary component for liberation and social change:

> Dialogue with the people is neither a concession nor a gift, much less a tactic to be used for domination. Dialogue, as the encounter among men to name the world, is a fundamental precondition for their true humanization. . . .
>
> Dialogue with people is radically necessary to every authentic revolution. . . . A true revolution must initiate a courageous dialogue with the people. Its very legitimacy lies in that dialogue. . . . To impede communication is to reduce men to the status of things and this is a job for oppressors, not for revolutionaries. . . .
>
> Some well-intentioned but misguided persons suppose that since the dialogical process is prolonged, they ought to carry out the revolution without communication . . . and once the revolution

is won, they will then develop a thoroughgoing educational effort. No! The educational, dialogical quality of revolution . . . must be present in all its stages."[7]

Communities should draw upon local resources whenever possible in organizing these meetings. It is not necessary to bring in high-priced consultants and guest speakers. Local college professors and public schoolteachers, principals, and counselors, business leaders, and independent entrepreneurs have lots of valuable insight into how to make organizations function. On the other hand, some communities may wish to bring in a well-known person as a catalyst for the local movement.

Also, those who convene the conversations should acquire training and seek counsel from professional group facilitators about how to run effective group meetings. They must not enter the process with the intent of preaching long sermons to people. They must anticipate and prepare to deal with difficult subjects like sexuality or abuse. And they must be smart about how to keep a conversation dynamic, inclusive, and safe for all who participate.

Step Two: Collaborative Leadership
Assignment

Each organization leader in the village should demonstrate that he or she has worked earnestly to initiate partnerships or project collaborations with another organization.

It is time to pull the plug on our current organizational culture of inefficiency, duplication, and "silo survival." This is a widespread challenge and all kinds of thoughtful leaders are addressing it. Even at Emory University, our executive leadership is trying to lead change that transforms a good "*multi*versity" of strong, autonomous departments and schools into a great *uni*versity. Because the needs of African Americans are so urgent and great, and because our resources are so limited, we must insist that all leaders work together to maximize good outcomes for children and youth.

This amounts to a call for a new style of *charismatic, servant leadership*. Although the theme of "servant leadership" has been popularized in the broader society, it has not found deep roots or resonance with black leaders, especially clergy. Generally speaking, African American communities continue to venerate the "elders in the village" who are charismatic leaders (gifted persons) and look to them for information, analysis, guidance, and inspiration. Charismatic servant leaders bring certain gifts to the community that are valued by the people, including inspiration, hope, entertainment, joy, and the courage to act for the common good. But typically we do not expect charismatic leaders to work with others. Too often they work independently of everyone else. But since we have lost ground during the current leadership's watch, then we should muster the courage to demand that they serve us differently. Such leaders must work together as a council of elders and move away from detached, self-centered initiatives.

We have an admirable example of leadership cooperation in the Black Leadership Forum, which was founded in 1977 in Washington, D.C. The Forum's Web site describes "a confederation of civil rights and service organizations started by a nucleus of 11 leaders of organizations which included the National Urban League, National Urban Coalition, NAACP, Southern Christian Leadership Conference, Joint Center for Political and Economic Studies, National Council of Negro Women, NAACP Legal Defense and Educational Fund, Martin Luther King Center for Non-violent Social Change, Congressional Black Caucus, National Conference of Black Mayors and the National Business League."[8] But, as I noted earlier, the Forum has not focused on the village-renewal agenda that begins with promoting a culture of healthy relationships.

As leaders who have never worked together begin to collaborate, the community should take note of it and commit itself to supporting them financially. The bottom line is that those who have never written a check to a local or national nonprofit organization should prepare to write one, but they should send it only to an organization that is working collaboratively with others to serve our children in greatest need. Let's reward those who are taking such risks, and let's commend their governing boards who expect and support that work.

If Dr. King taught us anything, it was that courageous leadership can move mountains. One expression of his courage and faith was his commitment to building *multiracial, interfaith coalitions of conscience.* If citizens are to make an impact on the crises I have described, it will be essential to create coalitions that are broad, nonpartisan, and committed to renewing the foundations of our villages.

Step Three: Vision and Plan

Nearly every nonprofit organization, school, and religious organization has some vision or plan for reversing the negative trends cited by Marian Wright Edelman. All of them are "standard versions" of what should be done. They address the familiar categories for action: political, economic, cultural, educational, health, criminal justice, and so on. The fact that everyone has a version of the same hymnbook is a good start. That is good news and will go a long way toward revitalizing our anchor institutions and redeeming our children. But during my lifetime and for a variety of reasons, I do not believe that we have seen these organizations collaborate and cooperate in bold and sacrificial ways (Du Bois) to accelerate measurable progress on these issues. We haven't been on the same page of the hymnal.

For instance, in the first chapter we saw the themes of the Covenant with Black America (health, education, criminal justice, voting rights, and so forth). Then there is the National Urban League's Opportunity Contract, which offers a prescription for addressing the scourge of poverty and lays the groundwork for economic empowerment of African Americans and others in the four areas of homeownership, jobs, economic development, and our children. And there is also the Million Man March agenda, which speaks of health, education, economic justice, human rights, ending police misbehavior, demanding reparations, and so forth. It would appear that we are "plan rich" but "execution poor."

There is no need to invent yet another revised standard version of the ten or two things we all should do to liberate the village. All of them are clearly important. Rather, I would suggest that we embrace the wisdom already elaborated and that we add a renewed focus on one simple issue: "What is in the best interest of our children, especially the least advantaged in the community and nation?"

That criterion should help to rearrange the priorities of many organizations. Once again, I think that we already have the tools and resources we need from experts like the Children's Defense Fund, Boys and Girls Clubs, Big Brothers-Big Sisters, and so on.

We need to craft a *comprehensive, strategic action plan* with timetables and accountability strategies. If a new local leadership regime emerges, neighborhood by neighborhood they should craft a comprehensive plan of action to renew families, strengthen houses of worship, support effective schools and colleges, and strengthen nonprofit groups. If those groups are engaged in the renewal of the village, they can make a compelling case for financial support and individual membership. If they are not doing the work of village renewal, they should expect to be ignored and to further lose prestige and influence. As leaders from local communities craft and implement their plans, they will be encouraged to report on activity, promising practices, and progress to a central source that can maintain an electronic inventory of this work that is available to the public. Hugh Price, former president of the National Urban League, observed, "We don't know our own strength. But, on occasion, I have seen the power of what synergy, a division of labor and collaboration can achieve. It's exhilarating."[9]

Assignment

Organization boards of directors and chief executive officers should endorse the idea of working with other organizations to eliminate child poverty and school underperformance.

For instance, the NAACP, along with a coalition of other sponsors, should convene a national gathering of organizational leaders who agree in advance to prioritize child well-being and healthy relationships as part of their next ten-year program. The NAACP also could convene and allow the Children's Defense Fund and other youth-serving organizations to intensify their work. Likewise, every member of the Black Leadership Forum and the major denominations, sororities and fraternities, other nonprofit organizations, and businesses should now privilege the agenda of promoting what is in the best interest of our children so that every child can show up on the first day of school prepared to learn.

The promising practices and rationales are abundant and compelling. According to the United Way of Metropolitan Atlanta, "every dollar invested in early learning saves $17 in future remedial education, welfare, and prison costs, and the drop out rate and juvenile arrest rate can be reduced by 26 percent and 60 percent respectively when quality child care is provided for children under age five."[10]

The Children's Defense Fund has launched a Cradle to Prison Pipeline® Initiative focused on poor and minority children who face unique risks and disadvantages that far too often shorten their childhoods and incarcerate them when they should be sitting in classrooms and playing in the schoolyard. This tragic pipeline also leads children to marginalized lives and premature deaths. Currently, the initiative's activities are aimed at helping to:

- pull families out of poverty;
- get families prenatal and health care;
- expand access to and use of early childhood education and development programs;
- prevent child abuse and neglect;
- provide all children needed mental health care;
- improve low-income and minority children's access to quality education;
- prevent youth from entering the juvenile justice system or incarceration.[11]

In this and in all of its programs, CDF brings a helpful matrix of distinctive but overlapping forms of care and discipline that they provide and encourage. They refer to these as giving every child a "Healthy start, head start, fair start, safe start, and a moral start."[12]

Step Four: Accountability and Action

We need to focus on building a culture of accountability that says it is okay for people to hold one another accountable for the well-being of our kids. Benjamin Canada, an educator and motivational speaker, speaks of the need to do Mentoring, Monitoring, and Ministering. Most nonprofit organizations do not appear to have a plan and a user-friendly way for the larger community to hold the organization accountable. Those organizations prepare elaborate funding proposals and claim that they serve those communities. But I offer here a concrete way to enlist young people in the accountability game.

Assignment

Every high school student who owns a cell phone should call one community leader per week to inquire about their progress and the status of their programs in serving the community more effectively.

What might it do for a local pastor, or parent, or school teacher to receive a weekly or monthly call from a student who respectfully but persistently asks, "OK, how are you doing this week with your assignment and piece of our village renewal? And if things are not advancing, can we help you get back on track?" Recruiting these young people may require the cooperation of school educators and officials and some resources from the philanthropic community.

This technology would also enable young people to text message reports on what they are seeing and hearing to an appropriate source who could monitor developments and even coordinate efforts to avoid existing duplication. Most important, this kind of monitoring and documentation would enable community leaders to discover gaps in the existing matrix of services that might be readily corrected. The identification of an organization to document and monitor this work regionally and nationally might be a project for a planning grant or a proposal to move this effort from talk to action.

Likewise, radio and television personalities enjoy high visibility and influence in the village. They should be regarded as the "talking drums" that communicate important information from community to community, helping to knit us into a national village. D.J.s should play a major role in helping to mobilize the community. Because they have large and loyal listening audiences, they should be more intentional about seeking to promote dialogue, reconciliation, coalition building, responsible individual agency, and holding themselves and others accountable.

Step Five: Sustaining and Fundraising

I would challenge the vast and resourceful philanthropic sector to invest in a renewed effort to coordinate efforts to renew families, congregations, and schools. As a former Ford Foundation program officer, I have some awareness of the culture of organized philanthropy in the United States. Often foundations are capable and willing to invest in high-risk, innovative initiatives that offer promise for the empowerment of local people, as opposed to giving money to a few elites in well-known and well-funded organizations. In fact, Barry Gaberman, former senior vice president of the Ford Foundation, noted in his 2006 plenary address to the Council on Foundations that foundations can:

1. Take risks and can afford to fail,
2. Take on sensitive issues public institutions will often step away from,
3. Take on activities not sustainable with only earned income and that require a subsidy since they are not governed by the tyranny of the bottom line,
4. Help sustain services desired by a particular segment of society; but that are not priorities for government,
5. Afford to think long term,
6. Be flexible and incorporate mid-course corrections to their programmatic efforts,
7. Act rapidly,
8. Test innovative and new initiatives that can be brought to scale,
9. Fund independent policy analysis as a check on the claims of the public sector, and,
10. Fund advocacy organizations.[13]

In 2005, there were roughly 68,000 grant-making foundations in the United States with total giving at $33.6 billion, "a record level and 5.5% ahead of the $31.8 billion given in 2004."[14] This plan needs organized philanthropy to step up and invest in a new approach to village renewal. Foundations that are already funding some component of the revitalization agenda should consider investing in the coordination, evaluation, and accountability work that will be important for the success of this initiative.

Assignment

Every foundation and charitable organization should devote resources each year to convene village leaders and challenge them to develop and implement concrete, measurable plans for improving children's academic and moral development. Also, they should support strategic conversations aimed at teaching and promoting healthy relationship skills, marriage, and family building.

Step Six: Documenting and Celebrating Progress

It is important to document the range of activity and progress made in these local initiatives. My hope is that local educational institutions will devote students and staff to begin the effort until funds can be raised to sustain that work. Local United Way organizations and community foundations should be invited to devote staff time and make grants to assist. With the omnipresence of personal technology, it is also possible to share stories of village mobilization via the Internet, phone text messages, and radio notices.

Hugh Price reminds us of the importance of inviting the community to celebrate its achievements. I grew up with a pastor, Bishop Louis H. Ford, who used to bestow enormous and beautiful trophies for academic achievement rather than athletic prowess. Every year he made a big deal out of reminding us to acknowledge those who had achieved in the library rather than on the playing field. Every village must find and implement more ways to celebrate academic and civic excellence in their midst.

In this book, I have attempted to elaborate the major steps that may be useful for renewing our villages. They include: (1) sponsoring a village-wide conversation about expectations and commitments for building good and just communities; (2) suggesting that we merge and consolidate the wide variety of organizational plans that are out there into a comprehensive strategic plan for community and national renewal; (3) promoting a new style of leadership and community accountability; (4) extending an invitation to the philanthropic community; (5) and the renewal of a multiracial, interfaith coalition that Dr. King nurtured and bequeathed to us.

I have also emphasized the need for our anchor institutions to become enduring institutions by cultivating qualities such as innovation, effective and resilient leadership, sharing essential information, and being true to their core values. Now, the burden rests with us. The families, churches, and schools that are in crisis can be renewed. They must be renewed so that they can engage in redeeming those who are in greatest need, such as formerly incarcerated people and at-risk children. We must allow our indignation with the statistics and trends to move us to organize and to mobilize. The children are waiting for us. In fact, there are countless children locked behind a dark and frightening place right now who hope that the village will move all barriers to their chances for a better life.

Villages need certain things to thrive. They need elders who will educate the community. They need producers who work hard each day to provide goods and services. They need nurturers, both women and men, to care for and nurture children and youth. And they need warriors who protect the community from external and internal threats. It's now time for all of us to accept our responsibilities and seize opportunities to uplift and to serve.

A SERMON ON VILLAGE RENEWAL: JOHN 11:1-48

In the Gospel of John, we find a family, or perhaps, the fragment of a family, for we hear nothing about their parents. We are left to speculate that the aging parents lived long and well and passed into the fading violet sunset of eternity. The text is almost cold in its simplicity and directness: "In the town of Bethany, the town of Mary and Martha and Lazarus." Three grown children huddled together against the harsh winds of life.

This reminds me of the plight of many families that are close knit as long as Granddaddy or Big Momma is alive. But once the matriarch or patriarch passes off the scene, often the remaining family members drift further into their own personal agendas and never come together to remember, to care, or to give.

But clearly that was not the case with these two sisters and a brother. There is a family here. They may be fragmented, but they are still a family. And note that Jesus spent considerable time with this family unit—often more time with them than his biological kin. Is that not like Jesus? He finds a family that is broken, a family that may be fragile but hanging together, and he joins himself to that family. And in the process, he makes them whole.

But there is also trouble in this family. For now one of the three survivors is sick and clinging to dear life while death stands impatiently at the door checking his wristwatch. The sisters are standing against death and trying to be as strong as they can be. But they are in distress. And in times of distress, just as they were taught to, they looked to the hills from whence cometh their help. They called for the Master.

Yes, once again, the women of the community, the praying women of the church interceded on behalf of a brother in trouble. Sisters are praying for the brother, and life and order and harmony swing softly in the balance of this delicate existential equilibrium.

While all sways in time and space, between life and eternity, they call the One who possesses command over death and the grave. Yes, if you've only got time to make one call—one call, that's it—it's a good idea to contact heaven and to plead your case in a brief time. The sisters call their other brother; their brother from another mother. They call Jesus.

Mary and Martha called for Jesus.

But let's take a look at these women for a moment. It's a good idea to understand the composition of community change agents. From all we know from the other Gospels, Martha was a woman gifted in the art of hospitality. I can imagine that she had always been a popular and gregarious girl. No matter how badly the kids at school might feel on a given day, they knew that if they could just get to Martha, she would make things alright. I imagine her to have been a colorful dresser and a wonderful cook. Look at her dressed in flowing gold and purple robes with a red scarf tied around her thick braided black hair. Every boy in the school wanted to date Martha. But, she knew how to say no and to make herself even more desirable by demanding that boys respect her. They called her "hard to get," but she was simply doing what her parents and her village expected and taught her.

And cook? Lord, the woman could cook! She was a virtuoso amidst an orchestra of steaming pots and pans. She was a little like your grandmother who, when you showed up at her house, made you sit and eat. Even though you weren't hungry or you were trying to lose weight, she said, "Sit down, child, you don't look good. If you don't eat, you'll lose weight!" And Martha knew the value of a mess of collard greens and corn bread, of fried chicken and candied yams, all washed down with ice-cold lemonade, followed by hot peach cobbler with a dab of vanilla Haagen Dazs ice cream melting on top. (I'm making myself hungry!) For some reason, Jesus liked visiting at Martha's table.

But then there was Mary. Something about Mary. Studious, contemplative Mary. You could always tell when she had been reading something profound. She would sit in a corner undisturbed by others and meditate on the implications of her learning. Mary could hold on to a word for a million years. How she loved to sit at the feet of Jesus and engage in deep theological analysis and textual exegesis.

So, while Mary couldn't cook, and Martha couldn't "book," brother Lazarus always respected their differences and never tried to compel one to be like the other. They were oil and water. Perhaps there's a clue there for parents who lean heavily on certain children to get them to become more like the other "high-performance" child.

Lazarus loved them and they both loved Lazarus. So you can imagine how they felt when Lazarus fell sick and landed so quickly at death's door.

Meanwhile, when the word reaches Jesus miles and hours away, he is busy doing ministry. And amidst the growing conflict between his work and his family, he does something extraordinary . . . he delays. The text reads, "He remained where he was for two days more."

At times, not always, God delays. It is a terrifying thought, isn't it? For, if God delays, we are likely to lose hope and yield to temptation. If God delays, even nature detours onto a destructive destiny. Summer winds that bring comfort become tornadoes that destroy hearth and home. Cool rains that nurture plants grow out of control and become mighty hurricanes.

Jesus tries to teach his disciples one of the most difficult lessons of discipleship, namely, that redemption can come from suffering. We heard that from Martin Luther King, Jr., didn't we? Lazarus's sickness and death are means to the higher end of exalting God's power, creating new community, and giving one person another chance to live.

Bishop Charles Blake says that Lazarus was dead but not dead long enough to certify that there was no hope of resuscitation. So, Jesus delays a few days longer, just to be certain that Lazarus was dead-dead, very dead.

Then, at the fullness of time, Jesus declares, "Now, let us go to Judea . . ."

When Martha learned that Jesus was near, she ran out to meet him. She protests, "If you had been here, our brother would not have died." Jesus engages her in a discussion that points her gaze higher to see God's purposes unfolding even now. She walks away uttering the faithful words, "I know that my brother shall live again. . . ." Jesus offers pastoral care and Martha is fine.

But then Martha told Mary that the master was nearby. When she ran out to see him, people thought she was going to the gravesite to grieve. She was headed not to the cemetery, however, but to the seminary where she would join the conversation about her brother's death.

When Jesus saw Mary, when her dark brown eyes met his, it was what Howard Thurman might have called "deep calling unto deep." In her eyes Jesus saw the questions, "Why our family? Why now? Haven't we suffered enough? Why do the good seem to die young while the evil flourish like the bay tree?" She asks the same question as Martha, "If you had been here, our brother would not have died." But Jesus seems to resist this effort to misplace blame. He seems to want her to realize that there are conditions in life over which we have little or no control.

A mature perspective accepts this and prepares for the inevitable.

Jesus then repeats the same words he offered to Martha as she made her indictment. But something strange happens. The same sermon didn't work for Mary. Is this a clue to us who often use "cookie cutter" formulaic approaches to meeting everyone's problems? It's as if Mary is saying, "Jesus, if you want to reach me, it will take more than words from a distance. You'll have to enter into my reality, walk in my moccasins. Feel my pain." And when Jesus goes to that place of deep empathy and as he observes the gathered masses who are troubled by despair, doubt, anger, and cynicism, he is disturbed in his spirit.

Then, in the shortest verse in the entire Bible (11:35), it says, "Jesus wept." The cool, calm face of the Son of God winced and broke into a torrent of tears. He didn't shed a discrete tear or cry softly—he wept!

I can imagine that his macho disciples were ashamed by this sudden display of grief. You can imagine Peter standing there trying to shield this spectacle from the masses: "Real men don't cry in public, and real men don't eat quiche!"

But Jesus allows himself the therapy of grief. It is as if he is saying to the church, "There are some conditions in the village that are so painful, the only appropriate first response is to grieve." And where our culture says, "I haven't got time for the pain," Jesus takes the time to grieve.

But then he does something strange; something out of order for one who is deep in grief. He asks the question, "Where have you laid him?" The question almost feels like Jesus is asking, "What have you done with the one who died before his time? What have you done with those who have dropped out of school before graduation? What have you done with the kids that have been incarcerated without proper representation and without the assistance they'll need to reenter the community? Where have you put them?"

The community stirs as he heads to the tomb. It was a cave, and a great rock lay against its opening.

Then, amidst growing tension and drama, Jesus looks at the community and commands, "Roll away the stone!"

Now in my homiletical imagination, I can see that great stone. It's shaped liked a piece of coal or even a diamond. It has facets and dimensions. And so I imagine that the rock has a political dimension. And all of the community members with political expertise—these politicians and lawyers put their shoulders on the political dimension of the rock. I imagine Jesus looks at them in their power and says, "I know you all are known for acting without consultation. But now I want you to wait for the rest of the people to join you."

The rock has an economic dimension, so all the community business leaders, those with capital and who work for economic justice, gather around and find their distinctive place on the rock. The rock has a familial dimension and so all those with skills in helping couples and parents gather around. You can see the crowd thinning out as they gather around the rock.

Then the elders and the disabled approach the rock uncertain about their value and their role. But Jesus smiles and says, "You have a role to play in this rock-moving mission. Just get close enough to touch the rock. We don't need you for your strength, we need you for your wisdom."

Soon, everyone has found a place on the rock, a place to practice his or her love. In fact, one young man with his shoulder against the rock, maybe a college student, looks up impatiently and asks Jesus, "Why aren't you helping us to push the rock?"

After a pause, Jesus says, "Because I am the Rock."

"I am the Rock of deliverance."

"I am the Rock of hope."

"I am the Rock of your salvation."

"And if you come together, if you do your part, if you'll work while you wait, if you'll sacrifice while you're waiting for me to show up, then I'll help you to help yourselves roll away the obstacles to your freedom."

So, if we're going to help Lazarus and bring joy to all of his kinfolk—

Let's roll! Let's roll! Let's roll!

NOTES

INTRODUCTION

1. Virginia Satir, *Peoplemaking* (Palo Alto, Calif.: Science and Behavior Books, 1972). This extraordinary book had a tremendous impact on me during my days as a seminary student.

2. Hillary Rodham Clinton, *It Takes a Village: And Other Lessons Children Teach Us* (New York: Simon & Schuster, 1996).

3. Ralph Ellison, *Shadow and Act* (New York: Vintage, 1995).

4. "The World's Most Enduring Institutions," a report from Booz Allen Hamilton, 2005 (http://www.boozallen.com/publications/article/659481?lpid=832435). Their list includes The U.S. Constitution, The Salvation Army, Oxford University, The Modern Olympic Games, Sony, General Electric, the International Telecommunication Union, the Rockefeller Foundation, Dartmouth College, and the rock group The Rolling Stones.

5. Mary Shelley, *Frankenstein* (Philadelphia: Courage Books, 1987 [1831]), 104.

6. Martin Luther King, Jr., *Stride toward Freedom* (New York: Harper & Row, 1963), 23.

7. The U.S. Census Bureau reports the rate of black poverty at 24.4 percent in 2003. http://www.census.gov/PressRelease/www/releases/archives/income_wealth/002484.html (December 2006).

8. See Shelby Steele, *The Content of Our Character: A New Vision of Race in America* (New York: St. Martin's Press, 1990); Glenn Loury, *One by One from the Inside Out: Race and Responsibility in America* (New York: Free Press, 1995); and John McWhorter, *Winning the Race: Beyond the Crisis in Black America* (New York: Penguin/Gotham, 2005).

9. William Julius Wilson, *The Truly Disadvantaged: The Inner City, the Underclass, and Public Policy* (Chicago: University of Chicago Press, 1987).

10. Jonathan Kozol, *Death at an Early Age: The Destruction of the Hearts and Minds of Negro Children in the Boston Public Schools* (New York: Houghton Mifflin, 1967).

11. Marian Wright Edelman, "What We Can Do," in Tavis Smiley, ed., *How to Make Black America Better: Leading African Americans Speak Out* (New York: Doubleday, 2001), 121.

12. Wright Edelman, in *How to Make Black America Better*, 123.

13. Jesse L. Jackson Jr., "Full Political Participation," in Tavis Smiley, ed. *How to Make Black America Better*, 101.

14. Carter G. Woodson, *The Mis-education of the Negro* (Trenton, N.J.: Africa World Press, Inc., 1990 [1933]), v.

15. Obie Clayton Jr., *An American Dilemma Revisited: Race Relations in a Changing World* (New York: Russell Sage Foundation, 1996). The book commemorates the fiftieth anniversary of Gunnar Myrdal's classic study of race relations, *An American Dilemma*. It contains chapters on the political situation, underclass population, blacks in business and professions, gender and social inequality, and the church and social change.

16. H. Richard Niebuhr, *The Responsible Self* (New York: Harper & Row, 1963). There are numerous other examples of this analytic genre, including Johnnetta Betsch Cole and Beverly Guy-Sheftall's *Gender Talk: The Struggle for Women's Equality in African American Communities* (New York: Random House, 2003).

17. Philip Foner, ed., *W.E.B. DuBois Speaks, 1890-1910*, 2 vols (New York: Pathfinder Press, 1970), 1:79.

18. I think especially of Cornel West and Kelvin S. Sealey, eds., *Restoring Hope: Conversations on the Future of Black America* (Boston: Beacon Press, 1997); and Walter Mosley, Manthia Diawara, Clyde Taylor, and Regina Austin, eds., *Black Genius: African American Solutions to African American Problems* (New York: W.W. Norton, 1999).

19. Smiley, ed., *How to Make Black America Better.*

20. Earl Graves, "Leveraging Our Power," in ibid., 110.

21. Ibid.

22. McWhorter, *Winning the Race,* 359.

23. Ibid., 360.

24. Juan Williams, *Enough: The Phony Leaders, Dead-End Movements, and Culture of Failure That Are Undermining Black America—and What We Can Do about It* (New York: Crown Publishers, 2006).

25. Ibid., 211, 215.

26. Jawanza Kunjufu, *Solutions for Black America* (Chicago: African American Images, 2004).

27. Ibid., 9.

28. Tavis Smiley, ed. *The Covenant with Black America* (Chicago: Third World Press, 2006).

29. Ibid., 235.

CHAPTER ONE: FAMILIES

1. Albert J. Raboteau, *Slave Religion: The "Invisible Institution" in the Antebellum South* (New York: Oxford University Press, 1978), 90.

2. Jessie Bernard, *Marriage and Family among Negroes* (Englewood Cliffs, N.J.: Prentice Hall, 1966), 9. Here Barnard includes an account that suggests that the few slave masters who permitted slave marriage utilized the practice of "jumping the broom."

3. Herbert G. Gutman, *The Black Family in Slavery and Freedom, 1750–1925* (New York: Random House, 1976), 6. Gutman includes the heartrending account of a husband and father who was sold to another master. He remarries and continues a correspondence with the first wife. He urges her to remarry and to "send me some of the children's hair in a separate paper with their names on it . . . tell them that they must remember that they have a good father and one that cares for them and one that thinks about them everyday."

4. Lorraine Blackman, Obie Clayton, Norval Glenn, Linda Malone-Colon, and Alex Roberts, "The Consequences of Marriage for African Americans: A Comprehensive Literature Reiview," a report from the Institute for American Values (New York, 2005), 9.

5. Blackman, Clayton, Glenn, "The Consequences of Marriage for African Americans," 8.

6. Don S. Browning, Bonnie J. Miller-McLemore, Pamela D. Couture, K. Brynolf Lyon, and Robert M. Franklin, *From Culture Wars to Common Ground: Religion and the American Family Debate* (Louisville: Westminster John Knox Press, 1997), 230.

7. Ronald B. Mincy, and Hillard Pouncy, "The Marriage Mystery: Marriage, Assets and the Expectations of African American Families," in *Black Fathers in Contemporary American Society: Strengths, Weaknesses, and Strategies for Change*, edited by Obie Clayton, Ronald Mincy and David Blankenhorn (New York: Russell Sage, 2003), 15.

8. "The Consequences of Marriage for African Americans," 9.

9. James P. Comer, Norris T. Haynes, Edward T. Joyner, Michael Ben-Avie, eds., *Rallying the Whole Village: The Comer Process for Reforming Education* (New York: Teachers College, Columbia University, 1996), 5.

10. William H. Cosby, Jr., *Fatherhood* (Garden City, N.Y.: Doubleday & Company, 1986), ix.

11. Michael Eric Dyson, *Is Bill Cosby Right? Or Has the Black Middle Class Lost Its Mind?* (New York: Basic Civitas Books, 2005).

12. Barbara Ehrenreich, "Corporate Home Wreckers," *The Progressive* (March 2006); http://www.progressive.org/mag_ehrenreich0306 (October 18, 2006).

13. Eleanor Holmes Norton, quoted in Spender S. Hsu, "Marriage Fund for Poor Proposed," *Washington Post*, July 22, 2005, B5.

14. Mincy and Pouncy, "The Marriage Mystery," 18.

15. Adelle M. Banks, "Pastors Issue Open Letter Urging Attention to Black Family Crisis," Religious News Service website posting, July 20, 2005.

16. The Seymour Institute for Advanced Christian Studies, "God's Gift: A Christian Vision of Marriage and the Black Family" (Boston: The Seymour Institute, 2005); http://www.contemporarypolicy.org/Site/Books/BookGodsGift.htm (October 18, 2006).

17. Glenn C. Loury, "Structure vs. Culture in Sociological Studies of the Black Family," Paper prepared for the Conference on Black Fatherhood, Morehouse College, Atlanta, Ga., November 5, 1998, 18.

18. Ibid. , 18.

19. Glenn C. Loury, *The Anatomy of Racial Inequality* (Cambridge, Mass.: Harvard University Press, 2002), 104, 105.

20. Daniel Patrick Moynihan, *The Negro Family: The Case for National Action* (Washington, D.C.: U.S. Department of Labor, 1965).

21. William Julius Wilson, *The Truly Disadvantaged: The Inner City, the Underclass, and Public Policy* (Chicago: University of Chicago Press, 1987), 64; Gutman, *The Black Family in Slavery and Freedom,* xviii and xix.

22. Andrew Billingsley, *Climbing Jacob's Ladder: The Enduring Legacies of African-American Families* (New York: Simon & Schuster, 1992), 18-35.

23. Orlando Patterson, *Rituals of Blood: Consequences of Slavery in Two American Cities* (Washington, D.C.: Civitas, 1998), 25–44.

24. Ibid., 41.

25. Ibid., 25.

26. Ibid., 48.

27. Ibid., 43.

28. Ibid., 47.

29. Mincy and Pouncy, "The Marriage Mystery," 22.

30. Kenneth B. Clark, quoted in Wilson, *The Truly Disadvantaged,* 73.

31. Nicholas Lemann, *The Promised Land: The Great Black Migration and How It Changed America* (New York: Random House, 1991), 4.

32. Wilson, *The Truly Disadvantaged,* 65.

33. Ibid., 56.

34. Working with Dr. Cheryl Townsend Gilkes, a sociologist at Colby College and a Baptist preacher, and a team of other colleagues, we convened groups of clergy at the request of Carole Thompson, a senior program officer at the Annie E. Casey Foundation in Baltimore. The results of these consultations can be found in two reports, both titled "Healthy Marriages in Low-Income African American Communities," published by the Annie E. Casey Foundation: Robert M. Franklin, "Part 1: Exploring Partnerships between Faith Communities and the Marriage Movement" (2003); and Robert M. Franklin and Stephanie C. Boddie, "Part 2: Expanding the Dialogue with Faith Leaders from Making Connections Sites" (2004). Both are available in PDF format at http://www.aecf.org/publications/browse.php?filter=21 (October 18, 2006).

35. Franklin, "Part 1: Exploring Partnerships between Faith Communities and the Marriage Movement" (2003).

36. As cited in the Region IV Healthy Marriage Initiative Resource Guide, U.S. Department of Health and Human Services, Administration for Children and Families, Washington, D.C. (2006), 6.

37. Patterson, *Rituals of Blood*, 56.

38. Ibid., 62.

39. Ibid., 63.

40. Ibid.

41. This third explanation is amplified by a provocative article by Joy Jones, "Are Black Women Scaring Off Their Men?" *Washington Post*. Sept. 1, 1991. Available online at http://www.gillistriplett.com/rel101/articles/scaring.html (October 18, 2006). Jones suggests that the problem may not be with men as much as with the behavior and attitudes of women. She offers advice to women that may offend as many people as it helps:

> In too many cases, when dealing with men, you will have to sacrifice being right in order to enjoy being loved. Being acknowledged as the head of the household is an especially important thing for many black men, since their manhood is so often actively challenged everywhere else. Many modern women are so independent, so self-sufficient, so committed to the cause, to the church, to career or their narrow concepts that their entire personalities project an "I don't need a man" message. So they end up without one. An interested man may be attracted but he soon discovers that this sister makes very little space for him in her life. Going to graduate school is a good goal and an option that previous generations of blacks have not had.
>
> But sometimes the achieving woman will place her boyfriend so low on her list of priorities that his interest wanes. Between work, school and homework, she's seldom "there" for him, for the preliminaries that might develop a commitment to a woman. She's too busy to prepare him a home-cooked meal or to be a listening ear for his concerns because she is so occupied with her own.
>
> Soon he uses her only for uncommitted sex since to him she appears unavailable for anything else. Blind to the part she's playing in the problem, she ends up thinking, "Men only want one thing." And she decides she's better off with the degree than the friendship. When she's 45, she may wish she'd set different priorities while she was younger. It's not just the busy career girl who can't see the forest for the trees.

42. Patterson, *Rituals of Blood*, 160 (emphasis added).

43. Mincy and Pouncy, "The Marriage Mystery," 22,

44. Ibid., 22.

45. "Cohabitation, Marriage, Divorce, and Remarriage in the United States: Data from the National Survey of Family Growth," Series 23, No. 22 (Hyattsville, Md.: Department of Health and Human Services, Centers for Disease Control and Prevention, National Center for Health Statistics, July 2002), 3.

46. A Philadelphia-based company, Motivational Educational Entertainment (MEE), has recorded the attitudes of teenaged men and women from ten U.S. cities, on sex, relationships, marriage, and sexually transmitted diseases. The content of those conversations places a chilling exclamation point on the fact that these teens reflect our general society's lack of interest in commitment and love. Although most of the young men celebrated the macho, "player" lifestyle with multiple female partners, they did acknowledge the value of having one "special lady" in their lives. They distinguished between "shorties" with whom they would have casual sexual relationships, and "wife-ees," the special young lady with whom he might have a long-term relationship that could include children. Their testimonies underscore the need for mentors, coaches, and teachers who can build upon their homegrown notions of a "wife-ee" and lead them to more fulfilled relationships that include nurturing successful children, generating and passing along one's wealth, and maintaining a stable family network in which one would eventually grow to become a respected grandparent and great grandparent. http://www.meeproductions.com/index.cfm (October 18, 2006).

47. Robert M. Franklin, "Healthy Marriages in Low-Income African American   Communities: A Thematic Summary," a report published by the Annie E. Casey Foundation, March 2004.

48. W. Bradford Wilcox, *Then Comes Marriage? Religion, Race, and Marriage in Urban America* (Philadelphia, Pa.: University of Pennsylvania—Center for Research on Religion and Urban Civil Society, 2002), 22.

49. Ibid.

50. "Who Benefits More from Marriage—Men or Women?" *Jet* (June 2001), 14–18.

51. Ibid.

52. My wife and other African American women remind me that in discussing this topic it is important not to overlook the "sister networks" that function to some extent as husband-father surrogates. She listed the various small groups of women who gather with their children to carpool, share babysitting needs, lend money, offer counsel and advice, share meals, and generally offer sisterhood and empathic support to one another. When these networks work well, women (including married ones) get at least some of the support they need when men are not available. None of these women would say that men are not necessary. But all would affirm that there are ways to make things work when brothers are MIA (missing in action). Given such sister networks, how can the case for marriage succeed?

53. Patterson, *Rituals of Blood*, 165.

54. U.S. Census Bureau study, 2005, summarized in a news article by Ely Portillo and Frank Greve, "Interracial Trend Far-Reaching Especially for Young People," *Atlanta Journal and Constitution*, July 23, 2006, A8.

55. Ibid.

56. Ibid.

57. Maggie Gallagher, "Can Government Strengthen Marriage? Evidence from the Social Sciences" (New York: National Fatherhood Initiative, Institute for Marriage and Public Policy, and the Institute for American Values, 2004). Available in PDF format at www.marriagedebate.com/pdf/ Can%20Government%20Strengthen%20Marriage.pdf (October 18, 2006).

58. Welcoming remarks by Ralph Smith, Vice President, Annie E. Casey Foundation, Baltimore, December 2003. I presided at the meeting attended by fifteen marriage education professionals, eight African American clergy, foundation staff, consultants, representatives from the Administration for Children and Families (HHS), and scholars on the African American family such as Dr. Robert Hill (WESTAT) and Dr. Linda Malone-Colon (Hampton University).

59. Hsu, "Marriage Fund for Poor Proposed."

60. Nisa Islam Muhammad, ed., *Raising the Bottom: Promoting Marriage in the Black Community* (Evansville, Ind.: GMA Publishing, 2005), 121–22.

61. CDC, "Cohabitation, Marriage, Divorce, and Remarriage," 13.

62. Linda J. Waite, Don Browning, William J. Doherty, Maggie Gallagher, Ye Luo, and Scott M. Stanley, "Does Divorce Make People Happier? Findings from a Study of Unhappy Marriages (New York: Institute for American Values, 2002), 1. Available in PDF format at http://center.americanvalues.org/?p=14 (October 18, 2006).

63. The Web site of the Faith Trust Institute of Seattle, a multifaith, multicultural organization that provides resources and advocacy to religious congregations on preventing sexual and domestic violence.offers a helpful summary of frequently asked questions related to this difficult issue. See http://www.faithtrustinstitute.org/ (October 18, 2006).

64. Faith Trust Institute website, http://www.faithtrustinstitute.org/index .php?p=Domestic_Violence&s=28.

65. Ibid.

66. Kathryn Edin, *Promises I Can Keep: Why Poor Women Put Motherhood before Marriage* (Berkeley: University of California Press, 2006).

67. When I shared this finding with members of the clergy focus group at the Annie E. Casey Foundation, they too were surprised and noted that very few of them had said much about domestic violence in their sermons or lectures. Fortunately, there are organizations such as the Faith Trust Institute producing valuable print and video resources aimed at various faith communities and ethnic-racial communities. And, thankfully, they address one of the most taboo, sensitive topics in congregational culture: What happens when clergy themselves are the abusers?

68. Randall Bailey, Kelly Brown Douglas, Cornel West, Michael Brown are contributors to *Frequently Asked Questions about Sexuality, the Bible, and the Church* (San Francisco: The Covenant Network of Presbyterians, 2006).

69. I have written about this in an exciting project supported by the Lilly Endowment; see "Christian Profamily Movements: The Black Church, Roman Catholics, and the Christian Right," in Don S. Browning, et al., eds., *From Culture Wars to Common Ground*, 219–46.

70. Carolyn McCrary, Lecture delivered at the Interdenominational Theological Center, 1999. McCrary is a womanist pastoral care professional who proposes that the term "primary parent" be substituted for "single parent" as a way of affirming the responsible parent who is present rather than defining her (or him) with reference to the absent partner.

71. Among them are: (1) Diann Dawson, a lawyer and social worker who now serves as director of regional operations for the U.S. Department of Health and Human Services, Administration for Children and Family, and is the senior African American administrative leader of federal efforts to promote healthy marriage. (2) Dr. Linda Malone-Colon, a marriage researcher who has taught courses on relationships at Hampton University and is now engaged in research on relationships and marriages. (3) Dr. Lorraine Blackmon of Indiana University, who has over thirty years of clinical practice in mental health, domestic violence, marriage, and family counseling. She directs the African American Family Life Institute in Indianapolis and has her own eight-week-format curriculum. (4) Nisa Islam Muhammad, founder of the "Wedded Bliss Foundation," and an author, motivational speaker, and creator of the national "Black Marriage Day." (5) The Reverend Dr. Rozario Slack, a staff member at First Things First, a marriage and family promotion agency in Chattanooga. Dr. Slack has also teamed up with his wife, pediatrician Dr. Angela Slack, to produce a series of valuable marriage enhancement DVDs titled "Ten Great Dates for Black Couples," a program adapted from a popular model created by David and Claudia Arp. (6) The Reverend Dr. Sherone C. Patterson, a Dallas-based United Methodist pastor whose book and relationships workshops are titled "The Love Clinic."

72. See note 30, above.

73. Morehouse, the alma mater of Dr. Martin Luther King Jr. and numerous other influential black leaders, is the only all-male, historically black college in the United States. This bastion of African American male achievement was the perfect venue for a conference designed to examine issues pertaining to the future of marriage and parenthood in black communities. In contrast to other conferences on the topic, whose proceedings slumber between the covers of academic journals, the conference organizers, Obie Clayton, (Morehouse), Ronald Mincy (Ford Foundation, now Columbia University), and David Blankenhorn (Institute for American Values), decided to produce a report titled "Turning the Corner on Father Absence in Black America: A Statement from the Morehouse Conference on African-American Fathers" (Atlanta/New York: Morehouse Research Institute/Institute for Family Values, 1999). Available online at http://www.americanvalues.org/html/r-turning_the_corner.html (October 18, 2006).

74. Ibid., 9.

75. Ibid., 4.

76. Ibid., 4.

77. Ibid., 5.

78. Ibid., 4.

79. Ibid., 5.

80. Cornel West, *Restoring Hope: Conversations on the Future of Black America* (Boston: Beacon Press, 1997), 201–202.

81. Ibid., 201, 202.

82. Walter Mosley, "Giving Back," in Walter Mosley, Manthia Diawara, Clyde Taylor, and Regina Austin, eds., *Black Genius: African American Solutions to African American Problems* (New York: W. W. Norton, 1999), 48

CHAPTER TWO: CHURCHES

1. I am using the terms *black church* and *congregation* interchangeably although the concept of congregation is a sociological category that includes official religious communities in the many religious traditions.

2. Albert J. Raboteau, *Slave Religion: The "Invisible Institution" in the Antebellum South* (New York: Oxford University Press, 1978), 87-89.

3. See C. Eric Lincoln and Lawrence Mamiya, *The Black Church in the African American Experience* (Durham, N.C.: Duke University Press, 1990); Anthony B. Pinn, *The Black Church in the Post-Civil Rights Era* (Maryknoll, N.Y.: Orbis Books, 2002).

4. "Black Megachurches' Mega Outreach," resource for journalists; see http://www.religionlink.org/tip_040908bzones.php (October 18, 2006).

5. Michael Owen and R. Drew Smith, "Congregations in Low-Income Neighborhoods and the Implications for Social Welfare Policy Research," *Nonprofit and Voluntary Sector Quarterly* 34, no. 3 (September 2005): 316–39.

6. Michael Joseph Brown, "*Manus Pastorum*: A Calling to Be Creatively Out of Step," in *The A.M.E. Church Review* 121, no. 398 (April-June 2005), 72, 73.

7. "Preaching to the Pocketbook," *All Things Considered* broadcast, National Public Radio (August 7, 2006). Available online at http://www.npr.org/templates/story/story.php?storyId=5624473 (October 18, 2006).

8. From James Weldon Johnson, "Lift Every Voice and Sing," in *Saint Peter Relates an Incident* (New York: Viking Penguin, 1963).

9. The Learning Annex Real Estate Wealth Expo; information on 2006 and 2007 conferences at https://www.learningannex.com/reales-tate/realestate.taf?coursenum=&menu=&refer=&ccode (October 18, 2006).

10. "Black Wealth Initiative," *Black Enterprise* magazine Web site, http://www.blackenterprise.com/wealth/wbk.asp (October 18, 2006).

11. http://www.blackenterprise.com/wealth/20.htm (October 18, 2006).

12. The concept of "shared prosperity"was developed by the nonprofit organization, Demos: A Network for Ideas and Action. For more information on this network of thoughtful activists engaged in policy change aimed at a more inclusive democracy and more just economy, see http://www.demos.org/home.cfm (October 18, 2006).

13. R. Drew Smith for the Leadership Center at Morehouse College, "Beyond the Boundaries: Low Income Residents, Faith Based Organizations and Neighborhood Coalition Building," Annie E. Casey Foundation report (November 2003), 13. Available in PDF format at http://www.aecf.org/publications/browse.php (October 18, 2006).

14. Joint Center of Political and Economic Studies Web site; the report is available in PDF format at http://www.jointcenter.org/publications1/PublicationsDetail.php?recordID=137 (October 18, 2006). The study drew upon survey data taken from a random sample of 750 congregations and clergy and from focus groups in Atlanta and Washington, D.C. I served on the advisory committee for the study.

15. Cornel West, *Race Matters* (Boston: Beacon Press, 1993), 51–70.

16. Tavis Smiley, ed. *How to Make Black America Better: Leading African Americans Speak Out* (New York: Doubleday, 2001).

17. Carter G. Woodson, *The Mis-education of the Negro* (Trenton, N.J.: Africa World Press, Inc., 1990 [1933]), 34.

18. Earl Ofari Hutchinson, *The Disappearance of Black Leadership* (Los Angeles: Middle Passage Press, Inc., 2000), 20–21.

19. Woodson, *Mis-education of the Negro*, 34.

20. Ibid., 59.

21. Aldon D. Morris, *The Origins of the Civil Rights Movement: Black Communities Organizing for Change* (New York: Free Press, 1986).

22. J. Irwin Trotter, "Our Theologies of Preaching," *Quarterly Review: A Journal of Theological Resources for Ministry,* Fall 1995.

23. Franklin, *Another Day's Journey.* My analysis builds upon the research and analysis of Lincoln and Mamiya, *The Black Church in the African American Experience*; Wyatt Tee Walker, *Somebody's Calling My Name: Black Sacred Music and Social Change* (Valley Forge, Pa.: Judson Press, 1983); Harold A. Carter, *The Prayer Tradition of Black People* (Valley Forge, Pa.: Judson Press, 1976); H. Beecher Hicks Jr., *Preaching through a Storm* (Grand Rapids, Mich.: Zondervan, 1986); James Forbes, *The Holy Spirit and Preaching* (Nashville: Abingdon Press, 1989).

24. Interview with Reverend Suzanne Johnson Cook, July 10, 2005.

25. According to the Schomburg Center for African American Life, the AME Church reports over 8,000 churches with 3.5 million members, up from a membership of 2.2 million reported in 1989 by Lincoln and Mamiya in *The Black Church in the African American Experience,* 54ff. Note also that the denomination's official Web site indicates 2 million members in 7,000 churches during the 1990s: http://www.ame-church.com/about-us/history.php (October 18, 2006). The AME Church supports five colleges, one junior college, and two theological seminaries, Payne Theological Seminary in Dayton, Ohio (which appointed a female president, Dr. Leah Gaskin Fitchue, in 2004), and the Turner Theological Seminary of the Interdenominational Theological Center in Atlanta. Although the A.M.E. tradition began ordaining women clergy in 1948, only recently did it elect three female bishops, Vashti Murphy McKenzie, Carolyn Tyler Guidry, and Sarah Frances Davis. The AME church is led by twenty bishops, twelve general officers, and 8,000 ministers, nearly the same as the number of congregations.

The African Methodist Episcopal Zion (AMEZ) Church reports 6,000 churches and three million members (it reported 1.2 million in 1989). It supports two junior colleges along with Livingstone College and Hood Theological Seminary in Salisbury, North Carolina. The Zion Church has ordained women since 1898.

The Christian Methodist Episcopal (CME) Church reports 3,000 churches with 800,000 members (it reported 3,000 and 975,000 members in 1989). It supports five colleges (Lane, Paine, Texas, Miles, and Mississippi Industrial [now closed]). Lincoln and Mamiya remind us that out of 9.4 million United Methodists, 360,000 were black and 2,600 of the 38,000 churches were predominantly black (*The Black Church in the African American Experience,* 67). Black

United Methodists have supported and continue to sustain the Gammon Theological Seminary, which was the nucleus institution in the founding of the Interdenominational Theology Center in Atlanta in 1958.

26. Hugh B. Price, *Achievement Matters: Getting Your Child the Best Education Possible* (New York: Kensington, 2002), 47ff.

27. Ibid., 47.

28. Ibid., 48, 49.

29. Today, the National Baptist Convention, U.S.A., reports having over 30,000 congregations and their denominational Web site estimates 7.5 million members; http://www.nationalbaptist.com/Index.cfm?FuseAction=Page&PageID=1000014 (October 18, 2006). If this number is accurate, it would be the largest of the black denominations. However, the number is now disputed due to questions raised during Rev. Lyons's tenure. An affidavit from a secretary indicated that Rev. Lyons may have fabricated the 8.5 million number in order to mislead business partners and investors, and that the actual number of participating and paying members was closer to one million. C. Eric Lincoln reported that the church had 7.5 million members in 1989. Insiders like W. Franklyn Richardson of Grace Baptist Church in Mt. Vernon, N.Y., say, "No one really knows. We know that there are millions." Dr. Samuel Berry McKinney of Seattle observes humorously, "All black people are Baptist by nature. They may be other things by choice." Counting by that axiom would certainly justify the larger estimates.

The National Baptist Convention of America reports 2.4 million members in 7,800 local churches; http://www.nbcamerica.net/ (October 18, 2006). There is an interesting history of political conflict behind why these two denominations have similar names but different histories. In short, the two separated in 1915 in a dispute over control of the publishing house. Keeping track of the two is often confusing to outsiders. Another denomination, the National Missionary Baptist Convention, was one of the member denominations of the Congress of National Black Churches and appeared to have a strong presence in southern states but no demographic details are available for this component of the Baptist family.

The other major branch of the Baptist communion is the Progressive National Baptist Convention (PNBC). Its Web site indicates that it was the spiritual home for Dr. King and many progressive civil rights leaders such as Jesse Jackson, Benjamin Hooks, and William Gray (former president of the United Negro College Fund); http://pnbc.org/index.php (October 18, 2006). Dr. Lincoln's research indicates 1.2 million members in one thousand churches. PNBC ordains women and encourages its clergy to pursue theological education.

30. To learn more about the Azusa Street Revival, see the web article, http://en.wikipedia.org/wiki/Azusa_Street_Revival In 2006, I attended the 100th anniversary celebrations of the Azusa Street phenomenon. Following a late-night service at the magnificent West Angeles Cathedral at which Bishop Paul Morton preached, sang, performed, and generally "wrecked the church," Bishop Charles Blake invited me to attend a reception for clergy. Gathered inside the expansive office of Bishop Blake were some of America's most talented, dynamic preachers—Bishops Paul Morton, Kenneth Ulmer, Charles Blake, and Clarence McClendon. Most of them are fairly young, all of them appear on television, and all are quite popular with young people—and all of them are probably wealthy. (Funny story: Upon arriving at Los Angeles International airport, I told my driver, a middle-age Japanese immigrant, to take me to the Cathedral on Crenshaw Boulevard. He nodded and promptly drove me to the "casino." After clarifying my destination we traded jokes about which location would see more money exchange hands that evening.)

31. The Church of God in Christ (COGIC) reports 10,000 congregations with approximately four million members; http://www.cogic.org/ (October 18, 2006). Its presiding bishop, Bishop Gilbert Patterson, resides in Memphis, which is also the denomination's headquarters. He has a national television broadcast and is a popular preacher on the national circuit. According to Adherents.com, the Pentecostal Assemblies of the World (P.A.W.) reports 1,600 churches with one million members; http://www.adherents.com/Na/Na_509.html#3072 (October 18, 2006). In 2004, it elected as its presiding bishop a physician and pastor, Bishop Horace E. Smith.

32. "The Ten Point Plan," Boston Ten Point Coalition, http://www.bostontenpoint.org/tenpointplan.html (October 18, 2006).

33. Several Pentecostal scholars and scholars of Pentecostalism have called attention to this dimension of Pentecostal urban ministries, including David Daniels, Adrienne Israel, Alonzo Johnson, Eldin Villafanje, Samuel B. Hogan, Anjulet Tucker, Brian Rubin, Eric Williams, Leslie Callahan and Marlon Milner.

34. Charles Green, ed., *Globalization and Survival in the Black Diaspora: The New Urban Challenge* (Albany: State University of New York Press, 1997), 2. The United Nations Population Growth projections indicate that the level of the urbanization for the world as a whole is expected to increase to 65 percent by 2025. But in the less developed regions of the world, the growth factor will be 83 percent by 2025, up from 75 percent now. Today, seventeen of the world's twenty largest cities are in less-developed countries and of the seven megacities with a population of fifty million or more, five are in developing countries, including Mexico City and Sao Paulo.

35. Ann Bernstein, "Globalization, Culture, and Development: Can South Africa Be More than an Offshoot of the West?" in Peter L. Berger and Samuel P. Huntington, eds., *Many Globalizations: Cultural Diversity in the Contemporary World* (New York: Oxford University Press, 2002), 244.

36. Among the classics that can enrich our knowledge of life-changing works of charity and mercy are Mother Teresa of Calcutta's words captured in Sean-Patrick Lovett, ed., *The Best Gift of Love: Meditations of Mother Teresa* (Cincinnati: Servant Publications, 1993).

37. Among classic readings on this topic I would suggest Archie Smith Jr., *The Relational Self: Ethics and Therapy from a Black Church Perspective* (Nashville: Abingdon Press, 1982); Edward P. Wimberly, *African American Pastoral Care* (Nashville: Abindon Press, 1991); and Howard Clinebell, *Basic Types of Pastoral Care and Counseling: Resources for the Ministry of Healing and Growth* (Nashville: Abindon Press, 1984).

38. Eileen Lindner, ed., *Yearbook of American and Canadian Churches* (Nashville: Abingdon, 1994).

39. Among the best resources to inform effective and faithful management of faith-based social-service ministries are Peter C. Brinckerhoff, *Faith-Based Management: Leading Organizations That Are Based on More than Just Mission* (New York: John Wiley & Sons, 1999); Christine W. Letts, William P. Ryan, and Allen Grossman, *High Performance Nonprofit Organizations: Managing Upstream for Greater Impact* (New York: John Wiley & Sons, 1998); and Peter Frumkin, *On Being Nonprofit: A Conceptual and Policy Primer* (Cambridge, Mass.: Harvard University Press, 2002).

40. Classic readings should include Gregory Peirce, *Activism That Makes Sense: Congregations and Community Organizations* (Skokie, Ill.: ACTA Publications, 1997); Anna Julia Cooper, *A Voice from the South,* the Schomburg Library of Nineteenth-Century Black Women

Writers (New York: Oxford University Press, 1990 [1892]); Martin Luther King Jr., "Letter from Birmingham City Jail" in James M. Washington, ed., *A Testament of Hope: The Essential Writings and Speeches of Martin Luther King, Jr.* (New York: HarperCollins, 1986), 289–302; and Marian Wright Edelman, *The Measure of Our Success: Letters to My Children and Yours* (Boston: Beacon Press, 1992).

41. Classic texts might include John Kretzmann and John McKnight, *Building Communities from the Inside Out: A Path toward Finding and Mobilizing a Community's Assets* (Skokie, Ill.: ACTA Publications, 1997); and Martin Luther King Jr., *Where Do We Go from Here: Chaos or Community?* (Boston: Beacon Press, 1968).

42. Children's Defense Fund mission statement, http://www.childrensdefense.org/site/PageNavigator/mission (October 18, 2006).

43. Edward K. Braxton, *The Wisdom Community* (Mahwah, N.J.: Paulist Press, 1980).

44. Martin Luther King Jr., "A Time to Break Silence" (4 April 1967 sermon), in Washington, ed., *A Testament of Hope,* 231–44.

45. Reinhold Niebuhr, Quote may be found at website: http://www.brainyquote.com/quotes/quotes/r/reinholdni116901.html.

CHAPTER THREE: COLLEGES

1. Juan Williams and Dwayne Ashley, *I'll Find a Way or Make One: A Tribute to Historically Black Colleges and Universities* (New York: Amistad, 2004), 10.

2. "Africans in America" PBS website, http://www.pbs.org/wgbh/aia/part1/1narr4.html.

3. James D. Anderson, *The Education of Blacks in the South, 1860–1935* (Chapel Hill: University of North Carolina Press, 1988), 1.

4. Ibid., 1.

5. Ibid., 2.

6. Ibid., 12, 13.

7. Ibid., 156.

8. Williams and Ashley, *I'll Find a Way,* 297.

9. Ibid., 301.

10. See the UNCF Web site: http://www.uncf.org/members/index.asp (October 18, 2006).

11. See the NAFEO Web site: http://www.nafeo.org/nafeo/about.php (October 18, 2006).

12. Williams and Ashley, *I'll Find a Way*, 303.

13. Ibid., 304.

14. Ibid., 10.

15. Ibid., 8.

16. Anderson, *The Education of Blacks in the South, 1860–1935*, 2.

17. Ira Berlin, Marc Favreau, Steven F. Miller, and Robin D. G. Kelley, *Remembering Slavery: African Americans Talk about Their Personal Experiences of Slavery and Emancipation* (New York: New Press, 1998), 280. For decades those recordings were stored in the Library of Congress. But in 1998 a partnership between several scholars, the Library of Congress, and the Smithsonian Institution produced this book and audiotape.

18. Ibid., 281.

19. Anderson, *The Education of Blacks in the South, 1860–1935*, 2.

20. Ibid., 5.

21. Ibid., 5.

22. Ibid., 5.

23. Ibid., 7.

24. Ibid., 13.

25. Daniel Alexander Payne, "Welcome to the Ransomed," in Milton C. Sernett, ed., *Afro-American Religious History: A Documentary Witness,* (Durham: Duke University Press, 1985), 220.

26. Anderson, *The Education of Blacks in the South, 1860–1935*, 248, 249.

27. Thomas Lickona and Matthew Davidson, *Smart & Good High Schools: Integrating Excellence and Ethics for Success in School, Work and Beyond* (Cortland, N.Y.: Center for the 4th and 5th Rs [Respect & Responsibility], Washington, D.C.: Character Education Partnership), 3.

28. Ibid., 9.

29. Ibid., 10.

30. Jonathan D. Glater, "Colleges Chase as Cheats Shift to Higher Tech," *New York Times*, May 18, 2006, Section A, page 1, Column 4.

31. Ibid., 11.

32. Jawanza Kunjufu, *Countering the Conspiracy to Destroy Black Boys*, (Chicago: African American Images, 1995), 31.

33. "Black Men Fall Behind," in *USA Today*, February 16, 2005, 10A.

34. Rhonda Wells-Wilbon and Spencer Holland, "Social Learning Theory and the Influence of Male Role Models on Afrian American Children in PROJECT 2000," *The Qualitative Report*, Vol. 6, Number 4 (December 2001).

35. "Black Men Fall Behind," in *USA Today*, February 16, 2005, 10A.

36. Ibid., 10A.

37. Ibid., 10A.

38. Ibid., 10A.

39. "We the People: Blacks in the United States," Census 2000 Special Reports (Washington, D.C.: U.S. Department of Commerce, Economics and Statistics Administration, U. S. Census Bureau, August 2005), 10. Available in PDF format at http://www.census.gov/prod/2005pubs/censr-25.pdf (October 18, 2006).

40. Smiley, *Covenant with Black America*, 33.

41. Lickona and Davidson, *Smart & Good High Schools*, 6.

42. My favorite "Mays memory" dates back to the evening in 1975, when a small coterie of students and faculty gathered at a secret campus ceremony, where the president emeritus placed a Phi Beta Kappa pin on my lapel. Although long retired from Morehouse and from the presidency of Atlanta's School Board, he took delight in coming over to inspire us with his warm smile and challenging words.

43. Robert M. Franklin, "Black College Commencement," *All Things Considered*, National Public Radio broadcast (May 10, 2001). Available online at http://www.npr.org/templates/story/story.php?storyId=1122752 (October 18, 2006).

44. Freddie C. Colston, ed., *Dr. Benjamin E. Mays Speaks: Representative Speeches of a Great American Orator* (Lanham, Md.: University Press of America, 2002), 164.

45. Ibid., 165.

46. Ibid., 166.

47. Ibid., 166.

48. Ironically, in 2006 *Black Enterprise* magazine declared that Morehouse had fallen in its own rankings from number one to number forty-five, largely due to its apparent low graduation rate, a claim that was strongly refuted by retiring President Walter Massey.

49. Ibid., 166.

50. Ibid., 170

51. Ibid., 171.

52. Ibid., 173.

53. Ibid., 174–75.

54. Du Bois's original essay, along with interpretive essays by two contemporary authors, are found in Henry Louis Gates, Jr. and Cornel West, *The Future of the Race* (New York: Vintage Books, 1997), 147.

55. Anderson, *The Education of Blacks in the South, 1860–1935*, 276.

56. Ibid., 277.

57. Colston, ed., *Dr. Benjamin E. Mays Speaks*, 201.

58. Gareth B. Matthews, "Socrates's Children," in *The Philosopher's Child: Critical Essays in the Western Tradition*, edited by Gareth B. Matthews and Susan M. Turner (Rochester, N.Y.: University of Rochester Press, 1998), 12.

59. Daryl McGowan Tress, "Aristotle's Children," in *The Philosopher's Child*, 26.

60. Edmund W. Gordon, "Establishing a System of Public Education in Which All Children Achieve at High Levels and Reach Their Full Potential," in *The Covenant with Black America*, Tavis Smiley (Chicago: Third World Press, 2006), 26.

61. Ibid., 34.

62. Comments made during a panel discussion on "Black Men: Your Perception, Our Reality," at the NAACP Leadership 500 Summit in Destin, Fla., on December 9, 2006.

63. Letter from President JoAnn W. Haysbert, May 1, 2006.

64. Letter from interim President Castell Vaughn Bryant, July 25, 2006.

65. Telephone interview with Reverend Lisa Rhodes, September 30, 2006.

66. Interview with Dr. Otis Moss, Jr., July 18, 2006. Moss's fascinating idea about the multiple purposes of commencements reminds me of a testimony shared by professor of philosophy Berkeley B. Eddins. When he was a child growing up on Cannon Street in Memphis, he

and his friends would attend the commencement ceremonies for LeMoyne College (now LeMoyne-Owen College). He said that they found these ceremonies to be inspiring and showed them what was possible for black students.

67. Anderson, *The Education of Blacks in the South, 1860–1935*, 251.

68. Ibid., 250.

69. Web biography for Howard Thurman, *Wikipedia,* http://en.wikipedia .org/wiki/Howard_Thurman.

CHAPTER FOUR: STRATEGIES

1. W.E.B. Du Bois, *The Seventh Son: The Thought and Writings of W. E. B. Du Bois*, ed. Julius Lester (New York: Random House, 1971), 1:575.

2. Tavis Smiley, *How To Make Black America Better: Leading African Americans Speak Out* (New York: Anchor Books, 2001), 121ff.

3. Ibid., 123.

4. Blaise Pascal, 1623-1662, http://www.spirithome.com/prayer_c.html

5. Howard Thurman, "How Good to Center Down!" in *For the Inward Journey: The Writings of Howard Thurman,* selected by Anne Spencer Thurman (San Diego: Harcourt Brace, 1984), 93.

6. Du Bois, *The Seventh Son*, 1:575.

7. Paulo Freire, *Pedagogy of the Oppressed* (New York: Continuum International Publishing Group, 2002), 93.

8. From the Black Leadership Forum Web site: http://www.blackleadershipforum.org/about.html (October 18, 2006).

9. Interview with Hugh Price, October 16, 2006.

10. United Way Letter from Early Learning Commission, Atlanta, Georgia, July 24, 2006.

11. See the Children's Defense Fund Web site, http://www.childrensdefense .org/site/PageServer?pagename=c2pp (October 18, 2006).

12. Children's Defense Fund Web site, http://www.childrensdefense.org/ site/PageServer?pagename=About_CDF (October 18, 2006).

13. *Foundation News and Commentary,* May/June, 2006, vol. 47, no. 33, http:// www.foundationnews.org/CME/articles.cfm?ID=110&IssueID =3659.

14. "Giving & Philanthropy from Wilmington to Port St. Joe," *Notes from the Field*, No. 15 (Summer 2006), 7.

INDEX